POE

POE

James M. Hutchisson

UNIVERSITY PRESS OF MISSISSIPPI

JACKSON

Willie Morris Books in Memoir and Biography

www.upress.state.ms.us

The University Press of Mississippi is a member of the Association of American University Presses.

Frontis: Courtesy of the Library of Congress, Prints and Photographs Division

13 12 11 10 09 08 07 06 05 4 3 2 1

Library of Congress Cataloging-in-Publication Data

Hutchisson, James M.
  Poe / James M. Hutchisson.
    p. cm. — (Willie Morris books in memoir and biography)
  Includes bibliographical references and index.
  ISBN 1-57806-721-9 (cloth : alk. paper)
  1. Poe, Edgar Allan, 1809–1849. 2. Authors, American—19th century—Biography.
3. Critics—United States—Biography. I. Title. II. Series.

  PS2631.H88   2005
  818'.309—dc22   2004020123

British Library Cataloging-in-Publication Data available

To RACHEL
With Gratitude

Ancilium numquam deficiens

Who would fardels bear,
To grunt and sweat under a weary life,
But that the dread of something after death,
The undiscovered country, from whose bourn
No traveller returns, puzzles the will,
And makes us rather bear those ills we have
Than fly to others that we know not of?

—WILLIAM SHAKESPEARE, *Hamlet*, Act III, Scene I

It is evident that we are hurrying onward to some exciting knowledge—
some never-to-be-imparted secret, whose attainment is destruction.

—EDGAR ALLAN POE, "MS. Found in a Bottle"

CONTENTS

CONTENTS

ACKNOWLEDGMENTS

My debts in a project like this run rather deep, since I have been thinking about, writing on, and teaching Edgar Allan Poe for nearly twenty years. In that span, I have benefited from many stimulating conversations about Poe and his world with friends, colleagues, and students. These people include J. A. Leo Lemay, James L. W. West III, the late James W. Gargano, Dwayne Thorpe, William P. Keen, Benjamin F. Fisher, John Jebb, Susan Donaldson, David Shields, Scott Peeples, Julian Wiles, Tony Redd, and Harlan Greene. During the spring terms of 2002 and 2003 at The Citadel I taught courses on Poe in the Honors College; to those students I am grateful for their good humor, patience, and persistence in ferreting out the multitudinous meanings of the Poe texts we studied. My wife, Rachel, graciously gave of her ever-depleting reserves of time and energy to read an early draft of this book, even though, by the last page, she still couldn't understand how such an odd person as Poe had managed to write such fearsomely intelligent stories.

Anyone who writes on Poe, of course, is also indebted to the legions of scholars who have preceded him, since Poe is one of the most written-about authors in all of world literature. I acknowledge here a special debt, however, to the pioneering work of Robert D. Jacobs, whose book, *Poe: Journalist and Critic* (1969), first unearthed an extraordinary mine of material about Poe's existence as a workaday journalist and made a major argument about the importance of understanding Poe as a critic rather than only as, or in addition to, a writer of tales of the supernatural. Jeffrey Meyers's 1992 biography, *Edgar Allan Poe: His Life and His Legacy*, continued that line of thinking. Lastly, many of my arguments about the life of loss that Poe led and the importance of his era's culture of grief and remembrance are indebted to Kenneth Silverman's psychoanalytic biography, *Edgar A. Poe: Mournful and Never-ending Remembrance* (1991).

In writing this book I was ably supported by colleagues, staff, and students at The Citadel—in particular, James S. Leonard, head of the English department; Libby Walker, Sarah Brailsford, and Kathleen Triggs in the English department office; and Debbe Causey, Kathleen Turner, Betsey Carter, and David Heisser at the Daniel Library. Thanks are also due my research assistants, Jim Senter and Kristopher Johnston.

A semester's leave in the fall of 2004 provided much-needed time for finalizing the manuscript. Seetha Srinivasan at the University Press of Mississippi was more than patient with my requests to work on the book "just a little bit longer." Anne Stascavage and Carol Cox shepherded the manuscript through production efficiently and with great care. My thanks to all.

INTRODUCTION

Edgar Allan Poe (1809–1849) was an American original—a luminous literary theorist, an erratic genius, and an analyst of the human psyche par excellence. The scope and diversity of these achievements, as well as the compellingly dramatic character of Poe's life, have drawn readers and critics to him in droves, bringing him a vast popularity that he dreamed of but could never have even faintly imagined. Several score of books have been produced about him, including biographies, critical monographs, specialized studies, and even novels and plays.

This book seeks to capture the most central of those examinations of his life and work, offer its own insights, and present them in a concise, accessible volume. It is not intended for Poe specialists but rather for general readers—those who wish to see the broad outlines of Poe's life, learn something of his career, dip into the boisterous worlds of literary New York and Philadelphia in the 1800s, and understand why Poe wrote the way he did and why that was so important to American literature. It presents a critical overview of Poe's major works and his main themes, techniques, and imaginative preoccupations.

Readers already familiar with the details of Poe's life will see some aspects of his biography given more illumination here than in previous works. This portrait of the writer emphasizes Poe's southern identity; his existence as a workaday journalist in the burgeoning magazine era and his presence as a literary critic and cultural arbiter; his courtly demeanor and his sense of social propriety; his patronage of women writers; his adaptation and refurbishment of art forms as diverse as the so-called "gutter press" and the haunting rhythms of African American spirituals; his borrowing of imagery from popular social movements like temperance and Freemasonry; and his powerful posthumous influence on the sister arts and on modern writers from Nietzsche to Nabokov, in three distinct cultures—America, England, and France. Indeed, perhaps no other American author has been so thoroughly absorbed by later writers.

Although some have tended to shroud Poe's life in mystery and obscurity, the documentary record is, except for one brief period, full, colorful, and clear. His contributions to the development of American literature were many, beginning when he rose to public prominence as a writer and critic in the 1830s. From 1835, when he assumed the editorship of the Richmond, Virginia—based *Southern Literary Messenger*, until his death in 1849, Poe was arguably the main protagonist in the story of the building of American literature. He edited several periodicals, routinely wrote for many more, was a book reviewer known (sometimes infamously) up and down the eastern seaboard, and contributed original theoretical essays to the ongoing discussion about American letters. He was widely known as a literary journalist, a poet, and a writer in a mode that was just beginning to catch on in America, the short story.

In fact, in a review of Hawthorne's collection *Twice-Told Tales* (1837), Poe first rolled out a blueprint for story writing, impressing it with his seal of originality and hoping that generations to come would consult it in constructing their own architecture of the imagination. In "The Philosophy of Composition," Poe went further by setting down an aesthetic for poetry writing.

Poe's versatility is also admirable. He worked with equal skill in poetry, stories, nonfiction, essays, hoaxes, satires, and works of social criticism. He invented the modern detective story and is credited with doing largely the same for science fiction.

Poe lived for his art, regarding it as almost a divine calling. He once told a confidant, "Literature is the most noble of professions. In fact, it is about the only one fit for a man. For my own part, there is no seducing me from the path." He also maintained high standards—impossibly high, some said—for the development of art in America.

By seeking to play such an influential role in literary affairs, Poe became a revolutionary, never hesitant about swinging his fabled sword of criticism far and wide. He cut a swath through the established ranks of the genteel literary society that was then in power, seeking to topple them and install a new regime in their place. Unfortunately, he often drew more blood than he intended. Although earning the respect of the likes of Charles Dickens and James Russell Lowell, at the same time he called down on himself the wrath of the major power brokers in the writing world, who used their authority to exile Poe to the equivalent of a literary Siberia.

In personality, Poe was excessively polite, even courtly. His drinking, however, something that has contributed to a negative portrait of the writer, was another matter. Poe abused alcohol and was at times a binge drinker. Yet it is ironic that, from the earliest days after his death to the present, this is sometimes viewed as a moral issue when applied to Poe, but not when applied to other writers. Among twentieth-century American authors, uncontrolled drinking seems to have been the rule rather than the exception. Of the seven native-born Americans awarded the Nobel Prize for literature, five were "drunkards": Sinclair Lewis, Eugene O'Neill, Ernest Hemingway, John Steinbeck, and William Faulkner. (Others include F. Scott Fitzgerald, Jack London, Tennessee Williams, and such contemporary authors as John Cheever and Raymond Carver.)

These writers were diagnosed alcoholics. It is likely that Poe was also, since his father and brother were alcoholics, and a predisposition toward the disease is inherited. A physiological component was also present. His body had a low tolerance for alcohol, and many acquaintances testified that all it took to put Poe under, or, alternatively, to stir him up, was a modest-sized glass of wine. A closer look at these modern alcoholic writers also reveals that several were suicides, a temptation to which the often despondent Poe once or twice nearly gave in to, but without much resolve. Poe's career as a writer was also almost exactly coequal with the rise of the temperance movement in the United States, suggesting, on one level, why so many of his stories (at least thirty-two of them, as one scholar has calculated) involve inebriation. Unfortunately for Poe, that movement's iron hold on Americans' moral sensibilities made it easy and natural for the culture to accept, so quickly, the blackened posthumous image of Poe as a drunkard and reprobate.

It is also worth noting that the periods of Poe's heaviest drinking coincided with the lowest points in his life. He used drink as an anesthetic, to numb his sensitivity to criticism and travail. He lived through more adversity, pain, and sheer bad luck than most people would ever encounter, beginning with the early death of his mother, his being taken to live in a family where the father didn't want him, and his marriage to a young girl—barely a woman—who died a ghastly death vomiting blood and cringing with pain on the floor of a drafty cottage outside New York. Poe allegorized it in a famous story as "the Red Death." Readers know it by its less poetic but equally terrifying name: tuberculosis.

And although he wrote of the macabre, in his private life Poe usually led quite a prosaic existence, anticipating Flaubert's dictum that one should be bourgeois in one's life so that one could be mad in one's art. For Poe, the line of separation became less distinct in the latter parts of his life, as personal turmoil churned within him, but for the most part his day-to-day life was not extraordinary.

One wonders, perhaps, why Poe's imagination was so obsessed with such phenomena as people buried alive or brought back from the dead; self-torturing husbands so intent on never forgetting their lost loved ones that they remain with their corpses in the darkness of miasmic nights; otherwise ordinary people who suffer from a split self—like Doctor Faustus's good angel and bad angel—trying to reunite with dead wives, sisters, and mothers. Seen in context, this may not appear quite so bizarre. Because the practice of medicine was haphazard and hardly scientific, people actually were buried alive, having slipped into a coma or a similar death-like trance. As precautions against such error, some instructed their heirs to test their feet with a match and a knife before they were buried. Before technological advances in the manufacture of coffins, small bells that could ring at any unexpected movement were frequently attached to the bodies of the dead.

There was also a cult of death and remembrance in Poe's time that made dying, as J. Gerald Kennedy has noted, "a source of quiet fascination, even . . . contemplative pleasure." Mourning art proliferated, in the form of jewelry and samplers woven with locks of the deceased's hair.

Funerals became elaborate aesthetic spectacles, crowned by glass-sided coffins. Spacious new cemeteries were laid out to accommodate elaborate monuments and mausoleums. Death masks and portraits-in-death were all the rage, and graveyard poetry flourished. Magazines routinely printed articles about husbands so bereaved by the deaths of wives that they sat by the women's corpses, holding their hands, for days on end, and months later even ordered the graves exhumed so that they could kiss the dead flesh.

Alternatively, Poe's age was also mesmerized by pseudoscientific technologies and "discoveries" that promised to cheat death, or at least explain the causes of the cycle of human life—mummification, galvanic energy, automatons, revivification, metempsychosis, and phrenology were constantly written about, often in the periodicals that Poe worked for. Interest in discovery also drove Poe's age outside the bounds of the United States and into uncharted waters, like those nearer the South Pole. Arctic exploration and similar land expeditions were topics of public fascination.

Poe was also attracted to the so-called "nebular hypothesis" about the origins of the universe—the view that the heavenly bodies were created not by a single divine stroke but by the gradual coalescence of a thin, luminous substance diffused through space. In other words, the universe was still being created, and one day these single entities could be merged into a cluster of clusters and then into a single sun. This idea confirmed Poe's belief in an otherworld of repeated dyings and rebirths and of a return someday to the Original Unity or Nothingness in which the split self of the individual would reintegrate and reunify with his or her "mate." This theory accounts for Poe's persisting emphasis on organic unity in both his theoretical writings and his fiction.

Poe's hold on readers' imaginations is strong. This book explores the reasons for that, both in the context of his own life and the world of Victorian America.

POE

CHAPTER 1

CHILDHOOD

Boston, Richmond, England
[1809–1825]

N*ovember 29, 1811.* On the day after Thanksgiving, the *Richmond Enquirer* printed a plea for the citizens of the city to lend aid to one of its adopted daughters, Elizabeth Arnold Poe: "On this night," the paper read, "Mrs. Poe, lingering on the bed of disease and surrounded by her children, asks your assistance, and *asks it perhaps for the last time.*" Edgar Poe's mother, one of the best-known actresses in America, had reached the lowest ebb of a life that had seen its tide turn many times. She had been born in England, the daughter of actors who had put her on stage as a child. The Arnolds toured all over the country, appearing in Birmingham and in other theatre towns outside London. Minor players who hankered after greater fame, they emigrated to America to see if larger fortunes could be had there, arriving in Boston on the third of January 1796.

Three months later Eliza, as she was known, made her American stage debut at the Federal Street Theatre in Boston. In between the play *Mysteries of the Castle* and a musical afterpiece by William Shield, *Rosina,* Mrs. Arnold led her nine-year-old daughter onstage. With a voice often likened to that of a nightingale, Eliza sang the popular song "The Market Lass" and brought down the house. From there her success seemed ensured. She went on to play scores of roles on the American stage both in popular farces and in tragedies like *Hamlet, King Lear,* and *Romeo and Juliet.*

Yet her great success was offset by great misfortune. Both of her parents died when she was quite young—her father when she was only two, her mother of yellow fever when Eliza was eleven. At the time they were travelling with a troupe of fifteen players known as the Charleston Comedians. Eliza was taken into the care of the group's manager, Charles Tubbs. She carried on bravely for two years, but the life of an itinerant actress at the time was hardly respectable, and it was far from soft. Town after town, city after city rolled by on the dirt roads that the company traveled, putting up in one hostelry after another, contending with dirty linen, wet provisions, and, for Eliza, the lecherous gazes of older gentlemen in the halls where they performed.

But Eliza was a professional who concentrated on honing her craft. The theatre scene in America in the early nineteenth century was not all that different from what it had been in Shakespeare's day. The venues had become more elegant and commodious, but the atmosphere in the wings and in the dressing areas was just as frantically busy, and often as disorganized, as it had been at the Globe or the Swan.

Most of the production crew performed several different jobs all in the same evening, from lining up props to propping up scenery. To be successful as an actor, one had to have the same lightning-fast versatility, for there was no such thing as a play having a long run. Theatre managers changed the plays frequently, hoping to fill their houses by enticing audiences night after night with a new offering. Thus they hired only troupes who could "do" a large variety of standard parts. Eliza's mother had been trained in the repertory system in England, and she passed on her high degree of discipline and her strict professional standards to her daughter. By the time she was fifteen, Eliza knew about seventy parts.

She was also a beauty. Critics remarked on her luminous eyes, her raven-black hair, and her tiny figure, which made her strong voice all the more awesome. At age fifteen she married a teenaged character actor named Charles Hopkins, playing the Virginia circuit with him for about three years. But by colossal bad luck, at age twenty Hopkins suddenly fell ill and succumbed to yellow fever, the same disease that had befallen Eliza's mother. Now eighteen years old and completely on her own, Eliza resumed her career in Richmond. There she met David Poe, Jr., a twenty-one-year-old actor whom she often played opposite in the role of lover or wife. They married on March 14, 1806.

David Poe had been born in Baltimore in 1784, the son of a merchant who had fought in the Revolutionary War and, rather zealously, had also contributed some forty thousand dollars of his own money toward the cause. In local circles he was revered as a great patriot. (Although holding the rank only of major as deputy quartermaster for a Baltimore regiment, he was given the courtesy title of "General" and thereafter known as General Poe, something his grandson would later exaggerate for its cachet.) After his death, Lafayette visited the elder Poe's grave and was reputed to have called him *'un coeur noble'*—a noble heart. Young David had been training to follow his father and become a lawyer, but at some point he veered from this course and joined an amateur theatre group in Baltimore, the Thespian Club, where young men read and performed plays. While on a business trip to Norfolk, Virginia, David attended a play in which Eliza was performing. Seeing her onstage, he fell in love, and not long after—to the great consternation of his father—he cast off his few lingering pretenses at becoming a lawyer and joined Eliza's troupe. In the spring of 1806, they married.

Handsome and fit, David Poe marketed himself as an actor and a dancer, but in truth he had little talent in either area. Where critics universally praised Eliza, David came in for nothing but mean-spirited slander: "a more wretched Alonzo we have never witnessed," wrote the critic of the *Ramblers' Magazine* in September 1809, "his person, voice, and non-expression of countenance, all combine to stamp him—*poh!*" David Poe was sensitive and somewhat vain; he felt wounded by such slings, especially the vulgar puns on his name and references to chamber pots (*pot* in French). For these and other reasons David took to drinking with a vengeance and quickly gained a reputation in theatre circles as someone who welcomed a good fistfight as much as a bottle of ale.

Probably these same qualities made it inevitable that David would be unwilling to accept family responsibilities. The couple's first child, William Henry Leonard Poe, was born on January 30, 1807, in Boston, where the Poes settled for a time. Edgar was born on January 19, 1809. In December 1810 came a third child, an illegitimate daughter named Rosalie. By that time, David Poe had been gone for more than a year. Exactly why he ran off is not known, but he was certainly unsuited to family life. He may also have been envious of Eliza's talents and good reviews. Illness and poverty probably played large roles as well, undermining the marriage and creating an atmosphere of storm and stress. He died in Norfolk, apparently alone, on or about December 11, 1811.

From his father, Edgar would inherit a predisposition toward alcoholism and a sensitive nature that would not absorb personal wounds easily. Like his son, David Poe could also be vengeful; he went on record threatening to beat up any critic who ever made a negative comment about his wife's acting. Edgar would also retain something of the actor's flair for bragging and melodrama, exaggerating his talents and achievements to unbelievable degrees.

Alone again at age twenty-two, Eliza was left with only the comfort of her children to sustain her emotionally. Little is known of William Henry Leonard or Rosalie at the time. The middle child, Edgar, had the most inauspicious entry into the world, during a cold and moonless winter evening. He may likely have been his mother's favorite, especially since he inherited her diminutive figure, dark hair, and large, dark eyes. Certainly he was attached to her in stronger than usual ways. Later in life he boasted frequently of her "brief career of genius and of beauty" and memorialized her over and over again in his fiction and poetry, in a succession of portraits of frail but strong-willed women who lavish undiluted love and affection on their husbands and lovers.

The desertion of her own husband and the stress of having to provide for three young children on an actress's meager earnings eventually took their toll on Eliza. Travelling the circuit in various towns up and down the East Coast, in 1811 she had ended up in Richmond, ill and destitute. Suffering from pneumonia, or possibly tuberculosis, she underwent a rapid decline and passed away on December 8. In her brief life she had married twice, given birth to three children, and performed onstage more than three hundred times. She was twenty-four.

The women of Richmond society, who had grown to regard the abandoned Eliza as one of their "causes," mobilized to care for her young children. William Henry Leonard was sent to relatives in Baltimore. Rosalie was taken in by a local family, the MacKenzies. Friends of theirs, John and Fanny Allan, were persuaded to take Edgar, and on the day after Christmas, 1811, the boy moved into the Allans' rooms over a store at the corner of Main and Thirteenth streets, not as an adoptive son but simply as a foundling whom John Allan had agreed, grudgingly, to look after since the child had no blood relations in the area.

On the same day, the Richmond Theatre caught fire and burned to the ground, claiming twenty-two lives. The city mourned the loss of something that had meant much to them, just as the young boy Edgar mourned the double passing of his mother and her world. Poe inherited Eliza's strong work ethic, her determination to succeed—and her versatility, for just as one of Eliza's most notable assets was her ability to play both broad comic roles and inwardly intense tragic roles with equal precision and credibility, so too would Poe write in a variety of genres with consummate skill. Like his mother, Poe was every inch the professional.

As for his sense of place, it was not Richmond that Poe would later associate in memory with Eliza, but Boston. The only concrete remembrance of her that his mother left him in her will was a watercolor. It depicted Boston Harbor—an attempt, perhaps, to offer him some stability, some fixed point of identity and of place that he could internalize. On the back of it Eliza had written, "For my little son Edgar, who should ever love Boston, the place of his birth, and where his mother found her *best*, and *most sympathetic friends*."

Richmond in 1811 was a fast-growing city bursting at the seams with prosperity. Much of the new money came from coal, tobacco, and flour mills, and went directly into the pockets of a planter class of wealthy aristocrats. John Allan and his wife, Frances (or "Fanny"), did not quite fit this profile—Allan was a merchant who did a brisk, profitable business brokering goods and services with a partner, Charles Ellis. But through the commercial contacts afforded him by the House of Ellis and Allan, as his firm was called, Poe's foster father had scaled the social ladder and carefully cultivated an image as a civic leader. The city elite regarded the Allans as faithful churchgoers and generous benefactors to those more needy than they.

But even though John Allan had a reputation as one who "never turned a beggar from the door," he also had a strong streak of self-reliance that made him dislike dependency. Born near Glasgow, Scotland, in 1795, Allan, like Poe, had been an orphan. He had emigrated to the United States seeking to make his fortune and had lived a lean existence in which he had no one to help him but himself. Consequently, "Scotch" John Allan was all hard edges, with blunt facial features—square jaw, high forehead, and Roman nose—that seemed an outward reflection of the driven businessman within. He believed strictly in advancement through hard work and merit and in taking care of yourself. Such a philosophy probably doomed his relationship with Edgar before it had even begun, for the boy was completely without resources—and self-confidence—making him entirely dependent on his foster father. Allan was also single-minded, admitting no frivolity or "wasting" of time on vain or nonuseful pursuits, and was keen on self-improvement. As part of his bootstraps philosophy, he worked on softening some of the rough edges of his personality by speaking correct English and ridding his tongue of its heavy Scots accent. He also studied French—but only for its business value, not for love of learning.

Edgar would turn into the type of person John Allan despised—emotional, flighty, and unreliable, preoccupied with pursuits that had no material or financial value, like poetry and art. Poe never developed a bond with his foster father and later they became open enemies.

Some friends of the Allans later told biographers that the boy was baptised Edgar Allan Poe. But John Allan never legally adopted him, and once Edgar had left Richmond he always signed himself "Edgar A. Poe" or "E. A. Poe"—and occasionally "Edgar Poe"—but very rarely "Edgar Allan Poe" (that name was attached to him by his first biographer and erstwhile friend, Rufus Griswold). To omit the word "Allan" from his name was perhaps a symbolic act of independence, in which he aligned himself with his Poe ancestors from the North and his mother's happy days in Boston, not his faux "family" from the South and a childhood in Richmond that was often strained with the unrequited need to be loved.

Like Scott Fitzgerald and D. H. Lawrence, it was to women that Poe, in youth and in adulthood with equal ardor, continually turned to find this affection, approval, and sense of belonging. In contrast to the cold and aloof John Allan, Fanny, his wife, was sensitive and caring. She loved Edgar deeply, just as she would a child of her own and, almost certainly against John Allan's better judgment, persuaded her husband to pamper him a bit. In Richmond, Poe was privately educated at a dame school; he accompanied his foster parents on trips to resorts like White Sulphur Springs, and he was outfitted with an expensive wardrobe. Fanny too had been an orphan, raised by a guardian from the age of ten. She was now twenty-six, only a little older than Eliza, whom she resembled in her slight, girlish frame. Edgar took to her as a surrogate mother quickly, but to the emotionally volatile young boy, this became cause for fear rather than assurance, for when Poe was six and a half, John Allan took his family to England. He intended to expand his business by opening a branch house in London.

Sea voyages were perilous propositions. Ships were not built to withstand severe storms, maps and charts were often unreliable, and weather forecasting was almost nonexistent. The popular press routinely carried multiple column inches of sensationalized reporting about disasters at sea, with headlines that shouted words like "TERROR," "FAMINE," and "HORRIBLE DEATH." Such stories must have exerted an uncomfortable influence on a young boy's imagination, especially Edgar, who had a naturally excitable temperament. Fanny, who was frequently ill and thus in a weakened condition anyway, did not want to make the trip, and her fears must have affected Edgar as well.

None of this could have assured Edgar against the thing he feared most—losing his family again. And in fact while the House of Ellis and Allan prospered during the family's five-year stay in London, Fanny was sick much of the time, suffering one misery after another: attacks of catarrh, colds, sore throats, facial swelling, headaches, the croup, a fall.

Illnesses seemed to cling to her like parasites on a plant, although it might be said that her consistently poor health may have been a bulwark she erected to block the amorous advances of her husband. A gruff, insensitive type, John Allan most likely was used to getting and taking what he wanted. Fanny may have become, in a manner of speaking, professionally ill, as many nineteenth-century women were, choosing to take to the couch to escape boorish husbands, and to avoid childbearing, which at the time was potentially fatal. Nonetheless, Fanny's weakened condition made it difficult for Edgar to get as close to her physically as he wanted to be. She was often shut up in dark, airless rooms somewhere off in the flat, away from the family. Emotionally, Edgar may have been reluctant to offer Fanny his affection, afraid that he would lose her, too.

At age seven, Edgar enrolled for his first rigorous schooling, boarding first at the school of the Misses Dubourg (the family of John Allan's young clerk, George), on Sloane Street in Chelsea, about three miles from the Allans' rented flat in Russell Square. The schoolmistresses took good care of their charge, notifying Allan that the boy was "well & happy." A little more than a year later, Edgar was transferred to the care of the Reverend John Bransby, who ran the Manor House school in rural Stoke Newington, about four miles outside London. Here Edgar showed his first natural tendencies toward languages, excelling in Latin and Greek, pleasing his headmaster, a classicist by training who was said to be fond of quoting Shakespeare and Horace at length. Although Poe was a gifted and proficient student, he did not like schooling per se—early showings of his romantic temperament, which rebelled against rote learning and curricular regimens.

Poe's later lacklustre academic record may have been due to bad habits instilled in him by the English public school system, for it encouraged mechanical learning only, not genuine intellectual curiosity. The continuous memorizing of classical texts, without any attempt to explicate them or make them relevant to a young mind, may have put Edgar off education, and perhaps also planted seeds of rebellion against those in positions of authority.

Schools like Bransby's were known for their adversative philosophy of education, in which browbeating and sometimes outright cruelty were thought to build character and be good for the child's mental development. Poe later satirized these features of the school at Stoke Newington in "William Wilson," where he transformed an ordinary eighteenth-century square building into a "large, rambling Elizabethan house" (338) with endless winding stairways and passages that led nowhere. In the story, the exterior of the school resembles a prison, surrounded as it is by "a high and solid brick wall, tropped with a bed of mortar and broken glass" (339). And the original John Bransby, a genial man with side whiskers and a clerical collar, became someone with a "sour image" in "snuffy habilments" who ruled the school with a "Draconian" despotism (338). The young boy probably also did not react well to a second separation from his parents. Added to this was the cool reception he probably received from his schoolmates, whose country had just fought a bloody war with the American colonists.

With little warning, a financial slump hit London businesses in 1819; a sharp drop in the tobacco market was a major factor. Allan, once prosperous, suddenly found himself being dunned by creditors and hounded by complaining customers who were not getting their goods in a timely manner. Allan anxiously wrote his business partner back in Virginia for help, money, advice—anything that could avert the looming disaster, but by July the chain of business collapses had reached Ellis and Allan and the merchant was unable to meet his debts—nearly a quarter of a million dollars. Fortunately, Allan found his creditors to be reasonable men, and arrangements were worked out for him to pay off the debt. He returned to America on July 21, 1820, chastened but relieved. Fanny, hard hit emotionally by their financial woes and much the worse for the return trip, took to her room for some time, complaining of aches and fatigue.

As Allan set about putting his accounts to rights, Edgar continued his schooling, this time living at home. Until about age fourteen, he attended the academy of Joseph H. Clarke, and for two years after that he studied with Clarke's successor, William Burke, another Latinist who encouraged Edgar's gift for language. He read Horace, was adept at scanning poetry, and also in "capping verses"—an exercise in which one student would quote a line of Latin verse and the other had to quote another line beginning with the same letter. Edgar also studied French, committed hundreds of lines of English verse to memory, and tried his hand at writing poetry of his own—formal odes and lyrics in the eighteenth-century style with a rigorous metrical polish to them, quite an accomplishment for a teenaged boy. John Allan, however, discouraged Edgar in what he undoubtedly saw as foolish, "womanly" pursuits and instead urged him to study subjects that would prepare him for a career in business.

How fully Edgar responded to the political environment in Richmond is not clear, but as a still impressionable youth the social attitudes of the time and place must have been grafted onto his consciousness—race, class, the church, even statecraft. How much he assimilated such doctrine is also difficult to say, but his formative years were spent in the South, and in adult life Poe considered himself a southerner. His regional allegiances became important later in his career, especially in his relationships with other writers.

Certainly Richmond, as a sedate, bucolic environment, was radically different from the frenetic, ever-changing world of the theatre. Yet his identity as the son and grandson of actors was something he loved to assert. Poe was nothing if not theatrical—both skilled as a platform speaker and given to intense emotionalism in his private life. In several episodes during his Richmond boyhood Poe indulged his taste for melodrama. Around age fifteen or sixteen he successfully swam some six miles in the James River under a hot June sun and for at least part of the way against a strong tide. He would later brag about this display of physical prowess, especially in those times when he wished his public to think of him in Byronic terms—the latter poet having accomplished a similar fabled feat that became part of the lore surrounding him.

Another time, Edgar indulged a different tendency. The Marquis de Lafayette, the great hero of the American Revolution, visited Richmond in October 1824. At the time, Edgar was a lieutenant in a volunteer company of Richmond boys called the Junior Morgan Riflemen. He rode in a procession that followed Lafayette's carriage down one of the main streets of the city. Poe's attraction to the military would seem to be at odds with his poetic nonconformity and Byronic posturing, but he saw in the disciplined, hierarchical world of the military an outlet for his need or will to be in power, and to master his shifting, unreliable surroundings. He was also very likely reasserting his identity as the grandson of General David Poe, father of the father he had never known.

As he tried to take command of his destiny, Edgar also sought comfort and a sense of stability in Fanny, whom he had taken to calling "Ma." Yet Fanny continued to malinger, to fall victim to various illnesses, making her less than an ideal mother for Edgar. (John Allan recorded with characteristic bluntness that his wife was "never clear of complaint.") Thus turned away, Edgar developed an infatuation with a friend of the family, Mrs. Jane Stanard, who with eerie precision once again resembled both Eliza and Fanny. Like them, she too was frequently ill and eventually fell into a prolonged period of depression, brought on by an unhappy marriage. This eventually made her go insane, and she lived in this chaotic mental state for about a year before she died in 1824. Poe frequently visited Jane's grave in Shockoe Hill Cemetery.

Like Eliza and other nurturing figures in Poe's life, Jane Stanard remained with him in memory forever. He called her "the first, purely ideal love of my soul" and she inspired one of his most beautiful poems. In "To Helen" Jane Stanard became the ideal of feminine beauty, like the Helen who became a visionary classical ideal—perfect, statuesque, and unattainable:

> On desperate seas long wont to roam,
> Thy hyacinth hair, they classic face,
> They naiad airs have brought me home
> To the glory that was Greece,
> And the grandeur that was Rome.

The closing couplet of that stanza is among Poe's most memorable verses. It is also revealing of his views of women—as nurturing beings that he needed to assure him he was loved, and as alabaster-skinned beauties forever immortalized in memory, through art.

In 1825, the year after Jane Stanard died, Edgar became secretly engaged to Elmira Royster, the fifteen-year-old daughter of a neighbor. She too, however, turned out to be unattainable, since her father forbade the marriage. Edgar was an orphan, with no financial resources of his own, and no immediate future in a "solid" line of work, like banking or trade.

Without a caring home environment, Poe grew rebellious and surly—behavior that did not sit well with "Scotch" John Allan, who would not abide disorder or lack of harmony in his house. A clash was inevitable, as the foster father provided for him faithfully, paying his tuition, shelling out money for clothes and "trimmings," yet receiving "not a Spark of affection" nor a "particle of gratitude" in return. When Allan thought about all he had done for the boy, Edgar's unresponsiveness galled him even more: "Had I done my duty as faithfully to my God as I have to Edgar," he once wrote, death itself would hold no terrors for him.

In a letter to Poe's brother, Henry, Allan inaugurated what would become a steady series of tirades about Edgar's behavior. Taking in hand a recent letter from Henry to Poe, Allan wrote on the pretext of apologizing for Poe's not writing back sooner, for reasons unknown. "He has had little else to do for me," Allan wrote, "he does nothing & seems quite miserable, surly & ill-tempered to all the Family. How we have acted to produce this is beyond my conception—why I have put up for so long with his conduct is a little less wonderful."

Allan's dark mood was in part due to business losses. The collapse of the land and cotton booms had sent the country into a deep economic depression that lasted until 1824 and forced him in that year to dissolve his partnership. Yet in a miraculous reversal of misfortune, a deus ex machina descended onto the stage of Allan's life in March 1825 when, seated at breakfast with his uncle William Galt, the relative "suddenly threw back his head & eyes" and died on the spot. Said to be the wealthiest man in Virginia, Galt had an estate that seemed boundless—plantations in several counties, grist and sawmills, stock in the Bank of Virginia, and several hundred slaves. To John Allan came an inheritance of more than $750,000—a fortune.

Suddenly rich beyond measure, Allan got out of debt and acceded to the life of the landed gentry. Very quickly he found a house to suit his new position. A two-story brick structure with wide, wraparound porches, it was called Moldavia, and had once been owned by the wealthy milliner Joseph Gallego. The house was situated on the slope of a hill and advertised as affording the most spectacular views in the city. The interior was as awesome as the site itself—a mirrored ballroom with hand-carved mantel, a wide mahogany stairway, and an octagonal dining room, which the Allans completed with the most expensive fittings that could be found. Antiques and objets filled the house, yet the sum total of the furnishings barely touched Allan's overflowing coffers.

Edgar was approaching sixteen that summer, a late adolescent on the cusp of adulthood. He was trying to find his way in the world, determine where his destiny lay and with what talents he could capture it. The lack of a stable family structure and the fear of losing more people whom he loved preoccupied him. Money, being in such abundant supply, probably did not occupy much of his thinking, though soon it would, because none of John Allan's great wealth would ever come to him.

CHAPTER 2

THE BYRONIC YOUTH

University, the Army, and West Point .
[1826–1830]

In February 1826, Poe left Richmond for Charlottesville to enroll in
Thomas Jefferson's innovative "academical village," the University of
Virginia. Some sixty miles from Richmond, the university had been oper-
ating for only a year. It had been founded by the eighty-three-year-old
former president, who envisioned it as an Athens of America, an institution of higher learning unlike any other. Jefferson hoped to create an
environment where instructors and students would each pursue the art of
learning in a mutual endeavor, a society of scholars whose only commitment was to truth. Relations between students and teachers were close.
Jefferson (who died while Poe was at the university, in 1826) regularly
invited students to dine with him at Monticello, so it is likely that Poe had
met and interacted with him, probably more than once. Faculty and under-
graduates were also linked symbolically, through the campus's classically
inspired pavilions, which contained lodgings for professors above and classrooms below.

This was the ideal; the reality was dramatically different. John Allan
must not have known what life was really like there, or he would never
have sent Poe, for the university was the most dissolute environment
imaginable. It had no religious affiliation, unlike Harvard (Unitarian) or
Princeton (Presbyterian). It was nonsectarian and thus devoted to Jefferson's
Enlightenment-derived principles of reason and common sense. Students
were presumed to be able to monitor their own behavior, and they could

choose whatever courses they wished. Strict rules were laid down, but completely ignored.

Gambling, drunkenness, and fistfights were commonplace, and the violence wasn't confined to students. One professor of modern languages was observed horsewhipping his wife in the street. Another incident involved a young man who was beating his opponent handily but decided to attack his person even more barbarically, and so he bit him. "I saw the arm afterwards," Edgar wrote John Allan, "and it was really a serious matter—It was bitten from the shoulder to the elbow—and it is likely that pieces of flesh as large as my hand will be obliged to be cut out."

Because duels also frequently took place, in the southern manner, any given student could usually be found to own a pistol—"all the fashion here," Poe wrote. Reform eventually came about when a board of censors, comprised of "discreet" students, was set up to monitor behavior and report violations, but it was a long time in coming. During Poe's residency there, the faculty mostly waited in vain for the students to come around and follow Jefferson's liberal system of self-governance.

Despite the bizarre atmosphere of the place, Poe excelled in his studies. He had moved past his schoolboy rebellion and had begun to take great joy in discovering he had natural scholarly instincts. (Later, writers whom Poe edited or who were reviewed by him complained that he was pedantic.) He loved books and learning, music and languages. Edgar enrolled in courses in ancient and modern languages, excelling in the senior Latin and French classes. He also joined the Jefferson Society, a debating club, and became noted for his verbal facility.

Poe's intellect was well above average. One classmate testified that Poe rarely had to prepare his lessons in advance and that his memory was so acute that he required only a few minutes of study before class in order to give the best recitation in the group. At the end of the term, in December 1826, Poe was examined in all his subjects, along with students who had completed two years at the school, by two former presidents of the United States: James Monroe and James Madison, who had succeeded Jefferson as rector. In ancient and modern languages, Poe passed with highest honors.

Yet for all his ease in the academic world, he seemed to his classmates gloomy and morose, standoffish. Partly it was due to the loss of his childhood sweetheart, Elmira Royster, the year before. Poe assuaged some of his loneliness by writing poetry and drawing. One contemporary recalled that he would "with a piece of charcoal evince his versatile genius by sketching upon the walls of his dormitory, whimsical, fanciful and grotesque figures, with so much artistic skill, as to leave us in doubt whether Poe in future life would be Painter or Poet." This same acquaintance also testified to Poe's touchy, bristly, and sometimes pugnacious temperament, however: "He was very excitable & restless, at times wayward, melancholic & morose."

Poe was also affected by the wild and erratic behavior of his classmates. His mood swings were exacerbated by drink. "He would too often put himself under the influence of that 'Invisible Spirit of Wine,'" the same friend remembered; and another that "Poe's passion for drink was as marked and as peculiar as that for cards. . . . He played in such an impassioned manner as to amount to an actual frenzy. All of his card playing and drinking he did under a sudden impulse. . . . He would always seize the tempting glass . . . and without the least apparent pleasure swallow the contents, never pausing until the last drop had passed his lips. One glass at a time was about all he could take."

The last in the troika of sins that John Allan would use to condemn the young man and put an end to his education was gambling, something that the parsimonious Allan saw as venial, akin almost to murder. The university librarian, writing many years later, recalled a conversation he had with Poe in his room one night in which Poe "spoke with regret of the large amount of money he had wasted and of the debts he had contracted during the Session." By Poe's estimate, he owed his fellow card players two thousand dollars—more than twenty thousand dollars in today's currency—and had been forced to borrow sums at high interest by local moneylenders, most likely Jewish, which probably angered Allan even more.

Edgar's financial problems continued to accumulate, and the conflicts with Allan escalated. In addition to his gambling losses, Poe piled up a considerable amount of other debt. Defending himself to Allan, he claimed that the latter had not given him enough money to accoutre himself in the fine style of the young gentlemen with whom he attended class and that, after all, part of going to the university, in addition to acquiring knowledge, was acquiring savoir faire and a certain social position which one was expected to take upon graduation. "I will boldly say that it was wholly and entirely your own mistaken parsimony that caused all the difficulties in which I was involved while at Charlottesville," he later wrote Allan. "The expenses of the institution at the lowest estimate were $350 per annum. You sent me there with $110."

But Poe, wanting to emulate his more well-heeled classmates, began to dress expensively and, most likely, retain a servant—from among a pool of locally owned slaves—to clean his clothes, polish his shoes, and serve as all-around valet while he and his friends attended a nearly endless round of social affairs that usually involved drinking and gambling.

To the rock-hard, abstemious Allan the boy seemed not only to be living the life of a wastrel, but also to be spending money as never before. Thus was begun the second round of an ongoing battle that was shortly to reach its peak and conclude with Allan the victor. Letters and allegations flew back and forth between Richmond and Charlottesville, charges real and unfounded, rhetoric that was alternately conciliatory and charged with white-hot anger. Who had more just cause than the other will probably never be determined, but the result was that Edgar's academic career was over before it had really begun. In December 1826, Allan went up to Charlottesville, conducted a loud and public investigation into Edgar's ways, paid off the gaming debts he thought ought to be paid, and brought the young man back to Richmond, dejected and resentful.

Poe then went to work for a while in Allan's counting room, where he was supposed to gain some practical skills like bookkeeping, accounting, and writing business lettters, but another confrontation was inevitable. About two months after Edgar's leaving Charlottesville the strained relations between presumptive father and unwanted son snapped violently, and nearly two years of friction between them erupted. He had been pursued at home for his debts at the university, and Allan refused to pay them. Incensed, Edgar moved out of Moldavia to places unknown in the city. More letters were exchanged, with the most damning criticism coming from Edgar's pen: "You suffer me to be subjected to the whims & caprice, not only of your white family but the complete authority of the blacks." Poe's defensiveness would become a habitual reflex action, the beginning of a pattern in which he felt that people treated him shabbily, even persecuted him. And so he began to treat his defeats like accomplishments, an ironically fitting strategy for his career as a writer, one which would be all too true. The rhetoric with which Poe made his charges against Allan was appropriately formal and dignified, presented, as Kenneth Silverman perceptively observes, "in a tone of lofty resolve"—"you suffer me"; "you take delight in"; "You have moreover ordered," like Jefferson's language in the Declaration of Independence, in which the revolutionaries of his grandfather's generation had framed their criticisms of the king. Poe was asserting his independence once again.

When Allan finally replied, it was with derision and a particularly hurtful slight on Edgar's recent academic training, for Allan said that this was what reading novels and other literary indulgences had taught the boy. "It is true I taught you to aspire, even to eminence in Public Life, but I never expected that Don Quixotte [sic], Gil Blas, Jo: Miller & such works were calculated to promote the end." "Eating the bread of idleness," the dour Allan called it. Poe's foster father was a Scot and a Presbyterian. His gloomy, Calvinistic outlook on life would admit no such frivolties as literature.

Who was right and who was wrong will never be known. It does seem certain that Allan underfunded Poe when he sent him to Charlottesville. Why he did so could be answered several ways. Perhaps he wanted to impress on Poe the need for self-sufficiency; perhaps he wished Poe to fail at the university and so have to return to Richmond and work for him; he may have resented Poe's artistic and intellectual abilities and sought to undercut him; or, he may have been jealous of Poe's affection for Fanny and wanted poetic justice.

Perhaps accordingly, Edgar began spinning tales of the utmost woe, calculating that these would induce the proper amount of guilt in his foster father to make him give him money and reopen the doors of his home.

References to not having enough to eat and no place to sleep poured from his pen, but he received only stony silence in reply. It was not all that common in that time for foundlings and orphans to be taken in by families, as Poe was by the Allans. Most went instead to an orphanage or publicly funded school where they were educated in practical, "useful" trades. In fairness to Allan, Poe did owe him an immense debt; Allan provided Poe with a level of education that he would never otherwise have gotten, and Allan was most likely disappointed that Poe had not done more with it.

Then Poe disappeared. All of what happened is not known, but at least for several days he and a friend, Ebenezer Burling, joined the crew of a ship bound for England. Poe apparently used a false name, Henri Le Rennet (possibly a Gallicized version of Henry Leonard, a name he had also sometimes adopted to avoid his creditors). When Burling sobered up, however, he jumped ship and returned to Richmond. John Allan told his sister that Poe had "gone to Sea to seek his fortunes"; the reality was that his journey had taken him only to Boston, distancing him from Allan and imaginatively returning him to the bosom of Eliza, whose gift to him had contained written instructions that in that city he might find his "*best, and most sympathetic friends.*"

Poe arrived there in March 1827. He may have worked for a while in a merchandise house. He was definitely doing some writing, continuing his exploration of poetic form. Sometime in June or July 1827 his first book of verse appeared, issued privately by a young printer, Calvin F. S. Thomas, whose family may have known David and Eliza Poe. It was called *Tamerlane and Other Poems*. The slim volume (only forty pages) was also published anonymously, "*By a Bostonian.*" Its very small issue of only fifty copies attracted no reviews, but it gave Poe the confidence to continue writing. Today, these poems provide a revealing portrait of the artist as a young man, for Tamerlane is an orphanlike figure of uncertain parentage, with a "feigned name," solitary and wandering, abetted by an unquenchable thirst for power and command: "I was ambitious—have ye known / Its fiery passion? . . . / A cottager, I mark'd a throne / Of half the world, as all my own. . . ." The Byronic verse exudes a romantic pessimism founded on a disappointed childhood and the speaker's inner

21

nature of great passion and emotion. The poems also introduce some characteristics of Poe's fictive narrators, like the lack of identity and of place.

By this time, Poe had wound up in an unlikely spot: the army. Giving his name this time as Edgar A. Perry and his age as twenty-two, he had enlisted as a private for a five-year term in the First Regiment of Artillery. He was initially stationed at regimental headquarters in Boston Harbor, but in November the company moved to Fort Moultrie, South Carolina, on a rather desolate barrier island near the mouth of Charleston Harbor, where Poe would later set his prize-winning mystery story, "The Gold-Bug." Thirteen months later, the company moved again, to Fortress Monroe, located near the entrance to Chesapeake Bay at Old Point Comfort, a popular vacation spot for residents of Richmond.

During his two years in the army, Poe did well, remarkably so for this being his fifth change of environment—Boston and the theatre world of his childhood; London and boarding schools there; Richmond and a southern upbringing; the university; now the military. Perhaps Poe welcomed the regimented lifestyle that the military forced on him—a corrective to the too-liberal way of living at the university. Once again Poe distinguished himself, eventually rising to the responsibility of arranging for the company's food and supplies—not an exalted rank, but one that showed he was trustworthy and efficient. Approval ratings from his superiors were all high, and in his evaluations there was not even a hint of laxity or idleness, much less drinking, gambling, or consorting with women of uncertain reputation. He was promoted to sergeant major on New Year's Day, 1829, the highest rank possible for a noncommissioned officer.

In what would become characteristic for Poe, however, just after this he abruptly decided that the army was not the place for him and began inquiring about how to get out. For failing to honor his five-year contract, he could be sentenced to up to five years in the federal penitentiary. Fortunately for Poe, his commanding officer was a friend of John Allan and wished to see the two reconciled, so he promised Poe a discharge if Poe would apologize and allow himself to come back under Allan's authority. Poe was dubious about Allan's ability to reconcile, fearing that his coolness might harden into icy disapproval, though Poe did make an attempt.

Fate intervened to change the direction of Poe's emotions when on February 28, 1829, Fanny Allan died at the age of forty-three. She had been seriously ill for some time, beset by a variety of ailments that can only be summed up in the nineteenth-century way—as physical frailty, enabled by a weak constitution and its corollary, a weak spirit. Edgar received an emergency leave but arrived home one day too late for her funeral. She was buried near Jane Stanard in Shockoe Hill Cemetery.

Perhaps because of Fanny's death, Allan and Poe temporarily found common ground, as they had in Edgar's desire to attend a university, for now Poe wanted an appointment to West Point.

This seems a paradox, but it was typical of Poe to change his views abruptly, just as he would later sometimes recant earlier versions of a dispute with a colleague or retract a first judgment passed on a book or play he was reviewing. Poe had had a taste of authority in his creditable climb up the army ladder to the rank of sergeant major; desiring power over other people, he found the prospect of a bona fide officer's slot in the military hierarchy appealing. It may also have been the only believable effort at making up to John Allan that Poe could show, since in the back of his mind there must always have resided the long-term presumption that he would someday inherit at least of part of Allan's vast fortune.

Getting into West Point turned out to be a herculean task, taxing Poe's abilities to make good impressions on those in charge, as well as Allan's considerable string-pulling skills. The paperwork involved in making application to the military academy was daunting, and it required Poe to spin more fictions concerning his birth and parentage, for in truth Poe was a foundling with no real supporting family and no legitimate prospects for security, financial or otherwise. He was never adopted by John Allan and so he could make no claims to a stable background. In his application Poe averred that Allan had adopted him and made him his son and heir. To explain the absence of his parents, he placed them at the scene of the great Richmond theatre fire of 1809 and noted melodramatically that they had perished there. Allan became an accomplice in Poe's cover-up, stating in his own letter to the Secretary of War, John H. Eaton, that Poe had comported himself admirably throughout his youth and added that in his military career thus far, he had displayed nothing but "honorable feelings, and elevated spirit," making him the perfect officer candidate.

But although Allan had cleansed Poe of his youthful sins and indiscretions, almost none of their bitter animosities had completely washed away, for as Poe waited on the academy to make its decision, new clashes erupted with Allan on what by now were old topics—money and writing, for Poe had unwisely asked Allan to guarantee a potential publisher a sum of money against losses if they published his second book of poetry. Poe was never a very good judge of character, and if Allan's temper had earlier flared at the prospect of Poe even spending time (that is, "wasting" time) on writing, then it must have positively exploded when the young man asked him to subsidize his literary work. Prudently, Poe had gone to Washington to interview with Secretary Eaton, hoping to improve his chances of a West Point appointment, but while he was there a new barrage of letters flew back and forth to Richmond, none of them containing much hope for a permanent reconciliation with Allan, and the last of them ending with what was in essence if not in fact "a prohibition" against Edgar's returning to Richmond.

Poe thus found himself stranded and put in the position for the first time of depending on whatever charity friends or relations could offer him. As it happened, while in Washington he had briefly visited with his father's family in Baltimore and was able to board there for a while, albeit "in a most uncomfortable position." He asked for and was granted a small sum by Allan, though it came "with a taunt," as he interpreted it, that "men of genius ought not to apply" for "aid."

While waiting for news from West Point, Poe bided his time in Baltimore by shopping around the manuscript of his second collection of poems. Published in a small edition in November 1829 by the Baltimore firm of Hatch and Dunning, *Al Aaraaf, Tamerlane, and Minor Poems*, this time under his authorship, as "Edgar A. Poe," the slim volume consisted mostly of the poems in the first book, revised. With some minor additions, the book brought Poe only a little public attention. Most of the reviews were either indifferent or unfavorable, except for a gushing piece by the critic and novelist John Neal, a figure of limited literary talent.

The publication of the book may also have given Poe some small satisfaction in proving John Allan wrong—that is, that he, Edgar Poe, was talented enough to be considered a "real" writer. But Allan's earlier comments to Poe about how reading the classics and pining to be an author were wastes of time were, unfortunately, essentially true in early nineteenth-century America. Virtually no one at that time could live by the pen alone. Nearly all successful American authors, including Emerson and Longfellow, had other careers. Longfellow, for instance, was a foreign-language teacher until he had published enough to give him a financial safety cushion during his attempts to be a full-time writer. Emerson earned his income as a lyceum lecturer and occasional pulpit supply. It was not until the late nineteenth century—technically, almost until 1898, when an international copyright law was enacted—that the American publishing and bookselling industries could consistently support a class of full-time authors.

In the spring of 1830 came word at last that Poe had been admitted to West Point. That summer he decamped for the school, some fifty miles above New York City on the Hudson River, and fell easily into the old routines of formations, drills, and parades, as well as adjusting to the added demands of classes and homework. As he had in the past, he excelled in French, and discovered a new interest in mathematics. Again Poe thrived in the military environment, executing his duties with efficiency and grace and distinguishing himself as a student, earning the rank of the "Best" cadet in French one month and the same honor the next in math.

While at West Point, however, came the emotionally debilitating news that Allan had remarried, renewing Poe's fears that he was being systematically shut out of Allan's life and thus dimming his hopes of an inheritance. As displaced as he had previously felt, too, this most recent turn of events likely forced him to accept the fact that he had no home, just as he had no real family. "I no longer look upon Richmond as my place of residence," he wrote Allan. Poe acted emotionally rather than rationally and trained his anger again on Allan, renewing his barrage of criticisms. Chief among them was that Allan had promised him an education and then denied him one. Poe maintained the fiction that "I *earned*, myself, by the most humiliating privations" admission to West Point, when in truth Allan's considerable political influence was a large contributing factor. Acting perversely in order to wound Allan, Poe made another ill-advised decision, this time to leave West Point after eighteen months. He had vague plans for Tamerlane-like roving—joining the Polish army, establishing himself in Paris—all part of the Byronic persona that was the anchor of his inner existence, despite the outward show of military discipline and polish.

"Byronism," as it was known in the early romantic period, was largely a mood or temperament much in fashion in Poe's youth. It sprang from the antiheroic characters of George Gordon, Lord Byron, in whose poems readers came to admire the rebellious individualist, greatly misunderstood by a philistine society—gloomy, alien, mysterious—and also willful, self-determined, and superior, holding himself above the noisy, commercial fray. Poems like *Childe Harold's Pilgrimage* and *Manfred* were wildly popular in Poe's day, and Byron himself became a mythic figure. He was thought of as a dark outcast from the mainstream world who lived by his own moral code and pursued his passions regardless of the societal forces arrayed against him. This image—whether accurate or fabricated— had a persisting influence on American intellectual and cultural history.

Certainly it shaped Poe's thinking and behavior, but at this juncture it probably harmed him more than helped him, for getting out of West Point was just as difficult as getting in—perhaps more so, because under academy regulations a cadet could only be excused on charges of misconduct. Accordingly, Poe did not show up at roll call and incurred other misdemeanors to the point where he could be expelled. But before he could leave, he had to make good on the debts he had run up there. His stipend from the academy brought his bank balance to $85.09. His bills amounted to $84.85. On February 19, 1831, Poe left West Point for the city. A mere twenty-four cents remained in his pocket.

26

Like Chaucer's ascetic Clerk who would rather spend his money on books than clothes, Poe relished the life of the artist. He marshalled his skills at getting charity from his fellow cadets before he left, but not to give him means for food and drink. Rather, it was to cover the cost of printing a new edition of his poems. *Poems by Edgar A. Poe . . . Second Edition* was issued in April 1831. Poe dedicated the book "To the U.S. Corps of Cadets." It was the climax of the first stage of his literary career, and the culmination of his considerably developed views on the literary arts.

From his earliest and most idealistic aspirations in art to his final painful years as a rejected and even reviled writer, Poe always thought of poetry as the highest literary calling, and, although today most people regard him as a writer of horror stories, he always regarded himself as a poet, declaring that for him, "Poetry has been not a purpose but a passion" (18).

As a twenty-two-year-old with an incomplete education, Poe had well-defined ideas about verse writing, and he set them forth in a brief preface to the volume, enigmatically entitled "Letter to Mr. B—" (possibly Eliam Bliss, the book's publisher). Although not lengthy, this was the first of Poe's several critical statements about writing, and it is quite thoughtful and advanced. It is not only a gloss on his poetry, but it also helps explain why he chose the unorthodox subjects for fiction that he did, since Poe believed that the goal of literature was not to mirror reality but instead to pursue Beauty in its highest and widest sense. As Poe put it, "A poem, in my opinion, is opposed to a work of science by having for its *immediate* object, pleasure, not truth" (17), a statement that also shows how deeply he was indebted to the English romantic poets like Wordsworth, Shelley, and especially Coleridge, since Poe's comment was purloined almost without change from Coleridge's own aesthetic manifesto, the *Biographia Literaria*.

As much as he was indebted to the romantics, however, with their hostilities toward empiricism and their sympathies for revolution, Poe would also demonstrate a keen emphasis on craft, on method over muse and on form as much as on content. In this sense he more closely resembles not the romantics but their eighteenth-century predecessors, like Pope and

Young. In later poems Poe would become renowned for his deliberate efforts to create certain effects by the careful combining of sounds and images. To his detractors, very often this purpose overwhelmed all others, leaving his poetry rich in melody but poor in ideas. (Poe felt that music came closest to expressing "supernal beauty" and even defined poetry as "The Rhythmical Creation of Beauty" [78].) For this reason, Ralph Waldo Emerson is reputed to have derisively referred to Poe as "the jingle man."

Many of the verses in *Poems . . . Second Edition*, especially "Evening Star," the famous "To Helen," "The Valley of Death," "Irene," and "The Doomed City," reveal Poe's intense preoccupation with death, dying, and the afterlife. A reason is that his entire life history had been dominated by loss, and he used the therapy of writing to express his bereavement and to console himself through remembrance.

Kenneth Silverman's psychoanalytically oriented biography of Poe emphasizes the point that children who lose their parents at a young age are unable to go through the normal, adult process of grieving and then gradually coming to terms with their loss, eventually distancing themselves from the death and moving on with their own lives. Childhood places limitations on one's ability to grieve, so children tend to attach themselves more permanently to the memory of the dead mother or father and to magnify that parent's presence in their own lives, both before the parent's death and after. Sometimes, as in Poe's case, even in adulthood they can paradoxically accept that the loved one is dead but still retain the belief that the person has somehow survived the process of dying. The finality of death is denied, as it is in so many of Poe's macabre stories, many of which concern ways of arresting, forestalling, and/or cheating death. The most bizarre of them concern life-in-death: that is, the desire simultaneously to experience the process of dying and still not die.

Women are almost the sole focus of these poems, and of many of his stories—pure beauties like Jane Stanard of "To Helen." As much as the speaker of these poems is weary of his journeying and wants to return *home* (as Edgar wished he could return to the bosom of Eliza or, barring that, at least to Fanny Allan and Richmond), the wanderer is also forever melancholy, musing on the Hellenic beauty of the women he has lost and thus on the nature of death itself. These two preoccupations—beautiful women and death—were the cornerstone of Poe's works. In his 1846 essay on writing, "The Philosophy of Composition," Poe summarized his aesthetic goals by explaining that the "most poetical" of all possible subjects was "the death of a beautiful woman" (19).

Another reason Poe was obsessed with death comes from the culture in which he was raised. In Victorian America, death was an object of fascination, contemplation, and even pleasure. It became something of a cult, creating a cottage industry of mourning art (samplers, vases, jewelry), transforming the experience of dying from a private to a public event (death diaries, family chronicles, the reading of wills), making the funeral into an elaborate aesthetic spectacle, and paving the way for rural cemeteries that provided picturesque places of final repose. (Graveyard poetry was among the most prolific verse forms of the nineteenth century.) High mortality rates, especially child mortality rates, accounted for this rise and encouraged the growth of more affectionate relationships, which in turn made possible an unusual, even fetishistic, attachment to the dead body. Corpses would lie in state on the deathbed in the home for a period of many days, and mementos of the dead body proliferated—death masks, portraits "in death," and locks of hair woven into floral wreaths all reflected this preoccupation. All of this indicated a disinclination to part with the physical remains of the lost loved one and an interest in sustaining relationships beyond the grave. Death was not permanent; it was merely not corporeal. In Poe's "The Raven," the bird of ill omen futilely attempts to convince the bereaved young man that his lover will "nevermore" return to him. And much of Poe's later writing is driven by the question of whether or not the dead remain dead.

The poems in Poe's early volumes represent a remarkable achievement for a young man like Poe. By the time he was twenty-two, he had produced three volumes of poetry, much the exception in American literature of that time. Only William Cullen Bryant outdid him. The two other most famous poets of the age did not even come close to this accomplishment. Henry Wadsworth Longfellow, two years Poe's senior, did not publish his first poetry collection, *Voices of the Night*, until 1839. Emerson published none at all until 1847.

Ironically, at his death in 1849 Poe was hardly classed as a major voice in American poetry, unlike his peers, who presided over unveilings of statues, gave commencement addresses, and had their portraits hung in schoolrooms. In 1831, however, Poe had no inkling that a future of poverty, the lack of a stable home, and the losses of those who loved him were lying indifferently in wait. He had had a modestly good critical reception for his poetry, and new worlds were waiting for the literary wanderer to explore. With a shaky, adolescent-like confidence that tried to defy John Allan's dominion over him, Poe took himself next to Baltimore, where he fervently hoped that his real father's family would welcome him.

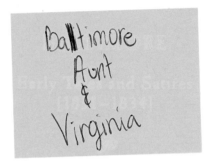

CHAPTER 3

P oe arrived in Baltimore in the spring of 1831 to find a city that prided
itself on its energy and industriousness, its forward-looking vision,
and its cleanliness and order. Small but comfortable brick row houses
lined the well-kept streets. Parks were built around circles and squares
with marble fountains and cisterns—a suggestion to Poe, perhaps, of
freshness, and of hopes to be fulfilled.

Poe's relations, the Clemm family, lived at Mechanics Row, Wilks
Street, in what is now Eastern Avenue. The house was almost unreal in its
tininess—like a doll's house—and the Clemms occupied only the top
floor. Poe must have been keenly aware of the change in station it represented for him, for the entire Wilks Street cottage would have fit easily into
one of the corners of Moldavia. The family included Poe's aunt, Maria
Clemm, recently a widow; her mother (Poe's grandmother), Mrs. David
Poe, Sr., also widowed; Maria's two children, Virginia, aged nine, and
Henry, Jr., aged thirteen; and Poe's brother, William Henry Leonard Poe.

Reuniting with his blood brother after so many years apart made Poe very
happy. Living with Henry—immediate family—gave Poe a sense of stability, of an anchor sunk into calm seas. Henry and Poe had much in common,
especially in their dreamy melancholia and dark romantic temperaments.
Both fancied themselves poets, and, sensing some psychic bond, during
their long separation they had tried to stay in touch. Even as a six-year-old
child in Baltimore, Henry was said to have spoken frequently of his brother

and expressed a strong desire to see him. Henry *had* visited Rosalie and Edgar in Richmond on at least one occasion, just before Edgar left home for the University of Virginia, but this was apparently the only time.

During his brief pass through Baltimore two years earlier, Poe had looked up to his brother, but he found Henry in as bad or worse shape than he, describing him plainly to John Allan in a letter of August 1829 as "entirely given up to drink & unable to help himself, much less me." Yet Henry was beautiful—slender, wan in a dreamy, expressive way, with dark eyes and a "singular" profile. Raised among the Baltimore Clemms, Henry had made several voyages to the Mediterranean, the Near East, and possibly also to Russia, as well as to the West Indies. He later romanticized his adventures, writing them up in a prose sketch entitled "The Pirate"; he also produced about twenty other stories and sketches in local newspapers and magazines. His poetry, like his brother's, was rooted in the early loss of Eliza. And like Edgar, Henry kept a lock of her hair as a remembrance. Poe clearly admired his adventurous older brother and may even have fashioned some of the romanticized fictions about his own life after Henry's. Their bond as orphaned brothers may also have manifested itself in a symbiotic way: Henry named the hero in one of his tales "Edgar Leonard," symbolically combining their two names.

Henry worked for a time in a Baltimore law office, but, as Edgar would turn out to be, he was easily susceptible to the effects of drink. Once alcoholism had gripped him, his decline was swift, and sadly, the two brothers' reunion lasted only six months. Henry died, apparently of disease brought on by alcoholism, on 1 August 1831, at age twenty-four.

Maria Clemm had been very fond of Henry, and she mourned his loss deeply. Henry had been the titular head of the family before Edgar's arrival, and she had depended on him heavily. After Henry's death, Maria took a larger role in the management of the family, in effect presiding over the Wilks Street house, and Edgar replaced Henry as the main object of her attentions. Maria in effect became Poe's surrogate mother (she was about three years younger than the age Eliza would have been had she lived), and she would turn out to have a stronger effect on him than the delicate young beauties like Fanny Allan and Jane Stanard who had fulfilled that role earlier in his life.

Physically, "Muddy," as Poe came to call her, was the opposite of Poe's earlier "mothers": she was heavyset and mannish-looking, with large eyebrows, a jowly face, and dark, somewhat mournful eyes that seemed automatically to importune whomever she fixed her gaze on to relieve her misery and give her money, for Muddy was indescribably poor. Having become accustomed to a life of privation, Muddy did not mind charity and regularly asked others for handouts. She never demurred in writing to distant relations and one-time brief acquaintances asking for financial help. She often presumed on imagined blood ties or friendships to try to get a loan, or even simple charity—a habit that Poe would pick up from her and rely on for the rest of his life. For example, around this time she wrote one Thomas Kell, an acquaintance of her late husband, that "for [Virginia's and Edgar's] sakes as well as for my own I venture to solicit a little assistance at your hands." She explained that ill health had prevented her from working for some time and that this had placed her and her children in a state where they were "enduring every privation. Under these circumstances," she continued, "I feel a hope that you will be inclined to give me some little aid. I do not ask for any material assistance, but the merest trifle to relieve my most immediate distress." A diplomatic and judiciously phrased plea, perhaps, but in her worst moments, Muddy could be a leech. The entire Clemm family, in fact, had about it the resigned, fatalistic aura of perennial poor relations.

Yet Muddy was also kindly and energetic, a fastidious housekeeper who kept the wax-neat rooms on Wilks Street as spotless as the deck of a navy clipper. She was also a worrisome, somewhat overprotective mother for Poe. She believed in Poe's talent, and upon his death she became one of his staunchest defenders against the slurs and other accusations of low morality that were flung against his reputation by Griswold and others. In the years to come, she would make great sacrifices on his behalf, assisting his career in whatever way she thought would help. She relieved him of all domestic responsibilities so that he could concentrate on his writing. She also conveyed messages back and forth between Poe and his editors, a servant to what she believed was Poe's genius. The Irish novelist Mayne Reid described her as "the ever-vigilant guardian of the house, watching it against the silent but continuous sap of necessity, that appeared every day to be approaching closer and nearer. . . . she was also the messenger to the market . . . bringing back, not 'the delicacies of the season,' but only such commodities as were called for by the dire exigencies of hunger."

Despite the appearance of the tidy rooms in the Clemm house, the living conditions in Baltimore that summer were stressful, especially as a cholera epidemic swept through the city, instilling fear of contagion and inviting death in a painful, gruesome form. Moreover, there was usually not enough money in the house to feed everyone. Maria undertook a serious campaign of letter-writing to prevail on friends for charity. And Poe, without a literary name to trade on yet, scoured the city looking for any kind of work imaginable. He applied for positions as an editorial assistant on a local newspaper and as a teacher in the city schools, and may even have worked for a time as a laborer in a kiln.

The family's misery forced Poe, again with great reluctance, to throw himself on John Allan's mercy, and again to no avail. In November Poe found himself arrested and put in the city jail as an insolvent debtor. His brother, Henry, had died owing some eighty dollars—a considerable sum at the time—to various tradesmen and creditors. The debt accrued to Poe as the de facto head of the household. Since Poe was unable to get a response from his foster father, Muddy wrote Allan on her nephew's behalf: "I feel deeply interested in him," she confided, "for he has been extremely kind to me as far as his opportunies would permit." Sometime in early December, Allan relented and wrote a friend, one John Walsh, directing him to buy Poe's way out of jail with twenty dollars he had sent. But the letter was apparently not posted until the twelfth of January of the following year. Poe languished in his cell for about five weeks—whether this was due to some spiteful, deliberate delay on Allan's part or just a clumsy miscommunication is not known. But of course it further nursed Poe's grievances against his foster father and pushed further away the possibility of a reconciliation.

In the early spring of 1832, Maria began to earn a little money by dressmaking, so the Clemms moved to somewhat better lodgings at No. 3

Amity Street. Most of the details of Poe's personal life at this time have been lost to view, but we do know that, thwarted in looking for work and harboring resentment against John Allan, Poe would, like most young men, frequently go out at night to carouse and drink. For this Muddy reprimanded him severely and worked to exert some positive influence on him, trying to keep him to the straight and narrow path.

Throughout Poe's life, people who knew him would have shifting and contrasting views of his relationship with the bottle. Few of them described what today would be called a drunkard, and some of them even stated categorically that Poe was rarely, if ever, inebriated. Lambert Wilmer, a local journalist and hack whom Poe befriended, left behind the most strident statement on the matter, one that defended Poe against the charge that he was a drunk. "During an intimate acquaintance with him," Wilmer wrote, "which lasted for more than twelve years, I never saw him intoxicated in a single instance." On one occasion, Wilmer conceded, he remembered seeing Poe with a "decanter of Jamaica spirits, in conformity with a practice which was very common in those days," but, Wilmer said, this was "the only time that ever I saw him drink ardent spirits." Wilmer's statement notwithstanding, Poe did drink, but most early recollections of him are of a moderate drinker—of someone who was not a wastrel, but of someone who often gave in to weakness, and someone who, with a genetic predisposition to drinking and a low tolerance for alcohol, would quickly become drunk.

Poe was also voluble and outgoing. Wilmer thought Poe "fluent, but not eloquent . . . an amiable colloquist"; in personal appearance Poe was "delicate," "neat," and even "effeminate," but not "sickly or ghastly." Other acquaintances recalled Poe's essential good looks, athletic build, and courtly manner. John H. B. Latrobe, an author and editor in Baltimore, described Poe as someone who "carried himself erect and well, as one who had been trained to it," yet he also discerned a theatrical flair, got up in spite of Poe's obvious poverty: "He was dressed in black, and his frock-coat was buttoned to the throat, where it met the black stock, then almost universally worn. Not a particle of white was visible. Coat, hat, boots, and gloves had very evidently seen their best days, but so far as mending and brushing go, everything had been done apparently, to make them present-able." Latrobe also sensed something elevated in Poe: "there was [a qual-ity] about this man that prevented one from criticizing his garments, and the details I have mentioned were only recalled afterwards," he noted.

Edgar also had the odd dalliance or two with young women of the city. One was with a seventeen-year-old named Mary Starr. Edgar was said to have sent her notes every evening, using his cousin Virginia as messenger, and then later appearing in person to sit with her on the front porch. Mary's brother, however, severely disapproved of Edgar as a suitor, with no steady work to support him and no career prospects to speak of. The relationship seemed never to have gotten off to the right start, anyway, and they fre-quently quarreled. One night Poe did not show up at her house, as expected, until nearly ten o'clock. He had been drinking, and after a time they began to argue. Mary ran back into the house through an alleyway and up the stairs. Edgar screamed after her to come back down, and when her mother appeared and interposed herself between Edgar and the stairwell, Poe apparently threatened to go after the young lady himself. But Mary's mother blocked the way and ordered him from the house, never to return.

Poe also had desultorily courted one of his cousins, Elizabeth Herring, addressing playful acrostics to her and penning love lyrics, too, but this relationship never really got started, once again because of her family's vehement objections to Edgar's character and circumstances. Perhaps this was why Poe formed a closer than usual attachment to his young cousin Virginia. Plump, cherubic, and rosy-cheeked, Virginia shared with the other Poe "women" an air of faint unreality, like a spectral presence from some benevolent otherworld of pixies, fairies, and angels. She was described as having dark brown hair and violet eyes, and—like Eliza—as being slight and petite, almost like a doll, although by most reports, Virginia looked older than her age.

Poe took an interest in Virginia's advancement (perhaps even recog-nizing the irony in her name being the name of his adopted southern homeland), tutoring her in languages and encouraging her interests in music. Of all the things Poe wanted for Virginia, as a father wants for a child, he wanted her to learn to sing, as his mother had once sung so beautifully. His initial relationship with his cousin seems clearly to have been that of teacher and student. He wanted to show her the path to an educated, cultured life, which was very much alive around them in Baltimore. Only poverty prevented him from taking her to the large theatre and concert hall and to hearing lectures by such famous native-son architects as Benjamin Henry Latrobe, painters like Rembrandt Peale, and writers like John Pendleton Kennedy. It is likely that Poe started to fall in love with Virginia, despite her tender age, and it is possible that they may even have married at this time. Most likely his attraction was grounded in the need for family, rather than in romantic or erotic love. He did, after all, call her "Sissy," in counterpoint to Maria's "Muddy" and perhaps in a manner of emotional compensation for the loss of his brother, Henry.

Perhaps it was Henry's example also that motivated Poe, upon first arriving in the city one year earlier, to call upon various editors and publishers and ask for literary work. He seems to have given this great effort and, as Maria had taught him, he was not reluctant to mention his ties to family members whose name might give him some credit in the city. In fact, another cousin, Neilson Poe, was a local journalist, and he visited the Clemm household frequently. Poe asked at least one editor, William Gwynn of the *Baltimore Gazette and Daily Advertiser*, if he might employ him in some capacity on Neilson's recommendation. Poe's volume of poems had been noticed by several New York critics, who praised them as "fraught with the treasure of thought and fancy," despite what to them were some absurdities and "obscurities" that they thought should have been "expunged" before publication. But these favorable comments seem to have carried no weight among Baltimore editors.

That spring of 1831, the Philadelphia *Saturday Courier* had announced a short story contest "in promotion of the Cause of LITERATURE" with a prize of one hundred dollars for the winning entry. Poe entered the contest a few months later. The prize went to a now-obscure local author, Delia S. Bacon, for a piece called "Love's Martyr." But the stories Poe had submitted impressed the editors, and five of them were published in the paper, beginning in January 1832 with a dramatic narrative, "Metzengerstein."

This tale employed what would become a compelling theme for Poe, ostracized by John Allan: aristocratic family members at war with themselves.

Characteristic of Poe's later work, the story, a precursor in many ways to the famous "The Fall of the House of Usher," has strong European overtones (it was originally subtitled "A Tale in Imitation of the German") and an indistinct but familiar setting that makes it feel faintly medieval. Other elements that would become trademarks for Poe are also present: a capacious house or castle that symbolizes the human body, the theme of revenge, and the overpowering presence of evil, which pushes the protagonist into self-destruction.

In the story, Baron Metzengerstein's parents have died, leaving him (like Poe) an orphan at a young age. He descends into depravity (like a later Poe alter ego, William Wilson) and makes an enemy of his neighbor, the Hungarian Count Berlifitzing, setting fire to his stable and killing the count (perhaps Poe is imaginatively recalling the Richmond Theatre fire of December 1811, which occurred three weeks after the death of Eliza Poe). However, the count's soul enters the body of his prize horse, which Metzengerstein uses as his own mount to get away from the fire. At the end of the story the enraged horse is seen carrying its rider off into oblivion.

The most Poe-esque element of this early story is its use of metempsychosis, the idea that the human soul may be transferred to an animal and that animals are thus trapped souls. This element of the story is in line with the tradition of the fable or French *fabliau*, in which an animal is given human qualities and serves as a moral counterbalance to the depraved actions of the human character. (In "The Rocking Horse Winner," a famous story reversing this motif, D. H. Lawrence animated the nursery rocking horse of a child who resorts to racetrack gambling to win his family's love.) Most important, the story inaugurates a long line of Poe tales in which the author fantasizes about ways of surviving death, here through the ancient idea of the transmigration of the soul.

The remaining four tales are seriocomic ones that treat related themes. For example, in "Loss of Breath," Poe introduces the paradox of the living dead. In the story, a criminal is tortured and hanged (anticipating later confessional tales like "William Wilson" and "The Cask of

38

Amontillado"). However, the gallows are ineffective; he still lives but is taken for dead because he cannot speak. If the loss of breath is a metonym for the loss of life, then Poe gives us a fantasy world, again, in which death can be reversed. Without speech or language, Poe is saying, we are effectively dead, a theme picked up in another short sketch from this period, "Silence—A Fable." Alternatively, the power of words is a strong enough force actually to prevent or at least forestall death.

This latter idea is the focus of Poe's most artful early story, "MS. Found in a Bottle." This tale of sensationalism and adventure at sea anticipates many later Poe stories and is deeply indebted to a favorite novel from Poe's childhood, Defoe's *Robinson Crusoe*, and even more so to Coleridge's famous "The Rime of the Ancient Mariner." In the tradition of the legends of the Wandering Jew (or the Flying Dutchman), the hero is (again like Poe) a young man (short, like Poe, at five feet eight inches tall) who has been estranged from his family. He survives a shipwreck and is picked up at sea by a lumbering, ancient vessel manned by an equally aged crew who do not acknowledge his existence. As the ship ventures farther south, it disappears down a vortex at the tip of Antarctica. The narrator relates his unearthly experiences in fragmented, diaristic entries that continue up to the moment of his presumed extinction.

Poe uses the voyage metaphor to great effect, for he invests it with an added significance not found in traditional sea stories that employ the journey as a symbol of self-discovery, like Joseph Conrad's *Heart of Darkness*. Poe adds to the voyage the dramatic tension of writing as a way both of staving off death and discovering what it's like—Poe's abiding obsession. The longer the author/narrator writes, the longer we as readers will get a story. Yet paradoxically, the act of writing is to get the narrator to the point of discovery, to reach the end of the story, and thus to die. The bottle may be thought of like the ship, as a vessel or a body, within which is the knowledge, the secret of the writer's imagination—the manuscript. Perhaps for Poe, language transcends ordinary existence and makes possible immaterial states of being.

Poe's other early efforts include "The Duke de l'Omelette," "The Bargain Lost," and "A Tale of Jerusalem." Later Poe planned to pull together these tales and eleven others and call them "The Tales of the Folio Club." He had written a brief narrative with which to frame them in which the tales were concocted by various members of a coterie of dilettantish gentleman authors with such comic names as Mr. Convolvulus Gondola, "a young man who had travelled a good deal," Mr. Horribile Dictu, and Mr. Blackwood Blackwood, "who had written certain articles for foreign magazines" (132–33). In the framing narrative (and also in the brief story "Lionizing," although not in quite so direct a way), Poe was constructing a satiric picture of the amateurish literary world that then existed in the new republic. At the time the pursuit of writing was hardly classed as a profession. Instead, it was generally thought of as a gentleman's avocation, something to do in one's spare time. To that end, numerous literary societies sprang up in cities like Baltimore, Philadelphia, and New York—Fenimore Cooper's Bread and Cheese Club, Alexander Hammond's Tuesday Club, and Baltimore-based ones like the Delphians, who briefly published their own literary magazine, *The Portico*. To Poe, who would soon embark on an earnest campaign as a book reviewer to elevate the standards of American art, these very societies, with their shaggy, amateurish efforts, were the ones impeding the creation of a truly vital and sophisticated national literature. The frame tale is eerily prophetic of the unenviable situation Poe would soon find himself mired in—having laid waste to such cliques in his writings, he would be blackballed by them when he went to New York and Philadelphia in search of literary work.

Yet as the name of one of the ersatz gentlemen indicates, Poe was also beginning to adopt the conventions of stories from the influential British literary journals, like *Blackwood's Edinburgh Magazine*: as one writer describes it, "the creation of a literary personality, the 'self-consciously learned pose,' the exploitation of the hoax, and the burlesque and horror tale as national fictional modes." Grotesque stories of life after death, evisceration, deathbed confessions, and weird narratives of extrasensory or out-of-body experiences were all the rage in such magazines, which Poe had studied carefully. He wrote to his future employer, Thomas Willis White, that successful magazine fiction consisted of "the ludicrous heightened into the grotesque: the fearful coloured into the horrible: the witty exaggerated into the burlesque: the singular wrought out into the strange and mystical." Poe admitted that some might take such work as being in bad taste. Yet (once again, presciently), he noted that "whether the articles of which I speak are, or are not in bad taste is little to the purpose. To be appreciated you must be *read*, and these things are invariably sought after with avidity." Poe added, "To be sure originality is an essential in these things—great attention must be paid to style, and much labour spent in their composition, or they will degenerate into the tugid [*sic*] or the absurd." This was one of the many paradoxes in Poe's personality: he stressed originality in art but could be imitative or derivative in his own writings.

Theories such as these would become the cornerstone of Poe's aesthetic, but for now, they did not really matter. Poe was writing solely to generate enough money to keep the wolf from the door, and even though these tales were reprinted in places like the *Minerva* of Baltimore and the *Literary Gazette* of Albany, New York, it's unlikely that he was paid for them. For now, fame seemed very far beyond his grasp.

In the summer of 1833, Poe submitted "MS. Found in a Bottle" to another contest, this one sponsored by the Baltimore *Saturday Visiter*, and this time he won—first place for fiction, and a prize of fifty dollars, and second place for a poem, "The Coliseum." But even this local success, in what would become a pattern in Poe's career, was not without a bizarre twist that cast a pall on the prize, for Poe had learned that John Hill Hewitt, the editor of the *Visiter*, had submitted his own poem, under a pseudonym, and that it was this poem that had won first place.

According to Hewitt, Poe ran into him on the streets one day and called out:

> *"You have used underhanded means, sir, to obtain that prize over me."*
> *"I deny it, sir,"* was my reply.
> *"Then why did you keep back your real name?"*
> *"I had my reasons, and you have no right to question me."*
> *"But you tampered with the committee, sir."*

"The committee are gentlemen above being tampered with, sir. . . ."

"I agree that the committee are gentlemen," replied he, his dark eyes flashing with anger, "but I cannot place you in that category."

My blood mounted up to fever heat in a moment, and with my usual impulsiveness, I dealt him a blow which staggered him, for I was physically his superior.

Like his father, David, Poe could resort to fisticuffs when he was sufficiently riled, and one of the injustices that angered Poe the most was that of other writers whose high reputations Poe felt were undeserved—as seen in his "Folio Club" sketches, which he described in part as a "burlesque upon criticism." Poe would many times have such run-ins with people more successful (and thus better-heeled) than he. Although Poe usually resorted to words rather than fists for his attacks, the outcome was usually the same: he was injured more by the unfavorable public image that the scene created than by his opponent.

Switching from crossing swords to crossing paths, Poe encountered a literary acquaintance of a different and more important sort when he met John Pendleton Kennedy, one of the judges of the *Visiter* contest. Kennedy had discerned something of value in Poe's writing. He made overtures to the author and became one of the few people with whom Poe had a long-lasting friendship, as well as one of the few writers to whom Poe gave unqualified praise. Poe may have discerned in Kennedy's background some common bonds. Kennedy was of Scottish descent, as John Allan was, and, although a Baltimore native, he had married a woman from Virginia. Unlike Poe, however, Kennedy was genial, tolerant, and good-looking—a man of means and the very model of success, according to the increasingly commercial standards of the young country. He had begun life as an attorney, but grew tired of his practice and gradually devoted himself more and more to writing. Under the pseudonym "Mark Littleton," he published two pastoral romances, *Swallow Barn* (1832) and *Horse-Shoe Robinson* (1835)—the former a series of sketches and the latter a novel, both dealing with life in Virginia before the Revolutionary War. Later, Kennedy ventured into politics. Under President Fillmore he was secretary of the navy, and he supported the Union cause during the Civil War. Kennedy's most important quality, however, may have been his generosity. After the war had ended, Kennedy favored "amnesty and forgiveness to the weak and foolish who have erred, charity for their faults and brotherly assistance to all who repent."

These qualities perhaps made him a soft touch for Poe, who, upon receiving Kennedy's invitation to supper, sent his regrets, pleading the lack of a decent set of clothes in which to be seen, then in the next sentence asking for a loan of twenty dollars to enable him to accept. Kennedy provided Poe with clothes, food, and even lent him the use of his horse for exercise. But the most important roles Kennedy played in Poe's life were as a sounding board for his ideas, a sympathetic listener to his frustrations, and eventually a father figure, something Poe desperately needed to validate his goals and aspirations and to quell his insecurities.

Kennedy also obtained for Poe what had so far eluded him: literary work. Kennedy wrote to a publisher friend, Henry C. Carey, to persuade him to issue an edition of Poe's tales. Carey saw no profit in the venture and declined. He did, however, suggest that Poe place some of the stories in the annuals, a good outlet for story and sketch writers of the time, and, again through Kennedy's intercession, at least one of Poe's pieces appeared in The Gift—a respectable publication that paid him fifteen dollars. Poe still thought of himself primarily as a poet; it was Kennedy who gave Poe the idea to turn his talents to more lucrative prose pieces. Poe had been working desultorily on a play called Politian, set in ancient Rome but based on a recent sensationalistic murder and trial that had taken place in rural Kentucky—the so-called "Beachamp Tragedy" (later the subject of novels by William Gilmore Simms and Robert Penn Warren). Kennedy advised Poe to put aside such lofty, unsaleable projects, at least for the moment, and to get "drudging upon whatever may make money."

To that end, in May 1834 Kennedy recommended Poe to another literary friend, Thomas W. White of Richmond, who had recently founded a new magazine, the Southern Literary Messenger. Kennedy described Poe to White as "a highly imaginative fellow," "very poor," but talented—someone so gifted that he could "write something for every number of your magazine." He told White that he "might find it to your advantage to give him . . . permanent employ." Poe sent White some stories, among them the macabre marriage tale "Berenice"; White had some misgivings, but he accepted it nonetheless and, with Kennedy's encouragement, went on to print a tale by Poe each successive month in his new magazine and also send him books for review.

The relationship between Poe and Kennedy became close. Kennedy told a friend that he had found Poe "in a state of starvation" and that he had "brought him up from the very verge of despair." Poe clearly looked to Kennedy as one would to a father, and a later grateful comment from Poe to his mentor—"I know that without your timely aid I should have sunk under my trials"—was exactly the type of statement that Poe had repeatedly made to John Allan, in the hope that Allan would respond approvingly and help him, but of course he had not.

Poe needed a surrogate father, particularly now, for his relationship with Allan had dipped even below the line of cordial indifference. There was now absolutely nothing between them. Several times in Baltimore Poe had written Allan in desperation, apparently willing to do anything to regain Allan's favor. Gone was Poe's rhetoric of intellectual superiority and in its place had arisen a plain language of humility, conciliation, and regret. In April 1833 he had sworn to Allan that he had not been "idle—nor addicted to any vice," perhaps feeling guilty over his past recklessness. "For God's sake pity me, and save me from destruction," he wrote. And later: "When I look back upon the past and think of every thing—of how much you tried to do for me—of your forbearance and your generosity, in spite of the most flagrant ingratitude on my part, I can not help thinking myself the greatest fool im [sic] existence,—I am ready to curse the day when I was born." Receiving no reply, Poe then launched into a series of letters that invoke fate and a divine presence: "if you refuse God only knows what I shall do"; "I beg and intreat you in the name of God to send me succour"; and "for the sake of Christ do not let me perish for a sum of money which you would never miss"—this last plea pathetically true. In two of these letters, Poe uses the salutation "Dear Pa," the only recorded instances of this in his long and painful correspondence with John Allan.

Allan rebuffed him. The man who never wanted a foster son left behind a vehement assessment of his charge on the reverse side of one of Poe's entreating letters: "Apl 12, 1833 it is now upwards of 2 years since I received the above precious relict of the Blackest heart & deepst ingratitude alike destitute of honour & principle every day of his life has only served to confirm his debased nature—Suffice it to say that my only regret is in Pity for his failings—his Talents are of an order that can never prove a comfort to their possessor."

After a long illness Allan died on 27 March 1834 and was buried, along with Fanny and Jane Stanard, in Shockoe Hill Cemetery. Poe had been to Richmond to visit him at least once, in June 1832, and possibly another time before that. Not gaining an audience, he tried again in February 1834 and succeeded, as well as meeting Allan's new wife, Louise.

But Poe received no inheritance. After his first wife's death, Allan had produced other heirs to his vast fortune. Three months after Fanny had passed away, Allan had remarried and fathered three children by his second wife. He also had illegitimate twins by his mistress in July 1830. In 1832 and again the following year, while Poe was scrambling to find enough work to care for the Clemm family, Allan revised his will and added a codicil. All of his children, legitimate and illegitimate, were mentioned in the will, but Poe was ignored.

Thomas White had offered Poe steady employment on the *Messenger*, and so, ironically, in August 1835, Poe returned to Richmond to begin a long run of producing stories, book reviews, and other pieces. This would keep him busy, and Muddy's and Virginia's presence would help soothe him, but his emotional balance would also be hit hard by living in the very place from which John Allan had sent him packing.

CHAPTER 4

RETURN TO RICHMOND

Marriage, the *Southern Literary Messenger*, and
The Narrative of Arthur Gordon Pym
[1835–1837]

It was a propitious moment to become associated with a fledgling magazine in the United States, for the whole tendency of the age, as Poe would later note, was "Magazine-ward." The magazine was a relatively new medium in America—created in part by the rapid growth of printing technology and the spread of public education—and was fast approaching its peak, from about a hundred or so periodicals in 1825 to some six hundred by 1850. In New York alone in 1849, the year of Poe's death, there were more than fifty periodicals, with some half million readers. The *Southern Literary Messenger* was the first of four magazines that Poe would work for. Each stint would be short-lived—no more than two years or so—but Poe would leave each magazine, and each of its owners, richer than before he came. Poe, for his part, would remain poor.

The *Messenger*, like most American magazines of the day, was quite different from the rather stuffy "journals" of England and the continent. British periodicals like *Blackwood's Edinburgh Magazine* and the *London Quarterly Review* usually published essays on specialized topics for highly literate, well-educated audiences. American magazines offered readers something more brisk and variegated. Readers wanted short tales and brief articles that could be digested, for example, on a train trip or while waiting for the ferry. It was the form of the magazine, with its audience desiring something that could be read in one sitting, that in part moved

Poe to formulate his famous theory of the tale. Although Poe outwardly criticized "the rush of the age," dealing out "the condensed [and] the readily diffused" he partly had these "limitations" in mind in formulating his aesthetic. But Poe also enhanced the artistic possibilities of the "true Magazine spirit" (1414–15). In fact, the great project of his life would be to publish his own magazine and use it to elevate the standards for American art.

When Poe arrived in Richmond in August 1835, White took him on in a part-time, temporary capacity. The periodical had had two editors since its founding the previous spring; the current one, Edward V. Sparhawk, a poet and journalist from Maine, left in late November 1835. Poe then came on board full time. He had no official title (the December 1835 issue refers to him only as "a gentleman of distinguished literary talents" assisting the proprietor), but in most respects he was the editor in chief, advising White on the merit of articles submitted for publication, editing copy and checking proof, and keeping tabs on the competition.

Born in Williamsburg just after the Revolution, White, of English ancestry, was the son of a tailor. At age eleven he was apprenticed to the publishers of the *Virginia Federalist*, and before he had reached age twenty he had secured a position as compositor for a Norfolk newspaper. He later established a successful printing business of his own in Richmond, publishing among other things the "Confessions" of Nat Turner, the slave who led the Southhampton Insurrection in tidewater Virginia in 1831. White also encouraged authorship by printing several books by local writers. Some of them, like James Ewell Heath, he pressed into service as contributors to the *Messenger* when he commenced its publication. White was typical of most of the magazine editors Poe encountered in his career—having started out as a printer, he had no training in writing, editing, or marketing and advertising. Poe seems to have had an instinctive feel for these matters, for by the time he left White's employ, in early 1837, the circulation of the magazine had quadrupled, making it well known throughout the United States.

Poe's editorial duties limited his time for imaginative writing, but between 1835 and 1836 he published seven of the original "Tales of the

Folio Club" in the *Messenger* as well as three extraordinary new tales. "The Unparalleled Adventure of One Hans Pfaall" is among the earliest examples of what today we think of as science fiction. The French novelist and utopian thinker Jules Verne (1828–1905) is usually considered the father of this genre, but Poe's experimental stories actually predated Verne's by thirty years or more. (In homage to Poe, Verne retold "Hans Pfaall" as *From the Earth to the Moon* [1865] and "The Balloon Hoax" as *Around the World in Eighty Days*; and he penned a "sequel" to *The Narrative of Arthur Gordon Pym*, entitled *The Sphinx of Ice*, taking up the story where Poe left off.) Poe's work also influenced other practitioners of the form, notably H. G. Wells, William Morris, and H. Rider Haggard.

Poe's story was probably inspired by two hot air balloon ascensions in Baltimore in 1833 and 1834 (the latter financed in part by the father of Poe's one-time sweetheart, Elizabeth Herring), although balloon ascents had been ongoing since their invention in France in 1783. Poe worked on the story for over two weeks, according to a detailed account that he gave to John Latrobe. The latter recalled Poe's complete imaginative immersion in the story, and his striving to make the fantastic seem believable:

> *[Poe] was engaged on a voyage to the moon, and at once went into a somewhat learned disquisition upon the laws of gravity, the height of the earth's atmosphere and the capacities of balloons, warming in his speech as he proceeded. Presently, speaking in the first person, he began the voyage . . . and leaving the earth, [he became] more and more animated, [as] he described his sensation, as he ascended higher and higher, until, at last, he reached the point in space where the moon's attraction overcame that of the earth, when there was a sudden bouleversement of the car and a great confusion among its tenants.*

Sparhawk puffed the story in the June *Messenger* as being of "irresistible interest"; however, the ambitious piece is actually rather weak. It takes as its premise a secret scheme by one Hans Pfaall, a mender of bellows in Rotterdam, who borrows money under false pretenses and constructs a helium-based contraption that he flies to the moon. Was Poe tempted to such flights of fantasy, in his desperation and his poverty?

48

Probably in part. This too accounts for the juvenile nature of much of the story, which does not once display the sophisticated narrative technique with which we associate Poe's mature work. Poe himself later admitted that the story was too unrealistic—"the chief interest," he conceded, had to "depend upon the reader's yielding his credence in some measure as to details of actual fact."

Poe had not yet found that delicate balance seen in his best work—treading the line between improbability and the delicate art of making something just believable enough to be accepted. And, as in some later works such as *The Narrative of Arthur Gordon Pym* and *The Journal of Julius Rodman*, in this story Poe's tone distractingly wavers between the realistic and the fantastic. "Hans Pfaall" is noteworthy, however, as the first instance of Poe's use of the imaginary voyage. This motif would become one of his most potent vehicles for analyzing human psychology and for delving into the issue of man's reaction to the unknown.

The other new stories, "Berenice" and "Morella," are more interesting. Both concern marriage between two people who are drawn to each other by an irresistible force that is unnatural and inexplicable. Both stories also inaugurate the trademark narrator of much of Poe's supernatural fiction. This person professes to be of aristocratic lineage, but has no concrete history that he can provide to the reader, often because he cannot remember much of his past. He is characteristically outcast or disinherited (as Poe thought of his own situation with John Allan). Just as the narrator cannot quite remember his origins and ancestry, so too can he not explain the actions he undertakes in the tale—they are presented only as manifestations of some aberrant psychological streak in him. Finally, the narrator deliberately remains at a distance in most personal relationships, to the point where he is a recluse, and—most significantly—he is obsessive and monomaniacal.

In "Berenice," the narrator and his cousin grow up together and eventually marry, yet their relationship apparently remains platonic. The ethereal beauties of such tales are much like the women in Poe's poetry— perhaps the southern idea of womanhood: "I had seen her," the narrator says, "not as the living and breathing Berenice, but as the Berenice of a dream—not as a being of the earth, earthy, but as the abstraction of such a being" (229). (The writer who is closest to Poe in this yearning for ethereal beauties is the Nicaraguan poet Ruben Dario [1867–1916], leader of the modernist movement there and author of a major article on Poe in 1893.) Cursed with monomania, the narrator realizes that he has lost all reason, and his disorder begins to force him to dwell on "physical changes" in Berenice (220). Their marriage is at the point of a rupture, and he weirdly begins to fixate (as with the description of the horse in "Metzengerstein") on her teeth, ascribing to them in his imagination a "sensitive and sentient power" (231). He murders her and later has no memory of doing so until a servant confronts him in a disheveled state, his garments "muddy and clotted with gore" and his hands "indented with the impress of human nails." In his study he finds an array of "instruments of dental surgery, intermingled with thirty-two small, white and ivory-looking substances" scattered about the floor (232–33).

"Morella," another tale of an unnatural union, is narrated by a similar type of character. This time, however, instead of a frail and youthful beauty, the object of the narrator's obsession is an older woman, someone who combines features of an intellectual mentor and a mother. The narrator has a childlike attachment to the older female, whose erudition holds him in awe. Once again, fate brings them to the altar, and destiny compels him to "adore" her (237). Marriage again reaches a breaking point, and the narrator begins to long for his wife's death. She informs him she is pregnant, and that she will live through her child. Morella dies upon giving birth, and the little girl grows up to look and act weirdly like her mother, for the narrator describes her as possessed of an intellect far advanced in years. He does not give the child a name until the moment of baptism. Then, for reasons which he cannot explain, he whispers the name "Morella." The child then says, "I am here," and dies.

Poe derived many features of such tales from Gothicism, the most popular fiction genre of the time and a staple of American, British, and Continental writing for more than half a century. The surface trappings of Gothic fiction—gloomy, claustrophobic interiors and decaying exteriors, reincarnated lovers, clairvoyants, premature burials and even putrid bodily decay—are found throughout much of Poe's work. But Poe did not merely appropriate Gothic properties. He enriched their textures, preserving the narrative drive of the genre while "embroidering the whole with philosophical speculation and lore that deepen the mood of dire awe, and with sense details that lend the improbable events a feeling of reality." Gothicism created a mood in a story that admitted the possibility of an alternate reality.

To find examples of Gothicicism Poe had to look no further than the British quarterly magazines. *Blackwood's Edinburgh Magazine* and the *London Quarterly Review* often published stories in a similar vein. Such tales originated among the German romantic writers, like Hoffman and Tieck; among mystic philosophers like Schlegel and Kant; and among the so-called "Sturm und Drang" (literally, storm and stress) writings, like Schiller's *Love and Intrigue* and Goethe's *The Sorrows of Young Werther*, which featured intense, hypersensitive characters, often obsessed by unrequited love, and often aliented from mainstream society. Poe seemed at times both to be modelling his fiction on such tales—using them as launching points for his own philosophical speculations about the nature of death—and at other times to be mocking or parodying these popular stories. Later, he satirized the American rage for *Blackwood's*-type writing in "How To Write a Blackwood's Article," in which an unknown author composes a botched story for Mr. Blackwood himself, using a formula that he gives her. There is no doubt, however, that Poe saw the potency of such a "formula" for attracting readers to magazines—the argument he used in response to Thomas White's objections over the unsavory subject matter of "Berenice." Poe told him that "the history of all Magazines shows plainly that those which have attained celebrity were indebted for it to articles *similar in nature—to Berenice.*"

Some elements of the tales, however, were also rooted in a tragic reality—that of women dying far too young, and of primitive medicine that could not accurately identify the state of death. Nineteenth-century science was sometimes unable to tell the difference between someone who was dead and someone who had instead lapsed into coma or catatonic shock resulting from injury or illness—undetectable by the crude and uneven medical examination procedure of the time. Thus there was a high frequency in Poe's life of actual instances of premature burials, which a sensation-mongering press churned up and made liberal use of in their stories. The fallibility of the diagnosis of death was one of Poe's recurrent themes. His stories are thus not so macabre when one considers them in this context.

In part, too, Poe was dramatizing nineteenth-century America's elaborate rituals of bereavement and memorialization of the dead. It was a culture that valued these rituals deeply, and ordinary people could be seized by bizarre behavior that was not unlike that of Poe's crazed characters: when the young wife of an acquaintance of Poe's died, for instance, the husband sat beside her dead body for more than twenty-four hours, caressing her face with his hand and stroking her hair. Many days after her burial, the husband had the casket opened and embraced the rotting corpse. Ralph Waldo Emerson's wife died before she was twenty; for over a year, Emerson walked to her grave each morning, regardless of weather. It was said that he also ordered her coffin opened and embraced the corpse.

The focus of such rituals centered more on the one left behind than the one taken in death. This theme of remembrance is crucial to understanding Poe and the series of tragic losses he suffered as a child and an adult. His characters' attachment to their lost loved ones (often physically, fetishistically) represents an unwillingness to accept the finality of death. Thus, figures appear in the tales who are revenants, reincarnations, and reiterations of figures in characters' earlier lives that have passed away. There is also the recurring paradox of the character making a strong effort to forget, an act which actually conceals the stronger need to remember. Poe's main fictional preoccupation is an insistent questioning of the finality of death. Is it the end? Does one lose one's identity in death? Death is usually treated as an illusion or a mistake, or, as in the case of "Morella," the beginning of another life.

A final preoccupation is with the essential oneness of two individuals or of ostensible opposites. In part this interest of Poe's explains the reanimation or reappearance of lost loved ones in distinct but similar corporeal form. It also gives us insight into Poe's life—a life of loss and thus of the perpetual, tenacious desire to reunite with the one whose passing is mourned. It paves the way philosophically for Poe's theories in *Eureka* and in later tales in which chaos results from people suppressing their natural impulses and seeking to join with one another, in variations on homosexual situations and hermaphroditic characters. Poe's characters often exist in a degenerate mental and physical state because they are denying the instinctive need to reintegrate the opposing forces of the human soul.

Surely something of the obsessive character of these fictional figures came from the demons that Poe felt possessed by in the interval between coming to Richmond to help White with the *Messenger* and the point where he established himself there permanently. Poe was wound tight by his emotions. The death of John Allan haunted him; poverty nagged at him; but it was mainly the heightened fear that he would again lose another family—Muddy and Virginia—that gnawed at his emotional core, like some demoniac creature from the damp turmoil of a nightmare. Poe's love for Virginia had intensified, quickly and almost unnaturally, during his months in Baltimore, and now that he had come to Richmond, he felt her palpable absence. Some posthumous recollections of Poe indicated that the two had actually been married when Poe briefly visited her and Muddy in Baltimore in the fall of 1835. This is not certain, but he may well have done so in an attempt to prevent losing her to a rival, his cousin Neilson, who apparently had designs on Virginia. Poe's emotional involvement with Muddy and Virginia was intense, as one can see in this letter he wrote Mrs. Clemm:

My dearest Aunty, I am blinded with tears while writing this letter—I have no wish to live another hour. Amid sorrow, and the deepest anxiety your letter reached [me]—and you well know how little I am able to bear up under the pressure of grief. My bitterest enemy would pity me could he now read my heart. My last my last my only hold on life is cruelly torn away—I have no desire to live and will not. But let my duty be done. I love, you know I love Virginia passionately devotedly. I cannot express in words the fervent devotion I feel towards my dear little cousin—my own darling. But what can [I] say? Oh think for me for I am incapable of thinking.

Poe's grandmother had died in July, leaving only a small estate. Although Poe desperately tried to find a way to claim parts of the inheritance (even recruiting John Pendleton Kennedy to act as his agent on such matters), they came to nothing. Mrs. Clemm, then, was concerned that they would have to find means of sustaining themselves. Neilson was a ready option. When Poe learned that Muddy had considered throwing him over, as it were, for Neilson, Poe immediately countered that White had "engaged to make my salary $60 a month, and we could live in comparative comfort & happiness—even the $4 a week I am now paying for board would support us all—but I shall have $15 a week & what need would we have of more?" Thus feeling that he had made a good financial case, Poe continued his argument by returning to his theme of emotional injury, telling Muddy:

> *The tone of your letter wounds me to the soul—Oh Aunty, aunty you loved me once—how can you be so cruel now? You speak of Virginia acquiring accomplishments, and entering into society—you speak in so worldly a tone. Are you sure she would be more happy. Do you think any one could love her more dearly than I? She will have far—very far better opportunities of entering into society here than with [Neilson]. Every one here receives me with open arms.*

"Every one here receives me with open arms": a not very reliable claim, since, after all, Poe had left Richmond a few years earlier under a cloud. Poe then added a postscript "for Virginia": "My love, my own sweetest Sissy, my darling little wifey, think well before you break the heart of your cousin. Eddy."

Poe was truly frightened, like a child who needs to know that there is someone who loves him and won't abandon him. These pleas for love and intimate attachment are essentially the same requests that Poe had made so many times of John Allan. Simply put, Poe needed unmitigated love and unqualified approval.

Another way to understand Poe's emotional state at this point is to note, as Julian Symons has, that throughout his life, he would be "endlessly susceptible" to women. He had had two brief dalliances in Baltimore, and in Richmond he had even cast an eye on Thomas White's young daughter, Eliza—aptly named. But for Poe, to be in love with a woman was to be, like the narrator of "Berenice," in love with the idea of a woman—an ideal—and for a woman to be ideal, she had to be as far as possible removed from reality. This would be Virginia—far too young to be a wife, or even to be aware enough to realize the depth of Poe's emotional involvement with her. Nonetheless, in October, Poe's crisis had passed, and Muddy and Virginia came to Richmond. Poe was temporarily content, and he worked hard at establishing a respectable, middle-class identity.

As in Poe's fiction, however, the reality was never quite real, never quite accurate. He married Virginia in a public religious ceremony on 16 May 1836, with Thomas White as a witness. White, who had a low opinion of Poe's morals to begin with, must have been struck, as most people were at the time, with Virginia's youth. Moreover, at the ceremony, the bride was stated to be "of the full age of twenty-one years," although in fact she was not quite fourteen. It was not illegal at that time in the United States for a girl to marry at age thirteen, but—as has been noted many times—the fact that her age was deliberately concealed suggests something of the extraordinary nature of Poe's attraction to her.

It is questionable whether Poe and Virginia ever had sexual relations. Some have said never (as if anyone could conclusively know); one reliable acquaintance claimed that Poe hinted to him that it did not happen for the first two years of their marriage. In "Eleonora," the narrator notes that he and his cousin and mother lived together innocently for fifteen years "before Love entered within our hearts" and became "physical passion" (470). Autobiographical elements in Poe's works depict marital relationships that are more mother and child or sister and brother than sensual—Poe's name for his wife, after all, was "Sissy." It is clear that Poe's priority with Virginia was to mentor her, to mold her character into the kind of woman he thought was ideal. In Richmond, as he had in Baltimore, Poe nurtured Virginia's intellectual abilities, continuing to tutor her in music and languages. He also wanted to protect her, to shield her from the emotional abuses and injustices that he had suffered under John Allan. Sexuality may not have been much on Poe's mind.

Edgar and Virginia must have made an odd pair when seen on the streets of Richmond, for there was not much to her, either in temperament or in physical presence. Poe, in contrast, cut a dramatic figure, with his thin and delicate lips, "effeminate" and charming demeanor, and somewhat cultivated but striking appearance of shabby gentility. Most arresting, however, was his dramatic forehead, which he emphasized in idealized self-portraits in fiction like "Mystification" (1837) and "The Fall of the House of Usher" (1839), drawing attention to his capacious frontal bone. Reviewing a book on phrenology (the pseudoscience that connected the contours of the skull with the powers of the brain) for the *Messenger*, Poe equated the prominence of the frontal bone with a superior intellect.

His neat appearance went hand in hand with his orderly domestic habits and likewise orderly working routines. According to one acquaintance, at home Poe's character "appeared in its most beautiful light. Playful, affectionate, witty, alternately docile and wayward as a petted child—for his young, gentle and idolized wife, and for all who came, he had even in the midst of his most harassing literary duties, a kind word, a pleasant smile, a graceful and courteous attention." Poe liked to write in the morning and then, in the afternoons, either go on rambles through the countryside or work in his flower garden, while Virginia studied and Muddy silently hovered in the background, cooking, cleaning, and knitting. In the evenings she would often sit silently while Poe poured out his writing to her, occasionally commenting but mostly remaining enigmatically quiet, brooding, and sympathizing with his erratic genius. Poe even wrote in an orderly hand: his penmanship was small and of italic shape, sometimes so neat that it looked set in type. He liked to write on half sheets of loose paper, then paste them together end to end and roll them up like a scroll. When asked to read from one of his manuscripts, he would let it fall to the floor, to flow open in a dramatic, poetic gesture.

Flaubert once famously declared that the writer should be "bourgeois" in his life so that he could be "mad" in his art. That description would fit Poe well at this time; he would create his tales of scarred psyches and brutalized imaginations in the evenings, after his "regular" writing job of producing editorials and reviews for the *Messenger* was completed. Yet most of what Poe was writing was criticism rather than fiction, for it was in Richmond that Poe began his career as a reviewer of books.

This was how Poe earned his living—as a workaday journalist and professional critic, not as a poet or a writer of horror stories. Poe wrote more literary criticism than anything else: from 1835, when he became formally associated with the *Messenger*, until his death in 1849, when he was contributing to several magazines in the Northeast, Poe wrote close to one thousand essays, reviews, articles, columns, and critical notices. Some were no longer than a paragraph or two, some ran to as many as a half-dozen pages, but taken as a whole, they constitute, as Edmund Wilson once said, "the most remarkable body of criticism ever produced in the United States." Yet sadly, as W. H. Auden remarked, much of Poe's best criticism will never be read because it lies buried in reviews of totally uninteresting authors. Novels by Robert Montgomery Bird, Baron de la Motte Foque, Bulwer-Lytton, Morris Matson, Charles Dickens, and Washington Irving—all were one and the same for Poe, who reviewed them each with meticulousness and zeal, as he did nonfiction volumes on such topics as the life of Cardinal Richelieu and the history of the Episcopal Church in Virginia.

What did Poe accomplish with his critical notices? A great deal. Poe set a national standard for book reviewing. He displayed an intolerance for "puffing" second-rate American books simply because they were American. He developed inchoate ideas about aesthetics that he would later expand into full-length critical essays that elaborated original theories about art. Motivated by an unsparing devotion to the idea that Americans should be taught to distinguish between ordinary or even commendable works and true masterpieces, Poe held up high standards that were usually at odds with the literary establishment. He would end up paying a heavy price for his candor.

Poe worked in a climate of intense literary nationalism, a grassroots movement to establish a literature that could be identified as uniquely American. After the Revolution, Americans began issuing calls to their fellow citizens to consider the question of a national culture, as illustrated in works of art. A native literature would solidify the country's autonomy and enable it to stand up to its British and Continental critics. Initially, it was the young age of the country and the lack of a sizable, interested audience to support writers and artists that prevented a national literature from developing easily. Another impediment was the flooding of the American book market by British books and periodicals that came without any barrier of copyright and were actually cheaper to buy in New York than in London. Pirated editions of Dickens and Scott were thick on the ground, making it difficult for American printers to be sold on the idea of issuing native works. So too with periodicals: reprints of the *London Quarterly Review*, the *Edinburgh Review, Blackwood's* and others could be had for only a few dollars a year—a suffocating cultural stranglehold on the United States by its mother country. The nationalistic literary fervor intensified after the War of 1812 and culminated in an infamous rhetorical question voiced by the British literary critic Sydney Smith in an *Edinburgh Review* essay that took up a recent book on culture in the United States: "In the four quarters of the globe, who reads an American book? or goes to an American play? or looks at an American picture or statue?"

This question was the most reverberative shot in a war of words that began to be waged on both sides of the Atlantic, with the British wheeling out their most powerful arsenal of rhetoric to denounce the fledgling American literature. (In one memorable image, it was described as "a child, techy and wayward in its infancy" and already prone to bad habits.) Counterattacks were led mainly by members of the New England literary establishment like William Tudor, editor of the *North American Review*, the Unitarian minister William Ellery Channing, Harvard professor Edward Everett, and, most famously, Ralph Waldo Emerson, whose 1837 address to the graduating Phi Beta Kappa seniors at Harvard, known as "The American Scholar," took up the whole question of a national literature in a memorable and philosophically trenchant way.

By the 1830s, when Poe came on the literary scene, much of the propagandistic effort had shifted to New York, where people like Lewis Gaylord Clark, Cornelius Matthews, and Evert A. Duyckinck spearheaded the movement. These literary men, now known only as historical figures, were in their day immensely powerful editors, critics, and anthologizers of native literature. They used their positions to raise public awareness of America's subordinate position in the global cultural scene and to spur authors to work. Magazines like the *Knickerbocker*, the *Democratic Review*, and the *Literary World* routinely ran manifestos and other editorial pieces calling for a native literature, and then ran fiction—almost all of it third- or even fourth-rate—that illustrated the precepts called for in the editorials. Thus began a cycle, and a critical practice, which became known as "puffing"—lavishly praising—inferior native books. Poe disdained the idea of such a mutual admiration society, and he used his position as chief critic at the *Messenger* to say so.

The main characteristic of the hastily produced native writing that so offended Poe was its simplistic Americanness. This particular brand of creativity had its basis in eighteenth-century associationalism, the belief that thought is composed of associated elements drawn from immediate experience and that this process is affected by time and place. With this principle as the guiding criterion, a national literature could be produced by anyone who simply wrote about what surrounded them—American history, the American frontier, American scenery, American Indians. These were rich, varied, and inexhaustible mines for American books, but to Poe they resulted merely in Americanized versions of Scott and Dickens—a *Pickwick Papers* or an *Ivanhoe* featuring a Yankee candlemaker with the Hudson River Valley in his backyard. In one critical review, Poe summed up his position with frankness and aplomb: "We are becoming boisterous and arrogant," he wrote, "in the pride of a too speedily assumed literary freedom."

We get up a hue and cry about the necessity of encouraging native writers of merit—we blindly fancy that we can accomplish this by indiscriminate puffing of good, bad, and indifferent, without taking the trouble to consider that what we choose to denominate encouragement is thus, by its general application, rendered precisely the reverse. In a word, so far from being ashamed of the many disgraceful literary failures to which our inordinate vanities and misapplied patriotism have lately given birth, we adhere pertinaciously to the . . . gross paradox of liking a stupid book the better, because, sure enough, its stupidity is American. (506)

The movement toward democracy had led the country into what Tocqueville called the tyranny of the majority. Poe wanted to hold up high standards for national art and wanted to be regarded as a fearless critic. It was easy for Poe to assume this stance, for he was never much for egalitarianism. He always thought of himself as something of an aristocrat—a disinherited one, to be sure—but noble nonetheless. (In a fanciful autobiographical memorandum Poe once furnished a magazine editor, he concocted an illustrious family heritage for himself, including a "connexion with many of the noblest in England.") This led him into some rather elitist notions about art and class. He had a high opinion of his own intellectual gifts, and he was not shy about telling others what their defects were. In his fiction, he wrote primarily about the privileged class—an imagined federation of nobles and titled gentlemen who resided in manses and castles in a quasi-medieval or Renaissance-era Europe. Very little about his writings, like his critical opinions, were directly "American."

Another reason Poe was antipathetic to the literary world was its New England bias. Although he published his first volume of poems as "a Bostonian," and although he associated Boston pleasantly in memory with his young mother, when Poe wrote his critical exordia, he was almost always, directly or implicitly, speaking as a southerner. He often wrote with disfavor of the works of Longfellow, Emerson, Bryant, Fenimore Cooper, and Washington Irving, because he opposed their native Puritanism, their jingoistic chauvinism, their (to him) shallow optimism, and their abidingly democratic view of society. To Poe, these men lacked artistic vision and critical earnestness. Their writing took no notice of the psychic realities of humankind—it presented instead only pastel-colored vistas of plains and gushing waterfalls, or, when it turned philosophical, of a sentimental faith in some divine being. Poe equated these themes with the North. In turn, Poe was often disproportionately kind to southern authors like Kennedy, William Gilmore Simms, and Philip Pendleton Cooke, many of whom, it must be said, were far less gifted than their northern peers and who, more to the point, employed essentially the same themes.

In many of these reviews, therefore, Poe spoke up for the injustice he felt had been dealt to authors born below the Mason-Dixon line. Writing of A. B. Longstreet's *Georgia Scenes*, for example, in the March 1836 issue of the *Messenger*, Poe spoke of the author as "endowed . . . with an exquisitely discriminative and penetrating understanding of character in general, and of Southern character in particular." He then continued: "Seriously—if this book were printed in England it would make the fortune of its author. We positively mean what we say—and are quite sure of being sustained in our opinion by all proper judges who may be so fortunate as to obtain a copy of the '*Georgia Scenes*,' and who will be at the trouble of sifting their peculiar merits from amid the *gaucheries* of a Southern publication" (778).

Similarly, later in his career, Poe would write of William Gilmore Simms that "Had he been . . . a Yankee, [his] genius would have been rendered *immediately* manifest to his countrymen, but unhappily (*perhaps*) he was a southerner, and united the southern pride—the southern dislike to the making of bargains—with the southern supineness and general want of tact in all matters relating to the making of money" (904). And of minor talents, like Edward C. Pinckney of Baltimore, author of what to Poe was "an exquisite poem" entitled "A Health," Poe would say: "It was profoundly admired by the critical few, but had little circulation:—this for no better reason than that the author was born *too far South*" (1440).

At the *Messenger*, therefore, Poe set out with the deliberate intent of kicking up the dust. "We wish, if possible, to take the public opinion by storm," he wrote one potential contributor; and to another, he asserted that he would "strike a bold stroke." Poe was immensely successful. The *Messenger* attracted national attention, and the enterprising Poe quickly called his success to the attention of his peers. To the publisher Harrison Hall, he wrote that the large number of testimonials appearing about the *Messenger* in other periodicals was "*such as have never appeared to any volume in the country*" and then added with false modesty, "I mention this *merely* as a matter of business." Of course, Poe mentioned it to a great many people.

One might argue, however, that the attention the *Messenger* got was merely a succès de scandale, the result of Poe's notoriety as a negative critic. In fairness, Poe truly believed that the critic's task was to distinguish good literature from bad and to consign the bad to oblivion, so he placed a strong emphasis on negative criticism. Most would say, however, that the emphasis was disproportionate. His models, the British critics, wrote anonymously or pseudonymously, and thus they were able to damn an author in one article and praise him in another—a practice that guaranteed controversy and high circulation figures. But Poe often went too far. Lacking diplomacy, Poe never knew when he had crossed the line, and when he should have stepped back. Frequently his critical articles began with valid points but then degenerated into ad hominem attacks, revealing Poe's bitterness toward others with what he regarded as undeservedly high reputations.

Nevertheless, Poe's presence as a national critic began to be felt quickly. By the December 1835 number, he was regularly using the reviews to make critical pronouncements: this issue of the *Messenger* established Poe's reputation as "the man with the tomahawk," an epithet that Poe earned for his strong negative criticism. In the September number he had ridiculed the anonymous *Mephistopheles in England; or The Confessions of a Prime Minister*, because of its "utter want of *keeping*" and its lack of a "just object or end." While Poe did not develop this point much further, it foreshadowed his eventual idea of art as a teleological construct in which a preestablished design and the execution of the design were of first importance. The ubiquitous Cornelius Matthews, whom Poe detested as nothing more than a spaniel trotting obediently alongside his *Knickerbocker* masters, like Gaylord Clark, was guilty in his epic poem *Wakondah* of penning "from beginning to end, pure trash." Another writer was said to have "negative merit"; still another was called "a public imposition."

His harsh judgment of these books, however, was tame compared to his annihilation of Theodore Fay's *Norman Leslie* in the December issue, where he made his next important statement as a critic—on the business of criticism itself. Poe had been looking for a way for the *Messenger* to "kick up the dust" in the magazine world; he found the perfect target in Fay's third-rate novel. Poe used this review to sound the first of several clarion calls for a rigorous and independent criticism in America (the other major statements appear in the "Prospectus" to his projected "Penn Magazine" [1840] and in a review of Lambert Wilmer's *The Quacks of Helicon* [1841]). His skewering of Fay touched off a skirmish with the powerful New York literary clique to which Fay belonged. Later, it escalated into an all-out war.

Norman Leslie had been "puffed" to excess by the New York *Evening Mirror*, the very newspaper where Fay was an associate editor. When the novel finally came to Poe for review, he must have been lying in wait:

Well!—here we have it! This is the book—the book par excellence—the book bepuffed, beplastered, and be-Mirrored: the book "attributed to" Mr. Blank, and "said to be from the pen" of Mr. Asterisk: the book which has been "about to appear"—"in press"—"in progress"—"in preparation"—and "forthcoming": the book "graphic" in anticipation—"talented" a priori—and God knows what in prospectu. For the sake of everything puff, puffing, and puffable, let us take a peep at its contents! (540)

Poe ridiculed every facet of the novel. He began with general matters, criticizing the unrealistic characters and convoluted plot; finishing that, he moved in on more specific literary transgressions and pinned them on the author, like Hawthorne's scarlet letter. Using abundant examples from the text, he faulted the style and diction of the novel—an early example of Poe's eventual method of close textual analysis, which he elaborated on in "Exordium to Critical Notices" (1842). Poe concluded that *Norman Leslie* was "the most inestimable piece of balderdash with which the common sense of the good people of America was ever so openly or so villainously insulted" (546).

The whole review, with its tone of jocose savagery, imparts a strong sense of Poe's cavalier challenge to the New York cabal with which he tilted the rest of his career. He certainly wanted to draw more attention to himself and to the *Messenger*, knowing that controversy would increase circulation. But he also wanted to foster an honest American criticism and to gibbet amateurish writing praised only because it was a native product. The irreverence, arrogance, and downright splenetic quality of this, the first of several attacks on literary coteries, owes much to the slashing reviewing styles of certain British critics, notably the infamous "Christopher North" (the pseudonym of John Wilson) and John Gibson Lockhart, two reviewers for *Blackwood's Edinburgh Magazine*, which was known for its ferocity.

Although Poe was definitely trumpeting himself and his abilities, he was also asking the country for dignity, restraint, and common sense in its opinions on art. He did not want to represent a feeble literary enterprise, but instead wanted American literature to be respected on the same footing with that of England and Europe.

Of course, Poe being Poe, he could not help but point out the injuries brought down on him by those who criticized his harsh reviewing style. To one correspondent he wrote that the persisting label of "tomahawk critic" was undeserved, because he did not denounce an unreasonably large number of books. And in the September 1836 *Messenger*, Poe reckoned that of the ninety-four books he had reviewed, in only five of them had censure been "greatly predominant."

The most important element of Poe's critical notices was the theoretical ideas underpinning them. Poe was arguably the first original literary theorist America produced. He honed his ideas in these reviews.

In the January 1836 *Messenger*, Poe led off with an omnibus review of the three leading sentimental poets of his day: Mrs. Lydia H. Sigourney, Mrs. H. F. Gould, and Mrs. E. F. Ellet. Nearly the entire review, however, was devoted to Sigourney (who would later call up Poe's sectional pride when a special posthumous edition of her work was published for the benefit of her children: "To Southerners, at least," Poe would write, "we feel that nothing farther need be said.") Although at this early stage of his career Poe showed only a little of his later characteristic anger at "popular" writers with undeservedly high reputations, he did seize on the fact that Sigourney was known as "the Mrs. Hemans of America," after the British poet Dorothea Felicia Hemans. This prompted Poe to lash out at provincialism, a recurring theme in much of his criticism. To Poe, the very fact that Sigourney had acquired that title made her "palpably convicted of that sin which in poetry is not to be forgiven" (875): Mrs. Sigourney lacked originality, and to Poe, imitation was the deadliest of literary sins. Poe found the volume to be unoriginal in structure, versification, subject matter, even phrasing. But what most irritated Poe was Sigourney's habit of prefacing nearly every selection with a motto or quotation of some sort which Poe thought gave the reader a predetermined "reading" of the poem; to Poe, interpretation should not depend on something outside the text (one way in which his criticism anticipates that of the post–World War II New Critics).

Poe's critique of Sigourney contains the first developed explanation of what he meant by "unity." The epigraphs Poe found so damaging were one example of how outside "forces" could corrupt unity: "the *totality* of effect is annihilated." Undue length, too, may violate unity:

> In poems of magnitude the mind of the reader is not, at all times, enabled to include in one comprehensive survey the proportions and proper adjustment of the whole. . . . But in pieces of less extent . . . the understanding is employed, without difficulty, in the contemplation of the picture as a whole—and thus its effect will depend, in a very great degree, upon the perfection of its finish, upon the nice adaptation of its constituent parts, and especially upon what is rightly termed by Schlegel "the unity of totality of interest." (876–77)

Whenever Poe used the term "unity," he always meant two things—the unity imposed by the writer on the work, and the unity felt by the reader. This "double unity" could only be achieved in the lyric poem and the prose "tale," both forms being short and thus requiring little sustained attention by the reader. In a novel, a narrative poem, or an epic poem it was impossible to achieve unity.

Poe drew this concept in part from several other theorists. First, in criticizing Sigourney's poetry for lacking "unity of impression," Poe was elaborating on the theories of organic unity put forth by August Wilhelm von Schlegel. For Schlegel a work of art was the same as a living thing: all parts worked to produce a joint impression on the mind. Second, Poe agreed with various of Coleridge's statements in *Biographia Literaria* that in reading a poem the pleasure derived from the whole is that which is "compatible with a distinct gratification from each component part" (10). Coleridge emphasized structural unity. Finally, Poe was indebted to the work of several Scottish aestheticians, including Hugh Blair's *Lectures on Rhetoric and Belles-Lettres*, Lord Kames's *Elements of Criticism*, and particularly the critical writings of Archibald Alison. In discussing length Poe had in mind the reader's inability to grasp the design of a long poem and his therefore being denied the pleasure or "unity of emotion" that Alison said the poem should impart.

Following his *Blackwood's* models, Poe also often pointed out the contrast between third-rate and first-rate books by writing reviews of each for the same issue; he therefore administered a corrective to the one by example and comparison. A case in point is the February 1836 issue, where Poe ruthlessly detailed the absurdities of plot and style in Morris Mattson's *Paul Ulric*, "despicable in every respect," as a way of indirectly praising the "artist-like eye, the originality, the fancy, and the learning" of Edward Bulwer-Lytton's *Rienzi* (142). In reviewing Bulwer's novel, Poe singled out and praised the very qualities that were lacking in Mattson's novel: clarity of purpose, artistry, technical skill, and ideation. Poe's review of Bulwer reveals another abiding component of his aesthetic: in praising Bulwer, whose novels were infamous for their "immorality," Poe was challenging the prevailing critical attitudes about the morality of art, thereby reaffirming his position as an objective critic.

Lastly, in his June 1836 review of Dickens's *Watkins Tottle* (now known as *Sketches by Boz*) Poe began to develop one of his most important theories, the aesthetic of the short story, or "tale." The novel, Poe said, could be sustained simply by effort and perseverance; the tale, however, depended on unity of effect, a quality which was "not easily appreciated or indeed comprehended by an ordinary mind." Tales had an advantage over novels because they could be "taken in at one view" (205). In commenting on "The Pawnbroker's Shop," Poe drew an analogy between each sentence of a tale giving a progressively more complete view of the overall work and the component parts of a painting adding up to a total effect (206). A novel, Poe said yet again, was not, properly speaking, an art form; it could be admired "for its detached passages, without reference to the work as a whole" (205). The painting analogy is congruent with Poe's principle of "totality of impression": thematic design should be emphasized over character, setting, and plot; those elements are simply the means by which that design is fulfilled.

In writing the reviews, Poe was hammering out his aesthetic ideas in a kind of critical workshop, fitting and refitting his evaluations from book to book, making adjustments in his specific insights until he found the precise form of expression for the general principle. These would later find full and coherent expression in critical essays like "The Philosophy of Composition" and "The Poetic Principle." Poe valued unity of design over diffuseness (and by extension, the short tale or poem over the novel); imagination over fancy; pleasure over didacticism; and technical skill over carelessness of form and structure. In later critical pieces, Poe would go on to apply traditional criteria to the language and metrics of a poem, yet at the same time seek out meaning as well as beauty. Championing originality, he would also try to discredit mere "imitators."

The *Messenger* won plaudits across the country. Although the creative pieces that Poe published in it were remarkable, the high praise given the magazine by other papers, which Poe unashamedly printed as "supplements" to each issue, were bestowed not on the fiction but on the trenchant and fearless literary criticism that Poe produced. With such success, it might be supposed that White fell in love with his young editor and promised him the moon, but such was not the case.

In the course of their association, White had usually expressed confidence in Poe—in fact, in a letter to Beverley Tucker, White called him his "right hand man." Poe, in turn, had told others that White was "exceedingly kind in every respect," especially with salary increases. Poe's annual stipend was at least eight hundred dollars a year-a handsome sum for the time. Poe worked extraordinarily hard, but to read his letters from this time is to see someone who was always urgently in need of money. He had purchased two hundred dollars' worth of furniture on credit—optimistically, it turned out—and carried a heavy load of debt. Expenses being high, Poe was left with just six dollars a week after the bills had been paid, and although he somewhat sheepishly asked relatives in the South for loans against future earnings (one scheme involved buying a house, renting it to Mrs. Clemm as a boardinghouse, and then being a paying tenant there himself), very little extra cash came in. Thus one strain between White and Poe must have been money. He later wrote the following to his cousin William Poe (14 August 1840): "The situation was disagreeable to me in every respect. The drudgery was excessive; the salary was contemptible. In fact I soon found that whatever reputation I might personally gain, this reputation would be all. I stood no chance of bettering my pecuniary condition, while my best energies were wasted in the service of an illiterate and vulgar, although well-meaning man, who had neither the capacity to appreciate my labors, nor the will to reward them."

White, for his part, felt at times that the magazine was no longer his own and that he had had to subordinate himself to Poe's instructions. He told Beverley Tucker at one point that he felt "cramped" by Poe "in the exercise of my own judgment, as to what articles I shall or shall not admit into my work. It is true," White conceded, "that I neither have his sagacity, nor his learning—but I do believe I know a handspike from a saw." Reasons for why White was so bristly around Poe may also have resided in problems of his own: in 1836, he had been beset by a printer's strike, which cost him a lot of money, and both he and his wife were in poor health; in fact, his wife had contracted a terminal illness.

Yet White mostly seems to have looked to Poe's character for explanations for their breakup. White was probably able to perceive the young man's critical acuity, but he had always had a low opinion of Poe's morals. Poe's marriage to the unusually young Virginia had disturbed him; he may have suspected that stories like "Berenice," which he was revolted by, contained more than a little something of Poe's bizarre turn of mind. But it was Poe's weakness for the bottle that bothered White the most. White was a firm believer in the bourgeois proprieties, and early in his relationship with Poe he cautioned the latter—in the best style of the temperance tracts of the time—that "no man is safe who drinks before breakfast."

Alcoholism in Poe's time was considered morally reprehensible. There was some thinking that genetic inheritance or early childhood exposure was primarily to blame, and Poe's father and brother were both alcoholics. Jane MacKenzie, Rosalie's adoptive mother, stated that on a visit to the Poe house shortly before Eliza's death she observed the children's nurse feeding them "liberally with bread soaked in gin" and that the "old woman acknowledged . . . that she freely administered to them gin and other spirituous liquors, with sometimes laudanum" to "make them strong and healthy" or to put them to sleep. Drinking was also regarded as a moral defect rather than a psychological affliction or chemical illness.

This perception was promoted by the fervent temperance movement— one of the largest social reform movements ever to take place in the United States. The earliest printed works of the movement focused on how alcohol affected one's health, including the immediate effects of drunkenness (like vomiting and headaches) and the perceived long-term effects of chronic drinking (like delirium tremens, "spontaneous human combustion," madness, and death). When the movement blossomed in the early 1830s, medical arguments were a powerful motivator in encouraging temperance, and many doctors belonged to temperance organizations. Temperance activists knew that alcohol could have a strong hold on people, and they used fear tactics to fight its deadly grip. Associating the devil and other demon figures with alcohol scared people away from liquor, which came to be known as "demon rum," "the devil's blood," and even "the dark beverage of Hell."

Many of the illustrations that accompanied popular books, songs, and placards for the temperance movement contained imagery that also shows up in Poe's stories. Alexander Anderson, for example, based his illustrations for "The Drunkards" from *Emblems of Mortality* (Charleston: Babcock & Co., 1846) on John Bewick's illustrations for an earlier edition, which were, in turn, based on Hans Holbein's sixteenth-century *Dance of Death*, a series of woodcuts showing various incarnations of a Grim Reaper skeleton figure.

The genre of temperance fiction, a sentimental brand of literature, was quite successful in Poe's time. Several purveyors of this brand of popular literature were friends of Poe's, notably John Laughlin, an alcoholic and an opium addict whom he had known in Baltimore (yet who continued to lecture on temperance and write popular novels), and the Philadelphia author Timothy Shay Arthur, whose novel *Ten Nights in a Bar-Room* was a huge seller and was later made into a successful play. There were melodramas with temperance themes and temperance halls that put on plays for the benefit of temperance organizations. Popular songs, including the well-known "Father, Come Home," used temperance as a theme. John S. Adams's *The Boston Temperance Glee Book* (Boston: Elias Howe, 1848) contained lyrics and melodies for numerous temperance songs, including "Touch Not the Cup" to the tune of "Long Long Ago" and "'Twas the Last, Last Rumseller" to the tune of "Last Rose of Summer."

The extent of Poe's own drinking has been much debated. Certainly there is a good deal of it in his fiction: it figures prominently in "MS. Found in a Bottle," "The Cask of Amontillado," *The Narrative of Arthur Gordon Pym*, "Hop-Frog," and several other minor stories like "King Pest" and "The Angel of the Odd." And although "The Black Cat" is as clinically precise a depiction of an alcoholic as one could find anywhere, Poe throws in a generous measure of moralism in taking his character down the road to self-destruction, as if to be sure he conformed to the temperance attitudes of the time. Poe supported temperance in his attempt to construct a life made secure and comfortable by the middle-class orthodoxies, yet for a variety of reasons, he could not restrain himself from drinking. Of course, there was always a tight connection between his binge drinking and the periods of greatest emotional stress in his life, his marriage, and his work.

But the biggest factor in Poe's breakup with White and the *Messenger* may have been the spectre of John Allan, which surely haunted Poe at almost every turn in his daily business, and which must have dealt a crippling blow to his emotional balance. Allan's death gnawed at Poe. As much as he hated Allan and sought to distance himself from him in different symbolic ways, there was also something of a masochistic attraction to him, a desire to be with the one who would injure him the most. One critic has found various anagrams of the word "Allan" in characters and miscellaneous names in Poe's fiction—Hans Pfaall, Amontillado, Tsalal, Ulalume. Poe by custom signed his name "Edgar A. Poe" or just "Edgar Poe," unmindful of any strong connection to the Allan line; yet around the time of his return to Richmond, he apparently for the first time signed two of his letters "Edgar Allan Poe"—only two of the eight extant letters in which Poe used that signature.

Simply returning to the city so soon after Allan's death must itself have been distressing, but every day Poe ran into acquaintances whom he had known before on terms of equality. These former friends no longer welcomed him here, for the second Mrs. Allan apparently did not like Poe, and it was thought that she poisoned the well as soon as he returned. These acquaintances from his youth led carefree lives, resting comfortably in the possession of vast sums of money and property. The prospects of beneficial marriages, lucrative business contracts, travel, and leisure were their futures. Poe's future was an uncertain territory of worry, debt, and insecurity about how much others valued the career he had chosen.

The physical environment of Richmond must also have churned up in Poe an unsettling mix of emotions. Moldavia, the Allans' manorial residence, was just around the corner from the house Poe had purchased. And every day he went to work on the second floor of the building at Main and Fifteenth streets, next to which were the former offices of Ellis and Allan. Feeling chained to his desk ticking off successive chores of editorial drudgery, Poe must have compared his present with his past. He might even have compared himself to another Edgar, the legitimate son of Gloucester in *King Lear* (a play in which Eliza had several times appeared, as the sincere and long-suffering Cordelia): a wrongfully disinherited child, an outcast reduced to penury by a vicious reversal of fortune.

By late 1836, White's worries about Poe's reliability became too much for him, and Poe was let go. His official announcement, stating that he had "retired" from the *Messenger*, appeared in the January 1837 issue. And so Poe withdrew from the first of his editing posts, the beginning of a pattern in which he was never able to hold down such a position for very long, and from which he always parted company in an atmosphere of tension, guilt, and failure.

Poe's break with the *Messenger* presumably brought on a long period of unemployment and poverty—presumably, because there is a gap in the biographical record for about twenty-nine months, from February 1837 to May 1839. Poe, Muddy, and Virginia apparently migrated to New York, where they lived in an old frame house in the Greenwich Village area, for perhaps fifteen months. They survived on the rent paid by the lodgers that the reliable Muddy took in. One of them, William Gowans, a Scotsman who later became a prominent bookseller, left a description of the household at 113 1/2 Carmine Street, depicting Poe as a particularly earnest and hard-working young man, "a good man as well as a good husband, for he had a wife of matchless beauty and loveliness." "During that time," Gowans continued, "I saw much of him, and had an opportunity of conversing with him often." Gowans recalled that Poe was not "the least affected with liquor," nor did he ever "descend to any known vice." He found the author to be "one of the most courteous, gentlemanly, and intelligent companions" he had ever met.

Poe tried to scare up literary work, but without success. With the country in the grips of a financial panic, many of the magazines on which he had earlier relied had temporarily suspended publication, or closed down for good. In any case, it is unlikely that the powerful editorial establishment which he had so brazenly challenged in the *Messenger* would have opened its doors to him. During several months in the city, Poe sold only two stories.

In the spring or early summer of 1838, Poe gave up on New York and moved his family to Philadelphia, second only to Gotham as a publishing center for weekly and monthly reviews. Philadelphia offered Poe a fresh start. In his mind, he may have associated it with his colonial ancestors and even with the cause of freedom from injustice and oppression. Second only to New York as a literary center, Philadelphia was where another Boston-born writer, Benjamin Franklin, the Renaissance man of American life, had opened his own printing office at the age of twenty-two and had published *The Pennsylvania Gazette* and his annual *Poor Richard's Almanack*. Like Poe, Franklin believed in the power of the written word to bring enlightenment to the people. Also like Poe, Franklin was remarkably adept at writing in a variety of modes: journalism, essays, satires, and hoaxes. Both were interested in science and in politics, on which both commented freely, unsparingly, and often mockingly. Both were industrious and energetic, and Poe could exercise the strictest self-discipline, like Franklin, when he needed to. Both were also sharp-eyed analysts of human nature, and believers in man's innate tendency to deceive.

Poe definitely knew Franklin's now mythic *Autobiography* quite well, for in mid-1840 he satirized its ethos in the story "The Business Man." Certainly, unlike the optimistic, forward-looking Franklin, Poe would at times profess little faith in the progress of the human race or in the perfectibility of man. Poe seems appositely to ridicule the Franklinian method of self-improvement through hard work in such tales of moral degeneracy as "William Wilson" and "The Fall of the House of Usher," and perhaps even directly to satirize Franklin in social-critical stories like "The Man That Was Used Up." But all that would be some time in the future. For now, Poe may have hopefully associated Philadelphia with Franklin's rise from poverty and obscurity to a state of affluence and celebrity in the world. He may have hoped to emulate Franklin's model of the self-made man.

And in fact, Poe's fortunes began to rise in Philadelphia. Poe sold what he afterwards thought of as his finest story, "Ligeia," to a Baltimore magazine for the agreeable sum of ten dollars. He afterwards published some poems in the same magazine, and in the winter of 1838 ghost-wrote a piece of hackwork for Thomas Wyatt, a British professor and lecturer, called *The Conchologist's First Book*. Poe put together this geology textbook by cribbing the information from a similar book published five years earlier. Poe added an introduction, and some library research may have gone into his descriptions of different animal species, but on the whole, the book was a work of plagiarism. When thus accused, Poe retorted angrily that all such books were a pastiche of common knowledge (not exactly rebutting the charge), and he lashed out at his accusers, threatening legal action. The episode foreshadows another paradox in Poe's personality, as he later would make "originality" a mantra for the highest literary achievement and would wage unfounded, silly campaigns against major writers like Longfellow on accusations of plagiarism.

During this time Poe must have been working on *The Narrative of Arthur Gordon Pym,* his only completed novel. A venerable publishing house, Harper and Brothers, brought it out in 1838, after two installments of the beginning of the book had appeared in the *Messenger* just after Poe left Richmond, in early 1837. *Arthur Gordon Pym* is a fascinating, frustrating, ultimately flawed book that soars to new heights of fictional ingenuity and descends to new lows of silliness and absurdity. It may also be second only to "The Fall of the House of Usher" in the amount of critical commentary it has generated by Poe scholars.

The plot of the book is aptly summarized by its lengthy subtitle, which hints at incredible calamities, hardships, and fears. It reads:

"THE DETAILS OF A MUTINY AND ATROCIOUS BUTCH-ERY ON BOARD THE AMERICAN BRIG GRAMPUS, ON HER WAY TO THE SOUTH SEAS, IN THE MONTH OF JUNE, 1827. WITH AN ACCOUNT OF THE RECAPTURE OF THE VESSEL BY THE SURVIVERS; THEIR SHIPWRECK AND SUBSEQUENT HORRIBLE SUFFERINGS FROM FAMINE; THEIR DELIVERANCE BY MEANS OF THE BRITISH SCHOONER JANE GUY; THE BRIEF CRUISE OF THIS LATTER VESSEL IN THE ANTARCTIC OCEAN; HER CAPTURE, AND THE MASSACRE OF HER CREW AMONG A GROUP OF ISLANDS IN THE EIGHT-FOURTH PARALLEL OF SOUTHERN LATITUDE; TOGETHER WITH THE INCREDIBLE ADVENTURES AND DISCOVERIES STILL FARTHER SOUTH TO WHICH THAT DISTRESSING CALAMITY GAVE RISE."

The novel details the exploits of a youth named Pym who stows away on a brig and thus is catapulted into a series of barbaric, nightmarish events—catalogued above—that at the end of the journey take him to the lowest reaches of the southern hemisphere. In unexplored leagues of the Antarctic Ocean the brig's crew enters a surreal realm of milky white water. A chasm opens in the water and they float inexorably into the reaches of a bizarre shrouded figure identified only as having skin "of the perfect whiteness of snow." One of the most intriguing parts of the book is the ending; Poe leaves open to speculation exactly what happens to Pym when he reaches this point. (In addition to the huge amount of critical writing the book has generated, it also inspired the imagination of Jules Verne, who took up the story where Poe left off, publishing a "sequel" to *Pym* in 1897 entitled *Le Sphinx des glaces*.)

The indeterminateness of the ending may be a reflection of the jackleg character of Poe's composition of the novel, for *Pym* began life as one type of book, and seems to have ended up as another. The two *Messenger* chapters appeared under Poe's byline, but when the book was published, Poe's name did not appear on the title page. He apparently tried to conceal his authorship of the book version by writing an elaborately contrived preface by "A. G. Pym" that explained why portions of the novel had earlier appeared in the *Messenger* over Poe's name. In the preface, which is pure hoax, Pym claims that after his adventures in the South Seas he ended up "in the society of several gentlemen in Richmond, Virginia," to whom he related his exploits, and they encouraged him to publish an account. Pym demurred, however, because, "having kept no journal during a greater portion of the time in which I was absent, I feared I should not be able to write, from mere memory, a statement so minute and connected as to have the appearance of that truth it would really possess." Pym also states that he thought the "veracity" of the narrative would be questioned and that "the public at large would regard what I should put forth as merely an impudent and ingenious fiction." Pym therefore allowed "Mr. Poe" to "draw up, in his own words, a narrative of the earlier portion" of his adventures "from facts afforded by myself, publishing it in the Southern Messenger under the garb of fiction." However, "the public were . . . not at all disposed to receive it as fable," so Pym therefore determined that his story "would prove of such a nature as to carry with [it] sufficient evidence of [its] own authenticity" (1008). Poe thereby explains the provenance of the magazine installments, but his ulterior purpose, as one critic has noted, is "to impart a definite plausibility to the comments of A. G. Pym by combining seemingly factual details with exactly the right tone of diffident equanimity."

The novel appears to us today to be the most postmodern of all Poe's works and thus the text that shows most clearly his influence on later practitioners of metafiction, creators of books within books and puzzles within puzzles. In this sense Poe's influence on the Argentine writer Jorge Luis Borges is obvious, particularly in the story "Pierre Menard, Author of *Don Quixote*," as well on the writings of the Italian author Italo Calvino (*If On a Winter's Night a Traveller*), on the Russian author Vladimir Nabokov's *Pale Fire*, on South Africa's J. M. Coetzee (*Foe*), and on such contemporary American writers as John Barth, Robert Coover, and Paul Auster, whose 1985 novel, *City of Glass*, features a detective protagonist named William Wilson. An even more recent example is the British poet James Lasdun's first novel, *The Horned* Man (2002), a tale of paranoia and imagined persecution to rival both Poe and Kafka. Among postmodern detective novelists, the French writer Alain Robbe-Grillet's indebtedness to the verbal trickery and shifting narrative identity that Poe experimented with is probably the most prominent, especially in his thriller, *The Erasers*. The linguistical curiosities of the novel are also similar to those found in Joyce and Nabokov. Yet on the other hand, the book is firmly grounded in the popular narrative genre of the fiction of the sea and of exploration, like Swift's and Defoe's works before it, and its influence can be seen on Melville in *Moby-Dick*, and on such later writers as Conrad and Kipling.

In writing *Pym* Poe had taken the advice of a literary friend, James Kirke Paulding (who had approached Harpers on Poe's behalf), that American readers preferred a "single and connected story" to a group of his tales, which were "too learned and mystical" for the average taste. The stop-and-start change of focus created some aesthetic anomalies, making the book a far from perfect work of art. There was also the question of whether Poe intended the work to be a legitimate novel or merely a hoax, gulling readers into thinking the book was a true-life account of actual Arctic explorations—popular reading at the time.

Antarctica had been discovered in 1820, and the exploratory impulse in America was running high, a trend reflected in Poe's earlier story "MS. Found in a Bottle." For *Pym*, Poe borrowed fairly closely from

Benjamin Morrell's best-selling *Narrative of Four Voyages to the South Seas and the Pacific, 1822–1831* (1832), as well as the widely read travel books of Jeremiah N. Reynolds, like his *Address on the Subject of a Surveying and Exploring Expedition to the Pacific Ocean and South Seas* (1836), which Poe had favorably reviewed in the *Messenger* in January 1837. The novel begins in a realistic mode, in the manner of Conrad and Defoe, but it abruptly shifts into obvious hoaxing, satire, and even ridicule, in the manner of Swift; it then ends with a kind of self-reflexive, circular narrative that anticipates much postmodern fiction. Still, *Pym* is an ingenious and endlessly fascinating work that can be read on many different levels.

Its baseline concern is with the classic theme of illusion. The novel posits a treacherous world in which nothing is as it appears to be; all the characters at some point deceive themselves and/or others; and reality is always the opposite of what one expects. Pym deceives his grandfather by stowing away on the *Grampus*; the ironbound box he hides in turns out to be not a place of safety and nourishment but of death; his dog, Tiger, once friendly, turns out to be rabid; the seemingly benign ship's cook tries to murder him; the natives try to scalp him; a friendly ship turns out to be a Flying Dutchman–type vessel of death; the fiendish Dirk Peters turns out to be friendly, and the friendly natives turn out to be fiendish. The novel even begins on a note of deception, for it confuses the author and the protagonist in the minds of its readers. Rhetorical contrivances erect a verbal hall of mirrors that reinforces the concept of illusion. Poe plays around endlessly with names and dates, places and proper nouns, some of them anagrammatic and some even autobiographical.

Sometimes the illusion theme takes the form of life and death simulating each other, a characteristic Poe idea. Premature burials, a staple of the Philadelphia-era fiction, occur in metaphoric ways, such as when Pym stows away in a crate that Poe invests with both womb-like and coffin-like associations. As in the earlier "Berenice," images of orality also abound: biting and oral mutilation are everywhere present. Psychoanalytic critics of Poe tend to point out that teeth devour, having the single capacity to take in, to incorporate objects whole. This raises the paradox of on the one hand the dread of being consumed, and on the other the welcoming of being swallowed up—both protected and nourished, as Pym alternately is in the book.

The structure of the novel has also generated much analysis, some of it aimed at dismissing the conjecture that Poe slapped the book together hastily and without concern for an overall thematic or organic unity. Without trying to account for Poe's intentions, however, we can at least note that the book employs the classic motif of the voyage or the journey as a metaphor for self-exploration. In this sense the book can be read as a flawed but interesting bildungsroman in the same manner as Mark Twain's *Adventures of Huckleberry Finn* or Conrad's *Heart of Darkness*.

Pym is as much a journey into the past and interior life of Edgar Poe as anything else. The character's name, Arthur Gordon Pym, is a kind of cryptonym for Edgar Allan Poe. Both Pym and Poe are New Englanders, Pym being born in Nantucket and Poe in Boston. Pym's father, like Poe's foster father, is "a respectable trader in sea-stores" and is educated in private academies (1009). Like Poe, Pym grows up expecting an inheritance which he does not get. Both journey south, from "Edgartown" to the island of Tsalal in Pym's case and to the American South in Poe's case. In both places, the island and Richmond, blacks outnumber whites. Pym arrives at Tsalal on January 19, Poe's birthday, his journey having run from June 27 to March 28, the dates of Poe's own journey from the South (Fort Moultrie, South Carolina) to the North (Cape Cod). And as one critic notes, the central event in the formation of Pym's experiences is the death of his friend Augustus, which may be linked symbolically to the death of William Henry Leonard Poe, who passed away on August 1.

Perhaps the most prominent of Poe's loved ones who appears in the book is Eliza. The maternal spirit hovers over the whole novel, as *Pym* is a book that is very much about nourishment, feeding, and being emotionally consumed. As Kenneth Silverman has pointed out, the characters spend a lot of time thinking about, talking about, and looking for food: cordials, sausages, ham, mutton, sea biscuit, rabbits, terrapin, crabs, birds' eggs, even barnacles. At strategic points in the novel, we are reminded of the way nature takes care of its own, through such maternal imagery as the tortoises carrying with them a constant supply of water "in a bag at the root of the neck" (1101). And Pym's final journey (which comprises nine months in his life) takes him through a warm, milky ocean in a precarious state of near-expiration, searching for a nourisher or provider—a mother, father, or some surrogate giver of love, which seems almost affectionately to embrace him at the end.

In this sense, too, the novel reveals Poe's concern for the breakdown of order. Pym strives desperately to keep chaos at bay, to keep control over wild, terrifying reversals of fortune, just as Poe was at this time (and for much of his life) trying to bring order and control to his erratic life and his up-and-down literary career. The characters concern themselves, at bottom, as Poe did, with survival: what they must go through is extreme and improbable, but so is much of what Poe had to do to survive and to support Virginia and Muddy. Hanging over all that uncertainty, too, was the final uncertainty, for the last scenes of the novel return again to the classic Poe preoccupation with where the final journey of life takes one. Is death final, or is it some vast, indeterminate realm where an ambiguous presence meets one, stirring an unsettling mixture of fear and trepidation, but also the thrilling potential of discovering the ultimate secret knowledge?

In the years between his break with the *Messenger* and his next editorial assignment, Poe was much like his hero A. G. Pym—adrift in an ocean of confusion and misdirection, trying to navigate his way through the choppy waters of the literary world with no compass to guide him. Like Pym, too, Poe would not accept finality. He continued to press on, in search of a new and better experience.

CHAPTER 5

PHILADELPHIA

Burton's Gentleman's Magazine
and the Great Tales
[1838–1840]

In the spring of 1839 some good luck fell Poe's way, through the promise of a steady if not substantial income from William Evans Burton, sa transplanted English actor and theatre manager who had gone into the magazine business in Philadelphia. Burton offered Poe ten dollars a week for two hours' work a day, "except occasionally," so that Poe would be free to pursue "any other light avocation" and not be burdened by editorial duties. It seemed a fair deal to Poe, and Burton must have appeared to be a reasonable man to work for. His letter offering Poe the job was brief and to the point: "I shall dine at home today at 3. If you will cut your mutton with me, good. If not, write or see me at your leisure." Poe accepted Burton's offer and went to work. Although the conditions of Poe's employment would seem to have been ideal, circumstances transformed them instead into a situation similar to the one Poe had just left, at the *Messenger*, and *Burton's* would simply be another brief stop on Poe's journeyman travels through the stressful and exploitative world of magazine journalism.

Born in 1804, just five years before Poe, Billy Burton was destined for the church, until at age eighteen he rebelled and decided to become an actor. After taking parts in amateur plays, in 1825 Burton joined a repertory company that toured the provinces and displayed a natural aptitude for comedy, soon appearing at the Haymarket. In 1834 he accepted an offer to work in America, appearing as Wormwood in *The Lottery Ticket* and Dr. Ollapod in *The Poor Gentleman* at the Arch Street Theatre in Philadelphia, one of the leading playhouses in North America. He also became a proficient interpreter of Shakespeare, and his performances as Falstaff and Sir Toby Belch were particularly admired. Burton wrote two plays and numerous magazine sketches and miscellanea, collected as *Waggeries and Vagaries* (1848), as well as a *Cyclopaedia of Wit and Humor* (1858). He also managed two theatres in Philadelphia, one in Baltimore, and one in Washington, acting frequently in them himself. Later, he moved to New York, becoming famous there, and with his wealth assembling one of the most imposing private libraries of Shakespeariana in history.

Poe and Burton were never destined to get along, however. One cannot imagine two more dissimilar personalities. Like most journalists and magazine owners of the time, Burton was mostly bluff and bluster, loutish and coarse-mannered, and something of a braggart—"were I to detail my daily avocations," he told a friend, "I do not imagine that I should be believed." He also lived fast and high, dressed expensively and dined in the best restaurants in the city, where the proprietors and maîtres d'hôtel rushed to greet him and fussed noisily over his appearance in their establishments. This could not have sat well with Poe, with his almost scholarly, ascetic devotion to art and literature. Poe's temperament, of course, was also completely the opposite of Burton's—his quiet voice, his tidiness and fastidious habits, his sombre wardrobe of Byronic black, and his small physique with its delicate face, tiny hands and feet, and the slightly dreamy, perplexed gaze of his eyes. John Monicure Daniel, in an article on Poe published shortly before his death, in August 1849, called him "keen visaged," and concluded that "His face is not an ordinary one." The same impression came from a later analyst, the editor and anthologist Thomas Wentworth Higginson: "It was a face to rivet one's attention in any crowd." Poe must have struck Burton as something of an oddity.

But Burton had an entrepreneurial flair and was quick to cash in on growing trends in society. He could also spot talent when he saw it, and Poe obviously knew exactly how to manage a magazine and make it profitable.

A typical issue of *Burton's Gentleman's Magazine* was like that of most monthlies—a miscellany of poems, fiction, and essays, plus feature articles on sailing, cricket, or hunting. The audience was the city gentleman of business and finance and of the club.

Like Thomas White, Burton published his magazine for the sole purpose of earning a handsome profit. He was sensitive to market concerns and audience tastes, and could make tough financial decisions when he needed to. When he first engaged Poe as editor, he told him frankly that "the expenses of the Magazine are already woefully heavy; more so than my circulation warrants. . . . Competition is high—new claimants are daily rising. . . . My contributors cost me something handsome, and the losses upon credit, exchange, etc., are becoming frequent and serious." Poe's motives in running a magazine were considerably different from those of his employers, but he often would not accept this simple fact. In truth, Poe felt that he would never properly fulfill any significant artistic ambitions until he had a magazine of his own, a dream project that he would soon undertake but never make a reality.

Since Burton acted in different plays at the same time that he was publishing the magazine, he wasn't a hands-on proprietor. He would occasionally write something for it himself, but left the business of soliciting contributions and editing them to Poe, who probably preferred it that way. As he settled into the routine of his editorial work at *Burton's*, Poe could by this time properly call himself a "magazinist," the nineteenth-century term for a working journalist, reviewer, and editor. He thus was not inhabiting the rarefied literary world that he thought he would, for even his tales he considered secondary to his real work, which was that of a poet. "With me poetry has been not a purpose, but a passion," he once said, and throughout his life Poe would always think of himself thus. The feature articles and gossipy tidbits that he put into print at *Burton's* were a far cry from this. And the seemingly endless series of menial tasks that fell to him—for Burton considered Poe merely an employee and gave him very few opportunities to display his talents in print—included things like proofreading, copyediting, compiling short fillers, and supervising the printing. Poe's correspondence at this time speaks of little else besides rates of pay and inches of column type. When he did mention something of the character of his work at *Burton's* to friends, as in this letter to Philip Pendleton Cooke, it was with disdain:

I send the Gent's Mag: (July, Aug:, Sep:) Do not think of subscribing. The criticisms are not worth your notice. Of course I pay no attention to them—for there are two of us. It is not pleasant to be taxed with the twaddle of other people, or to let other people be taxed with ours. Therefore for the present I remain upon my oars.

"As soon as Fate allows," he told his poet friend, he would have his own periodical.

Poe drummed up interest in the magazine, however, as never before. The November 1839 number carried a solicitation for contributions: "To render Burton's Magazine the most desirable monthly publication for the next year, the Proprietor, in addition to the promised articles from his powerful list of Contributors, ensures a series of Papers of Original value, from the pens of the best Authors in the United States. To perfect this arrangement, he offers A PREMIUM OF $1,000! in befitting sums, for articles of value, written expressly for the Magazine." A series of short tales "illustrating the events of distinct periods in the History of North America" would pay $250, $100 would go to a "Humorous or Satirical Poem," and $100 offered for the best "Essay on any popular subject connected with Science or Belles Lettres."

Such handsome fees brought in a bonanza of articles, and Poe boosted the circulation of the magazine, as he had that of the *Messenger*. But for his own efforts Poe was paid less princely sums—about three dollars a page for most contributions. Ironically, the extra revenue Poe generated for Burton furnished the capital for the actor to begin construction on a new project, the National Theatre on Chestnut Street near Ninth, in early May 1840.

The most involved bit of writing that Poe did for *Burton's* was an unsigned serial entitled *The Journal of Julius Rodman*, which was never finished, since Poe left Burton's before he brought the story to completion.

Like *Pym*'s account of exploration by sea in 1827, *Julius Rodman* is an adventure of exploration by land in 1792. Like *Pym*, the subtitle promises suspense and derring-do—*Being an Account of the First Passage across the Rocky Mountains of North America ever Achieved by Civilized Man.* By not giving himself a byline Poe probably wanted *Julius Rodman* to be received as a true account, like *Pym*. Also like *Pym*, the story is heavily padded with material from encyclopedias and reference works. (One can almost see Poe counting the words, column by column, as he strove to compile enough to buy his family that evening's supper.)

The book took its inspiration from recent overland expeditions, several of which are mentioned in the text, like Sir Alexander Mackenzie's *Voyages in 1789 and 1793* (1801); Washington Irving's *Astoria* (1836), which Poe had reviewed for the *Messenger*; and Benjamin Bonneville's *The Rocky Mountains* (1837). But surely the most significant inspiration came from the journals of Lewis and Clark, issued in 1814 but still very much fresh in the public mind. Poe probably followed Meriwether Lewis's exploits closely, since the latter was private secretary to a famous Virginian, Thomas Jefferson. The project never came to much, however. The only satisfaction that Poe may have derived from the work was that he successfully gulled a United States Senate aide into believing it to be an actual historical document, since a paragraph from the book was quoted in an 1840 report to the Congress on the Oregon Territory.

Although Poe downplayed the extent of his critical writing for *Burton's*, telling one friend that he was "merely penning an occasional paragraph, without care," he was actually producing more of the trenchant literary criticism that he had begun at the *Messenger*. He also, somewhat unfortunately, continued to "kick up a dust" by publicizing his high standards for literature, predictably inflaming his audience—and Billy Burton as well, who had cautioned him to be more conciliatory toward his "brother-authors."

Yet among the numerous ironies of Poe's reviewing career was that many of the writers he "tomahawked" in *Burton's* (and later, in its successor, *Graham's Magazine*) were third-raters. Poe frittered away his valuable intellectual capital on books of little or no value: the collection entitled *Writings of Charles Sprague* (May 1842), which Poe said had "negative merit"; Frederick Marryat's *Joseph Rushbrook, or the Poacher* (September), which gave Poe occasion to bemoan the lack of intellectual content in contemporary literature (325); and William Harrison Ainsworth's *Guy Fawkes; or The Gunpowder Treason* (November), which Poe found "a somewhat ingenious admixture of pedantry, bombast, and rigmarole" (101). Also to Poe's misfortune, he continued his ill-considered campaign of going after the major American writers with (to him) undeservedly high reputations—Irving, Bryant, and, in particular, Longfellow.

Poe reviewed Longfellow several times in his career; each time he grew more negative, almost to the point of being irrational. His attacks were motivated by an inability to accept the fact that Longfellow was famous, well regarded, and financially successful from being a poet, and he was not. As the symbol of New England literary culture, Longfellow was also an object of enmity for Poe because of sectional bias.

Poe's first review of Longfellow, in October 1839, was a one-paragraph notice of the prose romance *Hyperion*. Poe dismissed it as lacking both "shape" and "design," but his more important basic point was that Longfellow was capable of doing better. Poe held that true artists were obliged to keep at "the great labour requisite for the stern demands of high art," and that Longfellow had let slip this responsibility. Poe's comments illustrate his belief that the critic's duty was to be an arbiter of taste and a champion of quality, protecting the public from mediocre literature. Four months later, reviewing Longfellow's *Voices of the Night* in the February 1840 issue, Poe accused Longfellow of "purloining" the central image and overall design of his "Midnight Mass for the Dying Year" from Tennyson's "The Death of the Old Year." Kenneth Silverman notes that these reviews of Longfellow (like a biographical sketch of Bryant and an unpublished article on Irving from this same period), motivated by envy and sectional bias, were followed by hypercritical praising of these same authors as Poe wrote to them begging for favors and endorsements—a consistent paradox of Poe's career that became a habit of "easy lies and half truths." This first stage in Poe's using the reviews for personal attacks was a prelude to the Longfellow War in 1845.

But Poe's most revealing critique of Longfellow came two years later, when the poet's *Ballads and Other Poems* crossed his desk for review. In its distinctions between poetry and prose and in its separation of poetry from truth, this review summarizes Poe's entire aesthetic of poetry to this time and lays the groundwork, as Kenneth Hovey points out, for Poe's other criticisms of Longfellow, as well as for many of the ideas in his famous critical essay "The Poetic Principle." Poe stated that Longfellow's view of the aim of poetry was fundamentally wrongheaded: Longfellow regarded "the inculcation of *moral* as essential" to a poem (684). Poe had always objected to overt didacticism in literature. Poetry, as he said in an earlier review of two well-known poets of his time, Fitz-Greene Halleck and Joseph Rodman Drake, originated in the poet's state of feeling; the poem was the means by which the poet conveyed that feeling. "Beauty," he said, "has no dependence, unless incidentally, upon either Duty or Truth" (689), a position he substantially clarified and expanded upon in "The Poetic Principle": "It by no means follows . . . that the . . . precepts of Duty, or even the lessons of Truth, may not be introduced into a poem, and with advantage; for they subserve, incidentally, in various ways, the general purposes of the work:—but the true artist will always contrive to tone them down in proper subjection to that *Beauty* which is the atmosphere and real essence of the poem" (78–79).

By beauty Poe meant a "supernal" (687) or higher beauty (not merely the beauty of nature). The innate knowledge of or "sense of the Beautiful," Poe said, was a basic human quality (and "an important condition of man's immortal nature"). Poe saw poetry as having a basic transcendental function; poetry went beyond "the mere *record*" of "forms and colors and sounds and sentiments" to a higher plane: "It is not the mere appreciation of the beauty before us. It is a wild effort to reach the beauty above. . . . and the soul thus athirst strives to allay its fever in futile efforts at *creation*" (685). Poe thus saw "poesy" as "a response . . . to a natural and irrepressible demand" for an aesthetic product that comprised these (relatively "synonimous" [*sic*], as Poe put it, or at least complementary) elements: "the *novelty*, the *originality*, the *invention*, the *imagination* or lastly the *creation* of Beauty" (687).

Admitting that this type of Beauty defies precise representation, Poe stated that possibly the only way that the poet could evoke Beauty was through music; he reminded his audience that music was after all "one of the moods of poetical development," once again bringing his earlier aesthetic views (on Moore and Tennyson, for example) into a focused whole. In music, Poe said, "the soul most nearly attains . . . the creation of supernal beauty":

> It may be, indeed, that this august aim is here even partially or imperfectly attained, in fact. The elements of that beauty which is felt in sound, may be the mutual or common heritage of Earth and Heaven. In the soul's struggles at combination it is thus not impossible that a harp may strike notes not unfamiliar to the angels.

This link between men and angels led Poe to his ultimate definition of poetry as "the *Rhythmical Creation of Beauty*": rhythm and rhyme were simply verbal "modifications" of music (688). These statements are also fundamental to any understanding of Poe's epistemology, his faith in intuitive insight, and the symbolism of his moral allegories, his poems and tales of psychic conflict.

Poe then analyzed how Longfellow's poetry failed because it was aimed at instruction rather than beauty. Poe ended by taking a position on didacticism and moralizing: he had earlier stated that "a didactic moral might be happily made the under-current of a poetical theme . . . but is invariably an ill effect when obtruding beyond the upper current of the thesis itself" (691). Poe's ultimate formulation of the "poem written solely for the poem's sake" was rooted in his identification with the South and with its sense of history and time as cyclical. Unlike Longfellow, who wrote poems with positive messages, Poe saw time and truth as destructive to poetry and he resisted progressivism, because it might speed the decline of the South. Poe opposed Longfellow, just as he opposed other New Englanders, whom he later came to derisively call "the Frogpondians," as much in the name of the South as because he took issue with the quality of their work. Around this time, he wrote his Georgia cousin William Poe asking for financial assistance with the magazine he himself hoped to found and edit, remarking to him that "It is upon the South that I chiefly rely for aid in the undertaking, and I have every hope that it will not fail me in my need."

This partisanship had its ambiguities, as did so many elements of Poe's life. After all, he had been born in Boston, had saved the miniature of Boston Harbor his mother had left him as a reminder of where she had "found her *best* and *most sympathetic friends*," and he had published his first collection of poems "By a Bostonian." Nonetheless, Poe's criticism by the 1840s increasingly rejected "truth" in poetry because of the significant social implications that "truth" might hold. In this review of Longfellow and in "The Poetic Principle," Poe advocated "a beauty no truth could invade."

Poe often displayed elitist attitudes, particularly when it came to the venerated sanctum of high art. He regarded himself as part of an aristocracy of letters, an inheritance of his southern upbringing. Thus his critical writing, as well as much of his fiction, is antidemocratic, putting him at odds with the prevailing literary ethos of the country—not just the intense propaganda of the literary nationalists, but also of those Coopers and Irvings who wrote of the expansion of democratic vistas, of the frontier and the prairie as symbols of America's growth. When Poe did use American themes and settings, he did so satirically. We do not usually associate Poe with works of social criticism, but several stories from this period are in that vein. Most are extreme views, severe and even splenetic.

Some, too, like "The Business Man," attack one strain in the American character—here, democratic capitalism—while at the same time bringing to the surface subconscious animosities from his past and elements of his personality. "The Business Man" is a first-person account by a petty thief and con artist who presents himself as the desirable ideal of merchantile capitalism. He details roguish scheme after roguish scheme in which he separates innocents from their cash and belongings, all the time emphasizing his orderliness and exactness in method, perhaps a self-conscious jape by Poe at himself, with his mathematical preciseness in formulating criticism and dissecting grammatical structures. (Later, he would be famous for picking apart codes and ciphers.) "Method is *the* thing, after all," the narrator tells us—the same emphasis on craft and technique that Poe would later emphasize in "The Philosophy of Composition" (1846), his account of how he wrote "The Raven." The business man's schemes, from "Assault-and Battery" to "Mud-Dabbling," culminate in "the Cur-Spattering," in which his diminutive dog, Pompey, is an accomplice:

> *Pompey, having rolled himself well in the mud, sat upon end at the shop door, until he observed a dandy approaching in bright boots. He then proceeded to meet him, and gave the Wellingtons a rub or two with his wool. Then the dandy swore very much, and looked about for a boot-black. There I was, full in his view, with blacking and brushes. It was only a minute's work, and then came a sixpence. This did moderately well for a time;—in fact, I was not avaricious, but my dog was. I allowed him a third of the profit, but he was advised to insist upon half. This I couldn't stand—so we quarrelled and parted. (379)*

The story is also a not-so-subconscious attack on John Allan. The business man, named Peter Proffitt, several times draws a sharp distinction between Doers and Thinkers—speculative men of intellect and proponents of the life of art versus commercial, "Republican" men who are money-grubbers, part of a democratic rabble, that was at odds with Poe's aristocratic attitudes. "If there is any thing on earth I hate, it is a genius," says the character. "You cannot make a man of business out of a genius, any more than money out of a Jew" is a statement that recalls Allan's cutting remarks to Poe when he was at the university, forming his intellectual habits and artistic cast of mind.

Another attack on consumer culture came in "The Man That Was Used Up," which relates the life and career of General John A. B. C. Smith, a celebrated American hero who has been "used up," or grievously injured by wounds from the various military campaigns which he has led. Although still an imposing physical specimen (in contrast to the short and effeminate Poe), Smith is now composed mostly of prosthetic devices.

Poe drew the comic inspiration for this tale from several contemporary sources. One was the 1839–1840 presidental campaign of Benjamin Henry Harrison, whose slogan was "Tippecanoe and Tyler, Too." Jeffrey Meyers, one of Poe's biographers, thinks that the character may have been a reference to the English naval hero Horatio Nelson, who had lost an eye in combat in Corsica and an arm in Tenerife. The closest source for the character, however, was General Winfield Scott of Virginia, a relative of John Allan's second wife, who had once met Poe. Scott fought in the Seminole and Creek campaigns and was later Whig candidate for president. Finally, in creating the character Poe may also have been imaginatively recalling his own paternal grandfather, "General" Poe.

The phrase "to be used up" was slang in the nineteenth century for something talked up or written about ad nauseam; but Poe also means it in the sense of emotional exhaustion to the point of being blasé and depleted. After operations, amputations, and upgrades, Smith has become a mechanical man. Absurdly, society sees Smith as simply terrific, a "remarkable man"—a phrase that is repeated so much that it, like Smith himself, eventually rings hollow. Surely some of the injustice Poe felt at thinking himself possessed of a superior intellect and talent yet not attaining the high reputation enjoyed by "lesser" writers was behind this attack on the shallow-minded masses, who latch on to every new fad and gaze wonder-eyed at the latest pop culture icon, without ever really knowing whether that person deserves the accolades that are being heaped upon him. Smith's admirers have no real understanding of what makes him "remarkable"; they simply mouth the empty platitudes of their culture—catchphrases and buzzwords that they hear others say and that they read in print.

In the story, Poe also criticized the way the current "age of invention" had the truly frightening potential to overtake mankind's sense of its humanity and replace it with mechanical or technological marvels, destroying their inner spirituality. Poe disdained the age of technology and feared that it would remove mankind's heart and soul, a theme he also expounded on in the poem "Sonnet—To Science."

Like these tales, Poe's interesting but unfocused essay "The Philosophy of Furniture" takes up the subject of interior decoration in order to inveigh against the material acquisitiveness of ordinary Americans: "It is an evil growing out of our republican institutions," Poe writes, "that here a man of large purse has usually a very little soul which he keeps in it. The corruption of taste is a portion or a pendant of the dollar-manufacture. As we grow rich, our ideas grow rusty" (385–86). Poe goes to great lengths to point out the grotesqueries and gaucheries of much interior design. He does so in the name of good taste and quality, but he was also likely angered at such great displays of wealth and compared his humble lodgings with carpets "bedizzened out like a Riccaree Indian" and "astral lamps" with "cut-glass shades" (384). Poe's model for such households of excess was probably Moldavia, with its rococo architectural details and overly expensive furnishings. Poe starts the essay glancingly, by pointing out that "The Scotch are *poor* decorists" (382). Poe contrasts American excess, the result of lack of taste, with homes in England and on the Continent, which are no such "parade[s] of costly appurtenances" (382). How small and tight Poe's own spare existence must have felt to him when confronted (imaginatively or in person) with such profligate spaces. It may also suggest why the interior settings in most of his tales are so constricted and claustrophobic.

Some of Poe's theory of literature can be seen in this essay, too. Poe is particularly hostile to "the rage for glitter"—glass surfaces reflecting harsh, glaring light, "partly on account of [their] flashiness," but also because "the light proceeding from . . . these gaudy abominations is unequal, broken, and painful" (382). In other words, Poe is reacting against the disarrangement of parts in interior design: the lack of unity, symmetry, and order that were the hallmarks of his aesthetic theory. In "The Philosophy of Furniture," he was applying such ideas about literary creation, later made famous in his reviews of Hawthorne and in "The Philosophy of Composition," to residential architecture. He was also staking out his own independent literary territory, with its gloomy Gothic interiors, lit only by feeble rays of weak sunlight.

Poe's major fiction was not at all of a piece with American ideas and institutions. Poe did have the journalist's interest in whatever was new or faddish, and he sometimes drew inspiration from current topics and things that were in vogue. The tumultuous social changes going on in nineteenth-century America supplied the material for the daily fare of journalism Poe saw about him and that he himself sometimes produced. For the most part, however, Poe wrote apart from the swirls and eddies of social currents in America at the time. In fact, in most of his imaginative work, Poe lived in a world that had little to do with nineteenth-century America. His settings are devoid of technological marvels like internal combustion engines and steamboat travel and are inhabited instead by people who ride on horseback and live in quasi-medieval villages of a faintly European character. The interior settings also tend to be hermetic and even claustrophobic—quite in contrast to the wide-open spaces exalted by Cooper, Francis Parkman, and Irving and painted by Thomas Cole, Albert Bierstadt, and others of the Hudson River school.

Poe also contributed to *Burton's* two of his most prized tales, "William Wilson" and "The Fall of the House of Usher." They are neatly emblematic of Poe's fictive concerns—in their evocation of the supernatural, in their method of narration, and in their concern with the impossibility of repressing the self. In these and later tales Poe develops what is probably the animating principle of his aesthetic and his philosophy of life—the idea that mankind is forever searching for what Poe called Oneness, or the Original Unity, and that dysfunction, anxiety, aberrant behavior, and psychological perversions are the result of humans' separation from their other selves.

In both stories Poe investigates the concept of unity by employing the double—in German the "Doppelgänger" (literally, "double-goer")—the literary technique later used in such famous stories as Robert Louis Stevenson's *Strange Case of Dr. Jekyll and Mr. Hyde* and Joseph Conrad's "The Secret Sharer." In these tales a character is haunted by another being who is an exact image of himself physically but who represents a side of that character's self that is weak or lacking. In this sense, as Allen Tate said, Poe may be regarded as "the transitional figure in modern literature because he discovered our great subject, the disintegration of personality." "William Wilson" is a confessional narrative by a villainous character whose life has embodied a record of "unspeakable misery, and unpardonable crime" (337). Now guilt-ridden and contrite, he tells us that "Men usually grow base by degrees. From me, in an instant, all virtue dropped bodily as a mantle. From comparatively trivial wickedness I passed, with the stride of a giant, into more than the enormities of an Elah-Gabalus" (337). As further proof of his wickedness, this character describes himself as the "slave of circumstances beyond human control," the descendant of "a race whose imaginative and easily excitable temperament has at all times rendered them remarkable" (337–38).

In grammar school, Wilson discovers a classmate with the same name, visage, physique, and background as himself. This double shows up at different intervals in his life: at Eton and then at Oxford, and then again on the Continent during the narrator's travels. Each time the double shows up, the character is about to commit some trespass or sin. This conscience figure eventually provokes the character so much that he stabs him to death, "unresistingly" and "with brute ferocity." As he falls, the narrator sees that there is "not a thread in all his raiment—not a line in all the marked and singular lineaments of his face which was not, even in the most absolute identity, *mine own!*" (356). Having killed the ethical half of his self, he is now dead to the moral world—"*to Heaven, and to Hope!*" (357).

"William Wilson" may be Poe's greatest story of the criminal impulses of the human heart. It is similar to Dostoevsky's early story "The Double" (1846), yet the novelist Thomas Mann thought Poe's the better of the two tales, for Poe treated the topic "in a morally profounder manner, resolving the clinical in the poetic." Poe drew on at least two sources for the story. One was E. T. A. Hoffmann's tale "The Devil's Elixir," published in English by William Blackwood in 1824 and reviewed by John Gibson Lockhart in *Blackwood's Magazine* shortly thereafter. In Hoffmann's story, however, the character's double represents evil, while William Wilson's double is an influence for the good. A second source, which Poe acknowledged, was Washington Irving's article "An Unwritten Drama of Lord Byron," published in the same 1835 issue of *The Gift* in which Poe's own "MS. Found in a Bottle" appeared. Byron's unused plot concerned a character who also stabs his tormentor and finds him to be "his own image—the spectre of himself." At the end of the article, Irving appended a brief note: "The foregoing sketch of the plot may hereafter suggest a rich theme to a poet or dramatist of the Byron school."

In much of his fiction, Poe can be seen adapting and modifying known genres and subgenres. In his criticism, he flatly dismissed the vogue of certain forms of writing, yet he then went on to play around with them himself endlessly, testing their rhetorical boundaries. An immediate inspiration for "William Wilson," therefore, may have been the steady stream of criminal narratives, many of them of the "true confessions" variety, that poured off the cargo ships in all the port cities where Poe lived— Richmond, Philadelphia, and later, New York. Deathbed confessions, gallows narratives, and sensationalistic exposes of the exploits of such scalawags were commonplace, forming a whole subgenre of reading matter.

As David Reynolds points out, Poe's William Wilson is a variation on the type of coolly detached, oddly likable criminal who populated these criminal biographies and trial pamphlets. Manipulative cheats and anti-heroes like William Gilmore Simms's Guy Rivers and Martin Faber (both of whom Poe commented on in various reviews of Simms) and George Lippard's Devil-Bug profoundly influenced the sympathetic treatment of criminals not just in Poe's "William Wilson" and "The Tell-Tale Heart" but also the cretinous, unemotional Chillingworth in Hawthorne's *The Scarlet Letter* and the scientist-father in "Rappaccini's Daughter." So too with Melville's satanic Confidence Man. That novel even begins with a character on the riverboat peddling "the lives of Meason, the bandit of Ohio, Murrel, the pirate of the Mississippi, and the brothers Harpe, the Thugs of the Green River country, in Kentucky." The dark imagery of Poe's tales derives in large part from the pervasiveness of such popular literature.

If one is to play up the pious moralizing of the narrative and play down its possible subversive or parodic elements, it may even be possible to read the story as a version of the early American spiritual autobiography, like those by John Winthrop, Thomas Shepard, Edward Taylor, and Jonathan Edwards. "William Wilson" closely conforms to the traditional patterns in the spiritual autobiography up to the subject's actual conversion.

In such books, the subject progresses through three discrete stages in his journey to salvation. In the first stage, he evinces an early enchantment with religion, in Poe's story suggested by the awe struck in Wilson's heart by Bransby and the school. (The *"peine forte et dure,"* which Wilson refers to in speaking of the fear instilled in him and his classmates by Bransby [340], was a Puritan form of torture.) Stage two shows the character rebelling and taking pride in his lack of righteousness, as Wilson does repeatedly in his boasts. In stage three, repentance and absolution by the Holy Spirit, Wilson may been seen, in contrast, as rejecting salvation by metaphorically killing it, in the form of Wilson Two.

As he often did, however, Poe altered the material for special purposes, and one of those was to show the present being doubled by the past—specifically, Poe's past. He gave the character his own birthday, 19 January 1809 (and in successive versions gave the incorrect dates he sometimes deliberately gave out as well—1811 and 1813). He laid the early parts of the tale at the same school he attended as a boy in England, the Manor House, run by the Reverend Dr. Bransby, and in the next section settled the narrator at 39 Southampton Row, Russell Square, where the Allans lived at the time. The scenes laid at Oxford are also retellings of Poe's reckless behavior at the University of Virginia.

In fact, it is tempting to read the story as a confession of sorts by Poe, especially given his paradoxical character. The story anatomizes a character's dual impulses: to act destructively and irrationally and then to censure himself for his excesses. This theme is later seen in "The Imp of the Perverse," in which Poe speculates that there is some uncontrollable force within humans that makes them act against their wills, and against their better judgments. One can also see the tale as an allegory of the conscious and unconscious selves, an image that would fit Poe's life, too. Poe's conscious self was his logical, rational side—that aspect that made him such a good editor and manager of periodicals, solver of word puzzles, someone who delighted in ciphers, riddles, and was naturally drawn to what he called ratiocination, the basis for the modern detective story. In contrast was his unconscious self—the man who left his editorial offices and went home to write tales of the bizarre and unnatural, the man who was subject to drives and passions that he needed to release through his imaginative writing. Seen this way, Poe was a person who was very tightly wrapped. He seems to have struggled to control his emotions, and kept most personal relationships at arm's length, except for family like Muddy and Sissy, whom he embraced with passion. This unconscious self was kept at bay, perhaps, by Poe's conscious self, which lost itself in journalistic work, with its emphasis on facts, observations, and preciseness in editing. Of course, it is the unconscious self which interests readers today—the one who wrote "much of Madness / and more of Sin / and Horror the soul of the Plot."

Splits, fissures, and dichotomies are typical of Poe's plots, narrative structures, and characters. "William Wilson" seems to proceed moralistically, moving from bad deeds to worse ones. But it also proceeds by a kind of Ramist logic—a progression by dichotomies. Poe was always keenly interested in the war between mind and body. Wilson One seems to represent the baser, carnal desires of man as animal; Wilson Two the more elevated aspects of the self—the intellect, the soul, the spiritual being that keeps the other self in check. Poe believed that the tension between these opposing selves made it impossible to achieve a harmonious, fulfilled existence. Characters like Wilson typically deny one element of their selves—here, the mind. Wholeness thus cannot be achieved. Man needs to reintegrate the opposing forces of his personality, Poe seems to say, and thus achieve unity.

Lastly, the story is a "very Poe-esque protest against death," for it is the tale of a man who kills himself and still lives. Doubling serves Poe well in this regard, for to have a double means that one can "be here and not here, can die and still survive."

Poe's most prized tale, "The Fall of the House of Usher," is the classic expression of Gothicism in American literature. It can also be read as a synthesis of the recurring characteristics of Poe's fiction: interior and exterior settings with potent symbolism; premature burial; the mind/body dichotomy; doubling; and the unnaturalness of suppressing opposite halves of the self.

An unnamed narrator is summoned to the ancestral estate of a boyhood friend, Roderick Usher, who is suffering from a nervous malady that makes him experience "a host of unnatural sensations" and "a morbid acuteness of the senses." To this "anomalous species of terror," the narrator finds Usher "a bounden slave"; Usher tells him, "I shall perish . . . I *must* perish in this deplorable folly" (322). When Usher's twin sister, Madeline, passes through his chamber, like an apparition, the narrator sees that she too is wasting away from the grievous disease. She dies in the course of the story, and is promptly buried in the family vault beneath the house. Then, one evening when the narrator is reading Usher a medieval tale, "The Mad Trist," a scream is heard and Madeline appears outside the chamber door, in ripped and bloody burial garments. It is revealed that Usher has tried to bury his sister alive; she clasps her brother in a death embrace, and as the narrator flees the house in terror, it implodes, sinking into the dank, black tarn that surrounds it.

Houses were always potent symbols for Poe. The Elizabethan mansion of the Reverend Dr. Bransby, with its "terror inspiring" Gothic windows, winding passageways, and "incomprehensible subdivisions" (340), is used to suggest a confused reality for the young schoolboy. Moldavia, an imposing edifice, remained in Poe's consciousness as a bitter memory. And in "The Philosophy of Furniture," Poe commented specifically on the psychological suggestiveness of the arrangement of household furnishings and of décor. The house of the Usher family seems to rise out of its miasmic setting as the narrator rides up to it on horseback. Its "principal feature" is "an excessive antiquity" made worse by an overspreading of fungi across the façade (319). It totters on the verge of complete collapse, a "barely perceptible fissure . . . extending from the roof of the building in front . . . in a zigzag direction, [then becoming] lost in the sullen waters of the tarn" (320). We soon understand that the house and its inhabitants are one and the same—stained by time, used up, crumbling from within, and awaiting collapse.

Poe also uses the doubling motif to suggest that Roderick and Madeline are two faculties of the same soul, the collective soul of one being. The mansion can be read as a metaphor for their body. All three decline together, as the disappearance, or suppresssion, of one means the disappearance of the others. This occurs as Roderick tries to get rid of his opposite half, just as William Wilson does. But why does he do so? An answer may lie in Poe's portrayal of Roderick as an artist figure of sorts, someone who tries to live a life purely of the mind. Madeline, in contrast, represents the corporeal half of the self, which he tries to suppress. Her reclaiming him at the end of the story results in the completeness which is death. The "house" of Usher is meant to suggest both the physical dwelling and the family line, for there is more than a hint of incest in the narrator's observations about the Usher disease. Structurally, the split or schism is figured in the tale of Ethelred, which the narrator tells to Usher (doubling, in turn, Poe's relation to the reader, as author to audience), in the "reduplication in the still waters of the tarn," and in the image of the "fissure" that runs down the middle of the front exterior of the house itself.

One of the most lasting effects of the tale is the sense of claustrophia. Usher's chamber admits only "[f]eeble gleams of encrimsoned light," which "struggled in vain to reach the remoter angles of the chamber, or the recesses of the vaulted and fretted ceiling. Dark draperies hung upon the walls" (320). He feels that he has "breathed an atmosphere of sorrow. An air of stern, deep, and irredeemable gloom hung over and pervaded all" (321). So much is boxed or buried or hidden in Poe—this at a time when other writers were expanding American literature to take in vistas of seemingly boundless open spaces and their corollary boundless, democratic opportunities for themes. Poe, by contrast, confined himself to a rigid set of exact aesthetic criteria and technical specifications, and he put his characters in narrow, cramped, and confined spaces, often circumscribed by dungeon floors or cavern walls and often reached through a labyrinthine route of underground or out-of-the-way passages.

"Usher" might also be a symbolic depiction of the dying out of the southern aristocracy, since the mansion and its landscape evoke plantation images. In the tale, Poe employs the Gothic formula to construct a kind of jeremiad about the destruction of a culture; Madeline comes to bury the past, but she does not do so in order to make possible a future. Poe's house of Usher may symbolize opposition and fear of a world that he felt threatened the southern pastoral ideal and, possibly, the ideal of southern womanhood, as well.

In fact, whether directly or by implication, when Poe wrote he was very often writing as a southerner, speaking for the South. Much of the popular academic image of Poe nowadays is of an essentialist Poe—a pure man of letters devoted only to aesthetic ideals. However, Poe was the sole original voice coming out of the Old South at this point in the development of American literature, and although he rarely employed southern locales or character types, he did often weigh in on the issues of slavery, southern autonomy and separatism, and the obstinate oils and waters of northern and southern political attitudes. Poe was acquainted with, indeed connected to, the historical situation of Virginia in the 1820s and 1830s. As Poe's aesthetic and philosophical theories developed, an increasing disbelief in a cyclical view of history began to be folded into them. The Virginia dynasty of Washington, Jefferson, Madison, and Monroe had ended in 1825, and the intellectual leadership of the nation had moved elsewhere. "The glory of the Ancient Dominion," Poe wrote in 1835, "is in a fainting, is in a dying condition," a shadow of "things that *have been*." The 1830s marked the most turbulent period of slaveholder versus abolitionist antagonism and the Virginia legislative debates over emancipation (1831–32). Poe had moved north in 1837 by circumstance rather than by choice, and by 1841, he would lament that there was scarcely one "person of any literary distinction in the chief city of the Old Dominion."

It is possible to read several of Poe's stories as covert allegories endorsing the ethos of the antebellum South, particularly in their infrequent but obvious stereotyped characterizations of African Americans. Black characters, when they do appear, are either ignorant, stupidly happy, or darkly insidious: the murderous black cook in *Arthur Gordon Pym* and the docile servants Jupiter in "The Gold-Bug" and Pompey in "A Predicament," for example, come to mind. The social and racial dimensions of *Arthur Gordon Pym* are also frequently spotlighted, perhaps with some reason, as beginning in the 1830s various arguments for Anglo racial superiority gained currency in the United States. Pseudosciences like phrenology (which Poe accepted as true) and theories like that of polygenesis, the derivation of a species or type from more than one ancestor or germ cell (an idea which never gained acceptance in the South), fueled the arguments of proslavery apologists. Yet *Pym* seems to question the view that Poe is endorsing assumptions about race. Like many Poe texts, *Pym* proceeds by binary opposition. In most texts these are polarized archetypes like height and depth, water and aridity—or especially with Poe, the mind and the body. But in *Pym* they are racial—a Manichaean world where the colors black and white dominate but do not mix (white is the dominant color of the first half of the novel; black the other) until the final chapters, in the uncharted waters below the equator (the southern hemisphere). Here, the rigid system of black-white imagery breaks down from strict separation to a vaporous mist that is repeatedly described as "gray"—a blend of black and white.

In his reviews of novels, Poe often drew attention to the delineation of black characters, as in his notice of James Fenimore Cooper's *Wyandotte* (an author whom Poe otherwise disliked) when he mentioned the "admirably drawn" Negroes (486), or in his review of Robert Montgomery Bird's *Sheppard Lee* when he praised the "very excellent chapters upon abolition and the exciting effects of incendiary pamphlets and pictures among our slaves in the South"—a part of the narrative, Poe added, that ended with a "spirited picture of a negro insurrection" and the resultant hanging of the character named "Nigger Tom" (399).

Alternatively, an author who came in for uncensured scorn was Longfellow. In an omnibus review of Longfellow's works for the *Aristidean* in April 1845, Poe cut a swathe through much of the poet's shelf of books. Poe condemned *Poems on Slavery* as "intended for the especial use of those negrophilic old ladies of the north" who were so cosy with Longfellow and with William Ellery Channing, leader of the Unitarian church, to whom the volume was dedicated. In shredding the spurious assumptions behind the poem "The Slave's Dream," Poe noted that it was "a very commendable and comfortable thing, in the Professor, to sit at ease in his library chair, and write verses instructing the southerners how to give up their all with a good grace, and abusing them if they will not; but we have a singular curiosity to know how much of his own, under a change of circumstances, the Professor himself would be willing to surrender"

100

(762–63). More comments like this punctuate the review, assailing Longfellow for his sectional bias.

Was Poe a racist? Many scholars have hinged their arguments, pro or con, on Poe's possible authorship of a review in the *Messenger* of two books that endorsed slavery. The evidence for attribution of this piece is marginal and shaky at best. Those who want to see Poe as racist exaggerate the conclusiveness of the evidence; those who do not downplay it or ignore it entirely. Most likely, Poe agreed in principle with the attitudes he absorbed through his southern upbringing, though this does not make him overtly, in modern parlance, a "racist."

"The Fall of the House of Usher" is also the essential illustration in Poe's fiction of his theory of the "tale," or short story, which he began to develop about this time in a *Burton's* review of Edward Bulwer-Lytton's novel *Night and Morning*. It is significant for its definition of fictional plot (that is, structure or design); the definition prefigures the one in his more familiar review of Hawthorne's *Twice-Told Tales* that appeared in 1842. Poe's statement in the Bulwer review that a good plot is one "*in which no part can be displaced without ruin to the whole*" is an advance over his earlier definitions of plot and unity in the *Messenger* reviews. He expanded on (one might say exaggerated) Aristotle's theory that lack of unity will result in disjointedness by stating that it would be detrimental to the entire work, and he corrected Schlegel by saying that "most persons think of [plot] as simple complexity. It may be described as a building so dependently constructed, that to change the position of a single brick is to overthrow the entire fabric." "The greatest involution of incident," Poe said, would "not result in plot" (148–49).

One of Poe's greatest critical achievements was that he defined the tale, or short story, as we call it today. "A short prose narrative," he said in the Dickens review, "requiring from a half-hour to one or two hours in its perusal." This required high artistic control by writer and excited great interest in the reader. No "extrinsic" influences to distract reader or disturb its effect—the tale and the tale alone is important.

Poe held an Aristotelian view of form and technique that is perfectly illustrated by "The Fall of the House of Usher." The story begins and ends with similar rhetorical strategies that at the conclusion of the tale enact a symbolic closure, or burial, of the scene before us. "Usher" opens with the house seeming to rise out of a dank tarn to meet its visitor, then at the end seems to fall back, or devolve, into the primordial matter that has created it:

> *During the whole of a dull, dark, and soundless day in the autumn of the year, when the clouds hung oppressively low in the heavens, I had been passing alone, on horseback, through a singularly dreary tract of country; and at length found myself, as the shades of the evening drew on, within view of the melancholy House of Usher.*

> *While I gazed, this fissure rapidly widened—there came a fierce breath of the whirlwind—the entire orb of the satellite burst at once upon my sight—my brain reeled as I saw the mighty walls rushing asunder—there was a long tumultuous shouting sound like the voice of a thousand waters—and the deep and dank tarn at my feet closed sullenly and silently over the fragments of the "House of Usher."*

The story achieves unity by one dramatic effect, which takes place during a fierce windstorm at night; it is a correlative of the destruction going on within the house.

Another important essay was the "Exordium to Critical Notices." This manifesto contradicted the assumption that criticism could take any one of a number of forms—essays, sermons, history, philosophy, oratory— and further stated that criticism should be treated as a science rather than merely as an expression of opinion. Poe criticized the vogue of the review-essay and the shallow patriotism of literary nationalism, as well as the kinds of critical standards that would allow a Harrison Ainsworth or a Morris Mattson to be praised.

Finally, Poe added a significant element to his philosophy of criticism in defining what criticism should critique: it should be employed only "upon productions which have their basis in art itself" (1032). Although Poe had always advocated a rigorous, analytical criticism, he was by this point becoming more predisposed toward responsible (and objective) criticism, perhaps aware of his earlier impetuousness in the *Messenger* reviews. One indication of this maturity is his somewhat negative view of John Wilson's ("Christopher North") collected *Essays* that January. Poe criticized Wilson for some of the very qualities that characterized his own early reviews. This revised perspective places Poe squarely in the camp of the critical methodology that would in the 1940s come to be known as formalism or New Criticism, a belief that the task of the critic was to show how, through an analysis of language and form, a work of art expressed universal meanings.

It is hard to imagine Poe working any harder than he was, pushing his intellectual and imaginative abilities to the limit. He was producing what would become his classic tales of the supernatural, yet he was also refining his aesthetic theories at the same time, using his own fiction to illustrate them. To one correspondent he apologized for his delay in answering a recent letter—the "storm of business" that daily plagued him prevented a more timely reply.

Yet while some of Poe's best fiction was published in *Burton's*, he had great difficulty interesting a publisher in bringing out a collected edition of his works. He finally found a local house, Lea and Blanchard, but the terms were miserable—barely one step up from a vanity publication. The publishers agreed to issue an edition of 1750 copies "at their own risque and expense," from which they took sole profit. Poe was given twenty free copies as compensation. This collection of twenty-five stories, called *Tales of the Grotesque and Arabesque*, included almost everything he had so far put into print. He revised most of the tales meticulously and wrote a brief preface in which he downplayed the Germanic nature of the horror stories: "If in many of my productions terror has been the thesis, I maintain that terror is not of Germany but of the soul."

What did he mean precisely by the terms he used to describe the nature of this "terror"? In the preface, Poe refers vaguely to the "arabesque" tales as those based in horror; from this critics have inferred that the "grotesque" ones are the comic "Tales of the Folio Club." Both terms indicated an imaginative profusion and complexity, the opposite of the rule and order found in the classical Western view of art. To visualize the terms one should therefore think of canvases by Bosch and Bruegel rather than the work of Caravaggio or the Dutch genre painters. Both terms also conveyed the idea of a self split between the rational and the imaginative. "Grotesque" comes from the Italian *grottesca*, identified with nonrepresentational Italian "grotta paintings" that blended persons and animals with foliage, flowers, fruit—fantastic designs that were overfanciful, antithetical to the well-ordered, rational sphere. The word "arabesque" stems from Arabic designs—highly ornamental, intertwining and geometrically abstract patterns used in connection with pointed arches, soaring turrets, and minarets.

Poe hoped that the reviews of the book would bring his talent to national attention, but he was disappointed. The notices were generally favorable, but the book was ahead of its time and so did not sell well enough to sustain interest. Poe most likely was heartened by the fact, however, that the reviewers praised him personally. Joseph Clay Neal, in the *Pennsylvanian*, said that "Poe follows in nobody's track,—his imagination seems to have a domain of its own to revel in," and the reviewer for the Philadelphia *Saturday Courier* asserted that the author was "possessed of rare and varied learning" and compared him to Coleridge. Other reviewers were more impressed by the potential that the volume evinced than its actual achievement. One remarked that the stories "seem . . . the playful effusion of a remarkable and powerful intellect" and urged Poe not to rest on his laurels but to show that he "fully" deserved them "by actual performance." Only one review, in the *Boston Morning Post*, was negative—as severe as Poe's own censures: "A greater amount of trash within the same compass would be difficult to find."

In August 1841, a year and a half later, Poe tried to interest Lea and Blanchard in a new edition of the volume, with eight new stories added. He even volunteered (again) to forego any royalties, but the publishers quickly declined. "We very much regret to say that the state of affairs is such as to give little encouragement to new undertakings," they diplomatically wrote him, then added a bit more frankly: "As yet we have not gotten through the edition of the other work and up to this time it has not returned to us the expense of its publication."

In the magazine world, however, Poe continued to receive plaudits left and right. The *St. Louis Commercial Bulletin*, for instance, spoke of the "glowing pen of Edgar A. Poe, now assistant editor of *Burton's Gentleman's Magazine*" and praised Poe's "acuteness of observation, . . . vigorous and effective style, and . . . independence that defies control." "His is a high destiny," the piece concluded. Poe copied the article and rushed it off to his cousin Neilson, telling him to reprint in his newspaper—a puff—and when Neilson wouldn't do so, Poe angrily accused him of obstructing his success and recalled his attempt to lure Virginia away from him. Soon thereafter, Poe condemned Neilson in a letter to Joseph Snodgrass:

In your private ear, I believe him to be the bitterest enemy I have in the world. He is the more despicable in this, since he makes loud professions of friendship. Was it "relationship &c." which prevented him saying any thing at all of the 2 or 3 last Nos. of the Gents' Mag? I cannot account for his hostility except in being vain enough to imagine him jealous of the little literary reputation I have, of late years, obtained. But enough of the little dog.

Friendships in Poe's world were tenuous; they came and went as quickly as a spring snow.

Such turned out inevitably to be the case with Billy Burton. Like Thomas White before him, Burton had grown weary of defending Poe's scathing critiques of other authors, and he stopped printing them. "You must get rid of your avowed ill-feelings toward your brother-authors," Burton told his editor. "You see that I speak plainly—indeed, I cannot speak otherwise . . . your article on [Rufus] Dawes [a minor poet] is not written with that spirit of fairness which, in a more healthy state of mind, you would undoubtedly have used." To help Poe "regain a wholesome activity of mind," Burton advised more exercise. On what looks like a pretext, Poe got angry at Burton for an earlier harsh review of *Pym* in which Burton, noting the confused senses of fact and fantasy in the manner of the book's publication, wrote that "We regret to find Mr. Poe's name in connexion with such a mass of ignorance and effrontery." Poe himself had once called *Pym* "a very silly book," but he did not summon this assessment to mind when he fired back at Burton, "Had I written a similar criticism upon a book of yours, you feel that you would have been my enemy for life, and you therefore imagine in my bosom a latent hostility."

The inevitable break between the owner and his hot-tempered editor finally occurred in May 1840 when Burton, who had been spending more time at the theatre than at his magazine, realized that two interests were more than he could handle. Choosing the stage over the page, Burton put his magazine up for sale, and didn't tell Poe about it beforehand. Eventually it was sold to George Rex Graham, the Philadelphia publisher of a competing periodical, *The Casket*. Poe realized that the sale would probably mean he was out of a job, so he drew up a prospectus for his own magazine and started circulating it. Burton, in turn, was enraged. He thought that news of Poe's magazine would decrease the sale price of his own periodical, and he fired Poe on the spot.

Angered beyond sense, Poe stormed out of the office, then sent Burton a blistering letter that accused him of everything from philistinism to fraud. Burton believed that Poe had borrowed a hundred dollars from him and never repaid the loan, so he instructed his clerk to withhold three dollars a week from Poe's pay until the debt was settled; now he wanted full repayment. Poe responded: "You do me gross injustice; and you know it. As usual you have wrought yourself into a passion with me on account of some imaginary wrong; for no real injury, or attempt at injury, have you ever received at my hands . . . You are a man of impulses; have made yourself, in consequence, some enemies; have been in many respects ill treated by those who you had looked upon as friends—and these things have rendered you suspicious." Such a letter could do Poe no credit, for it is at the level of schoolroom sniping. (It also sounds very much like Poe's indignant reproaches of John Allan.) Poe preached dignity and restraint in literary criticism, but in personal matters he could be petty and defensive. Ironically, Poe's descriptions in this letter of Burton's behavior are apt descriptions of his own imaginings about being wrongly accused.

In Poe's defense, it must be said that he was serious about literature in a world that often treated it as little more than clubbish amateurism. His high-strung earnestness, his contempt for cant, shallowness, and willful stupidity probably amused his fellow journalists, laboring in the vineyards of cheap verbal plonk. Picture him in editorial offices and reporters' hangouts in Philadelphia: he must have cut an odd figure—sensuous-looking and pale-complexioned; dressed in black; courteous and soft in speech, yet, as several recalled, the courtesy had in it an undertone of irony which turned irritating and even arrogant very quickly. One can see the small, derisive smiles that must have appeared on the faces of those whom he interrogated and preached to about writing, how those same people, once they had turned their backs, must have rolled their eyes, thinking him an obvious crank. Poe was deadly earnest about what for others was just a way of making a living.

After being sacked, Poe wrote a sneering, bilious letter to Snodgrass calling Burton a scoundrel and trying to enlist Snodgrass's aid in a scheme to go down to the magazine offices in order to retrieve some manuscripts of his that he was alleging Burton had kept and lied about: "I would go down with you to the office, open the drawer in his presence, and take the M. S. from beneath his very nose. . . . What do you think of this plan? Will you come on? Write immediately in reply." Snodgrass had the tact not to reply, but even later, after the break was complete, Poe continued to nurse a grudge against his former employer: "Burton," he wrote Snodgrass, "that illustrious 'graduate of St John's College, Cambridge,' is going to the devil with the worst grace in the world, but with a velocity truly astounding. The press . . . have given him the cut direct. So be it—suum cuique. We have said q[u]ite enough about this genius."

For Poe, the dispute and subsequent break was a personal injury, an unconscionable attack on the citadel of high art and all that was sacred in the literary realm. Burton would be sorry that he took so rash a step, Poe claimed, for the future of literary criticism and American art hung in the balance. The split did not affect Burton, however, in the least, for it was merely a matter of business, and there were plenty of other interesting and profitable things to do with one's life. His parting words to George Graham were to look after Poe, and give him some consideration.

CHAPTER 6

GRAHAM'S MAGAZINE
"THE PENN," AND THE RED DEATH
[1841–1843]

After Poe had fallen out with Billy Burton, his initial plan was to start a magazine of his own, "The Penn," to rival Burton's and everyone else's. Its chief aim would be to offer "upon all subjects, an honest and fearless opinion." However, in December Poe became ill and was confined to his bed for several weeks, thus forcing him to delay the launch of the magazine. In February, a sudden financial crisis plagued the Philadelphia-area banks, and money was hard to obtain, thus forcing another postponement. Poe cited these as his reasons for not getting the magazine off the ground, but in truth the biggest reason for delay was a familiar one for Poe—lack of money. He had yet to enlist the financial support of people whom he could count on to provide the start-up funds. In fact, Poe would talk about and make concerted attempts to set this dream project in motion many times in the few remaining years of his short-lived career, but it was a dream that would never be realized.

For now, Poe was out of work, so he once again cast about for steady employment. Although he did not want to do so, Poe accepted a job back in his old office at *Burton's*, for in October Burton had sold his magazine to George Rex Graham, a local lawyer and amateur writer. At the time, Graham owned a small but flourishing magazine of his own, called *The Casket*. This magazine, which had been in business since 1826, was subtitled "Flowers of Literature, Wit, and Sentiment," a title which well describes its content. It was a middlebrow miscellany of sentimental and inspirational stories and articles—a cross between today's *Reader's Digest* and *Chicken Soup for the Soul*. A recent historian has described it well: "Across the pages of *Graham's* many stories and poems fluttered a veritable aviary of Keatsian birds; here quailed armies of orphans and widows beleaguered by Saracenic misfortune and there grew copses of sublime trees. The forest sheltered tribes of noble but safely expiring Indians; the hearts and villages welcomed back contrite souls who had wandered from middle-class verities."

Graham merged his *Casket* with the *Gentleman's Magazine*, paying Burton thirty-five hundred dollars, or one dollar per subscriber. Like Burton, Graham was a shrewd businessman and a hard worker. He had worked his way up from being a cabinetmaker to studying for the bar and was by this time quite well off and well respected. A boyish-looking, clean-shaven man, Graham was by all accounts gracious, friendly, and liberal with what he paid his authors—but not his editors, and although Poe started his new duties for Graham at a salary about three hundred dollars higher than he had for Burton, he still never profited from his labors. Graham started his new magazine with a combined total circulation of five thousand (by itself a huge figure), yet by February 1842, when Poe resigned the editorship, the magazine's circulation was forty thousand, making it one of the three or four most successful and important periodicals in American publishing history. Poe made George Graham a very rich man, but he reaped little in return.

On the positive side, Poe's duties at *Graham's* included less drudge work than at *Burton's*. An assistant editor took care of vetting manuscripts and corresponding with contributors, leaving Poe a good deal of time for his own writing. The magazine was high quality, with expensive engravings (many by the Philadelphian John Sartain, the best American engraver of the day) and fiction by well-known authors, among them Hawthorne, Bryant, Lowell, Cooper, and Oliver Wendell Holmes. Insisting on never-before-published contributions, Graham established an as-yet unheard of pay scale, "at least as liberal," Poe said, "as that of any publisher in America." Graham had to compete against nearly four hundred other magazines; to do so, he knew he had to offer authors very generous terms.

The magazine also ran essays on art, nature, and topics of current interest, but nothing controversial. There was a strong moral and pious element to the magazine as well as material designed to appeal to female audiences—fashion plates, articles on dress and etiquette, and other "domestic" matters. This diet could hardly have been palatable to Poe, but he stuck it out since he needed a steady income.

In fact, this was the most stable period in Poe's nomadic life. He was proud of his middle-class position in the world, and he often brought visitors home to dinner. He could show off the new harp and piano that he had bought for Virginia to encourage her interest in music, and the four-poster beds, thick red carpets, and white curtains purchased for Muddy, to provide comfort after a long day of housework. One journalist companion who visited the house wrote of "the little garden in summer, and the house in winter overflowing with luxuriant grape and other vines, and liberally ornamented with choice flowers of the poet's selection." He described Virginia as happy and full of life—"an exquisite picture of patient loveliness, always wearing upon her beautiful countenance the smile of resignation, and the warm, ever-cheerful look with which she greeted her friends."

The house was small but apparently had a sizable yard, for one of Poe's southern friends offered the gift of a pet fawn. Poe had to turn it down due to the difficulties of transporting the animal to Philadelphia, but thanked him for the sentiment—"precisely as if the little fellow were nibbling the grass before our windows." While Poe was at work in *Graham's* top-floor office on Third and Chestnut streets—the hub of the publishing district—Muddy and Virginia would go out shopping, then return to cook. After the day's work at the magazine was finished, Poe would sit at home writing. A tortoiseshell cat, Caterina, completed the household: a picture of complete domestic tranquility.

At work, Poe was his usual productive self. In literary criticism, he continued his campaign to topple the billboard-sized picture of American literature that his colleagues had constructed. During these years, Poe also matured as a critic, defining the role of the critic as mediator between a work of genius and an untutored public. He validated beauty and feeling as innate human needs that were fulfilled by poetry, rejecting the didacticism of Longfellow, Bryant, and others. In his critical essays on Hawthorne's short fiction, Poe defined the tale and firmed up his ideas about the unity of effect that a tale must achieve in order to be successful. In fiction, Poe produced for *Graham's* on average one tale per month—an impressive rate. Some of them, admittedly, were lesser works like "Never Bet the Devil Your Head" and "A Succession of Sundays." Yet here he also published the weirdly imagined but philosophically important "Colloquy of Monos and Una," which trods the by now familiar but still irresistible imaginative territory of resisting death. In the tale, Poe speculates about erasing the boundaries between existence and nonexistence and insists that all things are one, thus reiterating his insistence on some original cosmological unity.

These tales and others drew readers to the magazine like never before, but the most successful writing that Poe did for *Graham's* was his popular series on cryptography—the solving of ciphers and word-puzzles. This boosted circulation greatly and lent Poe another dimension of fame as an analytical and mathematical genius.

It was natural that Poe should be drawn to ciphers, given that side of him that showcased his orderly and disciplined mind, as well as his hyperlogical, analytical method of literary criticism. Many readers have also seen in Poe's interest in cryptography a natural corollary to his own puzzling stories, which in some ways are encoded "texts" that Poe challenges the reader to decipher. Poe's interest in the reciprocal acts of writing and reading, encoding and decoding, can be seen early on—in "MS. Found in a Bottle," for example, and *The Narrative of Arthur Gordon Pym*, in which maps, hieroglyphs, and flakings on cavern walls can be translated through knowledge of Ethiopian and Arabic alphabets.

Poe's interest in word-puzzles went back some years. At the *Southern Literary Messenger* in 1836, he had started a series called "Autography," or handwriting analysis. When that was successful, he urged readers to send in ciphers with the key phrase in Latin, Greek, French, Italian, or German, which he successfully solved. In the Philadelphia newspaper *Alexander's Weekly Messenger* in December 1839, Poe published an article,

"Enigmatical and Conundrum-ical," in which he solved a riddle that had baffled one of the paper's subscribers. As usual, Poe was tying into a topic of current interest. Numerous periodicals had run articles about a recently discovered system of "secret writing" developed by Charles I which had been found among the royal manuscripts in the British Museum; one of them was the well-known letter in which the monarch made concessions to the Roman Catholics of Ireland, contained in a coded note to the Earl of Glamorgan.

Most of these puzzles were simple substitution ciphers, in which a different alphabetical order (called litoreia) or series of numbers corresponding to letters was employed. None of Poe's challengers tried to stump him with puzzle-type cryptograms that used bizarre words and twisted syntax. In fact, most made it easy for Poe by taking as their plaintext (the original message of a cryptogram) some commonly known piece of writing like the Ten Commandments or the Lord's Prayer. Still, for someone with no extensive mathematical training other than his courses at West Point, Poe's success at solving the ciphers was impressive.

At *Graham's Magazine* Poe branched out a bit by moving from simple monalphabetics with word divisions to cryptograms that employed polyphonic substitution, a feat he would have his detective-hero Legrand repeat in the cipher-based mystery story "The Gold-Bug." Poe's success here created the legend of his ability to solve any cryptogram instantly, and he quickly exploited his renown with an article called "A Few Words on Secret Writing," published in the July 1840 issue of *Graham's*. Here he churned up more interest in his series. "This challenge [has] excited, most unexpectedly," Poe wrote,

a very lively interest among the numerous readers of the journal. Letters were poured in upon the editor from all parts of the country; and many of the writers of these epistles were so convinced of the impenetrability of their mysteries, as to be at great pains to draw him into wagers on the subject. At the same time, they were not always scrupulous about sticking to the point. The cryptographs were, in numerous instances, altogether beyond the limits defined in the beginning. Foreign languages were employed. Words and sentences were run together without interval. Several alphabets were used in the same cipher. One gentleman, but moderately endowed with conscientiousness, inditing us a puzzle composed of pot-hooks and hangers to which the wildest typography of the office could afford nothing similar, went even so far as to jumble together no less than seven distinct alphabets, *without intervals between the letters,* or between the lines. . . . *Out of, perhaps, one hundred ciphers altogether received, there was only one which we did not immediately succeed in resolving. This one we* demonstrated *to be an imposition—that is to say, we fully proved it a jargon of random characters, having no meaning whatever. (1281)*

When Poe's own difficult cipher could not be solved, he ran a contest, offering a year's subscription to the magazine to anyone who could solve it. A torrent of answers came in, and actually so wearied Poe that, after a while, he closed the contest and withdrew the offer.

Poe's series on cryptography was probably his most successful journalistic writing. However, its greater importance may be that it led him into creative writing that took as its subject an even more ingenious sort of puzzle-making and puzzle-solving detective fiction, or what Poe preferred to call "tales of ratiocination," or logical reasoning. Poe published three stories with a central detective-hero. Two, "The Murders in the Rue Morgue" and "The Purloined Letter," were set in Paris and featured one C. Auguste Dupin, a chevalier of the French empire and intimate of the city's nobility. The third, "The Gold-Bug" (in which cryptography plays an essential role in the solution to the mystery), featured a somewhat different character, a recluse named William Legrand, and was set in Sullivan's Island, South Carolina, where Poe had been stationed briefly in 1827 at Fort Moultrie. Two minor tales, "Thou Art the Man" and "The Oblong Box" also belong to the genre. After the success of "The Rue Morgue," Poe produced "The Murder of Marie Roget," a sequel, also a detective story, but one based on an actual murder—that of a clerk in a Manhattan cigar store, one Mary Rogers, whose corpse was found in the Hudson River. Poe took this real-life case and dramatized it as fiction, switching the setting from New York to Paris in order to use Dupin in it.

"The Murders in the Rue Morgue" was the very first detective story. (Poe's only near-model was the 1748 *Zadig*, by Voltaire.) Ever the journalist, Poe was the first to spy a trend in modern society and write about it, for crime was on the rise. There were no municipal police forces per se, only private "security firms" and groups of paid "watchmen" who were often as nefarious as the criminals they were paid to apprehend. Crime was a subject of much discussion in the papers, and the only professional police force then in existence was in London—"the bobbies," established by Robert Peel only twelve years earlier. American cities were just beginning to formalize police operations and to employ the methods of "scientific" detective work, such as forensic analysis. The gutter press and the criminal element fed off each other: newspapers like the "penny dreadfuls" were awash in gruesome details of murders and rapt descriptions of barroom brawls and back-alley knife fights in the less seemly quarters of the nation's cities.

"The Rue Morgue" inaugurated what we today think of as the classic formula of detective fiction. In it, Poe set down the pattern of the genre for all successive mystery writers, from Arthur Conan Doyle through Agatha Christie and the genre's "Golden Age" to contemporary writers like Ruth Rendell and P. D. James. This includes the Watson-like narrator, somewhat dull and not as intelligent as the detective he serves and admires and who tells the stories of their exploits with great admiration; the so-called "locked room" mystery, in which a murder has occurred in a space to which there are no visible entrances or exits that are not sealed; the somewhat eccentric but brilliantly cerebral detective, a la Sherlock Holmes, who is called in to do what the rather bumbling police are unable to do; the scientific analysis of evidence through deductive reasoning; and the systematic interrogation of suspects, culminating in the now-standard gathering of all suspects (often in the library of a country house) in which the detective delivers an "I-suppose-you're-all-wondering-why-I brought-you-here" speech, naming the perpetrator at the end.

However, Poe's Dupin differs from Holmes and his successors in at least two important ways. First, Dupin's motive is atypical. Later detective characters, as W. H. Auden pointed out in his classic essay

"The Guilty Vicarage," have altruistic motives. They do what they do in order to right injustice and to restore a fallen world to its prelapsarian innocence. Dupin, in contrast, is a dilettante who takes on his "cases" either for amusement—in "The Purloined Letter," it's to show off his skills in front of the nitwit police inspector—or to repay a favor—in "The Rue Morgue," the accused is a man who had "done him a good turn" once before. Legrand takes on the mission because he is greedy and wants the buried treasure (the subject of the mystery) for himself.

Second, Dupin's method is exclusively cerebral, unlike those who followed him in the detective fiction tradition. In the Holmes stories, for example, the detective often relies on reference works, newspaper clippings, and the advice of consulting experts in order to solve the crime. Such detective characters also often use plain common sense to adduce an answer. For example, in one story, Holmes figures out that a criminal suspect is so many feet tall because he has written something on a wall, and it would be written at eye level, thus giving an approximate measure of the person's height. (One of the few modern detective characters who can compare with Dupin in intellectual candlepower is Agatha Christie's Hercule Poirot.) Poe demonstrates Dupin's formidable reasoning powers in a scene early in the story where the detective tells his companion what another person has been thinking by following a train of thought from a topic his companion announced nearly an hour earlier, before they set off on a stroll through the city.

The tale proper concerns the brutal murder of a mother and daughter, Madame and Mademoiselle L'Espanaye, in the locked fourth-story bedroom of their apartment house in the Rue Morgue in Paris. (Although there was no actual Rue Morgue in that city, the title of the story, as Jeffrey Meyers notes, ingeniously links "murders" with "morgue" and conveys by association the idea of "morbid.") Dupin and his Watson-like narrator-companion read about the incident in the newspaper, and Dupin investigates. The Gothic house in which the women live resembles the house of Usher, as do other details of the story, such as the heightening of interest in the macabre details of the murder, which directs the reader's thinking to the mind/body dichotomy Poe so often explored. It comes

115

out that Madame L'Espanaye's throat was slashed with a razor, so that when the police attempt to lift up her corpse, her head falls back, and almost comes off. The daughter's body has been rammed feet first upward into the chimney. Several thousand francs in gold, delivered the day before, have not been stolen. The doors and windows to the room are all locked from the inside.

Testimony from witnesses, who heard screams from outside the building, is contradictory and thus inconclusive. All are of different nationalities, and none can identify the language that was heard coming from the building. All they are certain of is hearing either "a shrill voice" or a "gruff" one. Dupin deduces that the murderer could not have escaped down the central stairway of the building without being seen. He then reasons that the murderer was very agile, escaping through a sash in the window, which dropped of its own accord and became fastened, as it slammed shut, by a concealed spring. The nail in the bottom sash which looked fixed was actually broken at the head, making it therefore seem like the window was nailed permanently shut.

Based on the evidence of the coarse, reddish hair that Madame L'Espanaye is clutching in one hand, and the prehensile marks around her throat, Dupin concludes that the murderer was not human at all, but rather an "ourang-outang," which must have escaped from its owner. He advertises for the owner of the ape in the paper, and when the person comes forth (a sailor), Dupin convinces him to reveal all, knowing he is guiltless in the committing of the crime. In slashing the throats of its "victims," the ape was merely imitating what he had seen the sailor do—shave his face in the mornings. This fictional murder seems likely to have inspired a later, very Poe-esque work: *Native Son*, by Richard Wright. In that novel, the black character Bigger Thomas, who is later dehumanizingly described in the white press as ape-like, murders Mary Dalton by suffocating her (as in "The Tell-Tale Heart"), decapitating her with a hatchet (as in this story and in the parodic "A Predicament"), and then shoving her body into a furnace.

Poe most likely got his inspiration for the unusual "murderer" from the much publicized exhibition of an orangutan from Africa at Philadelphia's

Masonic Hall during August and September 1839. The *Pennsylvania Inquirer* for July 1 reported that the ape was "more perfect in its proportions, and in its resemblance to the human form, than any specimen of the kind, ever seen in this country." Despite its hero's feats of intellectual legerdemain, Poe did not think much of "The Rue Morgue," downplaying it to friends. Poe told his friend Philip Pendleton Cooke that "These tales of ratiocination owe most of their popularity to being something in a new key. I do not mean to say they are not ingenious—but people think they are more ingenious than they are—on account of their method and *air* of method. . . . Where is the ingenuity of unravelling a web which you yourself (the author) have woven for the express purpose of unravelling?"

Yet just as the appearance of the crime scene in the story gulls the police into seeing no rhyme or reason for the murder, so too does Poe in the story gull the impercipient reader into thinking that all there is to the tale is what meets the eye of the casual observer. As the narrator says just after the introductory paragraphs, a prefatory excursus on the nature of "the Bi-Partite Soul," "I am [not] . . . penning any romance" (402). The story uses doubling and homosexuality to suggest the imperfectness of the human animal, the essential irreconcilability of opposites, and the need to reintegrate opposing forces of the Self.

The narrator and Dupin are doubles for each other, as are Madame and Mademoiselle L'Espanaye. Each pair of characters lives on the fourth floor of gloomy, Gothic houses with "windows in their bosoms." As in "Usher," Poe uses the house as a metaphor for the body. Both couples' rooms are on the fourth and top story of an otherwise empty house, the top floor thus suggesting that the couples live only in the mind—therefore, both deny the body. Each (again like Roderick Usher) lives "an exceedingly retired life" in "perfect seclusion."

Poe suggests that each couple's relationship is a homosexual one. The narrator tells of his attraction to Dupin: "I felt my soul enkindled within me by the wild fervor . . . of his imagination" (400) and reveals that they only go out at night, sallying forth "into the streets, arm in arm" (401). Similarly, one of the residents in the L'Espanaye building says that the two women were "very affectionate towards each other" (406); another that the elder woman was "mannish"; and although they live in a large house where another room on the fourth floor "was crowded with old beds," the two women sleep in the same bed in the same room. Just as Dupin and the narrator "[admit] no visitors" (401), the L'Espanayes (in whose name is faintly echoed the word "lesbians") inhabit a house that "no one was spoken of as frequenting" (405). More sexual imagery occurs with the forced entry of the hinged gates to the house, which are opened "with a bayonet—not with a crowbar" (407), and the screams of protest from within the house, which cease abruptly after the gate is forcibly penetrated.

The point of such homoerotic suggestions was probably not to tweak the Victorian reader's sensibilities (that would have assumed, in the first place, that readers of *Graham's Magazine* were perceptive enough to pick up on such clues), but to present, in a similar but slightly different form from "The Fall of the House of Usher," Poe's theory of perverse psychology and his theory of humans' natural gravitation towards unity. The union of opposites, of male and female, suggests a complete whole, as in the archetypal symbolism of the hermaphrodite. In Plato's *Symposium* Aristophanes presented the idea that original humans, before Zeus split them, were both male and female. When today humans join together in sex, it is an attempt to recapture their original unity. Poe's stories are noticeably devoid of conjugal relations, even those of the so-called "marriage group," like "Morella," "Ligeia," and "Berenice." Sexual acts, when they are hinted at, are presented as difficult or impossible to achieve, one reason why Poe's male and female characters seem to exist on nonsexual planes—like mother and child, or sister and brother, as Poe himself seems to have with own wife, Virginia. For Poe, homosexuality in "The Rue Morgue," like twinship in "Usher" and the repression of the conscience in "William Wilson," represents man's imperfect attempt to achieve wholeness. On the other hand, the implied unity of opposites provided the ingredients of what to Poe constituted an achieved whole life.

These same themes are seen in "The Man of the Crowd," a story published a few months earlier. It is not a detective story proper, but it can be classed as a type of crime fiction. Like "The Rue Morgue," it also uses doubling, and it also addresses the problems of achieving final unity.

This story concerns a narrator with the typical Poe-character profile, someone who feels an "inquisitive interest in every thing" (388). He is an antihero, a pathetic and craven interrogator of the human condition, much like the narrator of Dostoevsky's *Notes from Underground*. Earlier ill, he is now in a condition of "returning strength" and in "one of those happy moods which are so precisely the converse of *ennui*—moods of the keenest appetency . . . and the intellect, electrified, surpasses . . . greatly its every-day condition" (388). Late one afternoon he is sitting in a London coffeehouse observing—in the anthropological method that Poe sometimes seems to favor—the different "tribes" or classes of people who frequent the place. (The character's hyperanalytic descriptions of the crowd suggest, on one level, Poe's sometime belief in the validity of phrenology.) The acuteness and intimate quality of the narrator's observations are disarming—one brutish but attractive man is described as having "thick sensual lips" (391)—indicating that, like Dupin and his companion, the narrator may be on the make for a homosexual fling. As the night deepens, the gas lamps cast feeble gleams of light into the bar, and the scene is given a "garish lustre" (392). In this miasmic environment, the narrator spies "a decrepid old man" who makes him feel "singularly aroused, startled, fascinated." When the old man makes to leave, the narrator is overcome with "a craving desire to keep [him] in view—to know more of him" (392) and "firmly resolve[s]" that "we should not part until I had satisfied myself in some measure respecting him" (394).

For the rest of the story, through the night, the narrator stalks the old man, following him until daybreak to another saloon, where, enmeshed in a throng of other layabouts and bar-goers, the man feverishly "presse[s] in and out of the flaunting entrance" until "with a half shriek of joy," he "force[s] a passage within" (396). The narrator cryptically concludes that the old man "is the type and the genius of deep crime. He refuses to be alone. *He is the man of the crowd*. It will be in vain to follow; for I shall learn no more of him, nor of his deeds" (396).

The tale is a chilling evocation of the underside of a busy city (by 1840 London was thronged, with a population of more than three-quarters of a million) and of man deracinated, aimless and wandering. Living in still rather provincial Philadelphia, Poe must not have felt all that much the rootlessness, isolation, and despair created by an urban environment, but in the story there is still a sense of real fear—of psychic scars caused by, as the narrator says, "our inability to be alone." The reference to temperance at the end of the story seems more a quickly contrived resolution to an indeterminate plot—perhaps Poe had fashioned something so enigmatic that he could not come up with any ending other than a conventional one? One wonders what contemporary readers thought of the story; today it remains one of Poe's least-known tales, underrated and underanalyzed.

The old man and the narrator who stalks him suggest once again the pull within man to reunify with one's other self, or alter ego. Poe uses images of overtly female or culturally feminine values of the time (a diamond flashing in a cravat pin) in juxtaposition with those of masculine or homosexual yearnings (a dagger, concealed within the old man's "bosom," suggesting the phallus). The relentlessness of the narrator pursuing the old man again suggests something of Poe's theory of perverse psychology—the instinctive but unanalyzable need to do something harmful or even criminous. And in the unceasing movement from place to place, ill-lit street to dim back alley, the story conveys a desire, or even a mania, for order that can't be satisfied, a rage for control. Lastly, the tale begins and ends with a quotation, often typical of Poe, that suggests an animating theme: "it is well said of a certain German book that '*er lasst sich nicht lesen*'—it does not permit itself to be read." Just as the old man is "unreadable" to the narrator but the narrator is nonetheless driven to interpret him, so too does Poe give us, here and elsewhere, stories that are encoded texts, books that invite scrutiny and analysis but give up their secrets, like the solution to the murders in the Rue Morgue, only by dint of patient and persistent inquiry.

During his tenure at *Graham's*, Poe met and developed relationships with two prominent writers, one American, the other English. The American was Rufus Griswold, a local author and editor to whom Poe took an early liking. The Englishman was Charles Dickens, whom Poe revered as a genius. However, as was often the case with Poe, both relationships began in cordiality and descended quickly into dislike.

The Poe-Griswold relationship is so intriguing and so involved that it is the virtual cornerstone of the great edifice of myth and legend in which most people's impressions of Poe are stored today. It was Griswold who so deeply maligned Poe after his death that serious study and appreciation of Poe was impeded for decades. Griswold, who became Poe's literary executor, spread lies about the author and blackened his reputation after his death by rewriting passages from his letters. Griswold's writings about Poe portrayed him as villainous, debased, and even sadistic, calling forth numerous defenses by Poe's admirers. Nonetheless, Griswold's opinion held sway. The story of how these two writers became locked in such tenacious verbal combat is a tale of inflated egos, political backstabbing, and literary derring-do.

Poe and Griswold first met in March 1841. Griswold had come to Philadelphia about six months earlier to write first for the *Daily Standard* and then for the *Gazette*. He had been born in Vermont in 1815, the son of a farmer and tanner, and had since his early teens migrated through a series of diverse jobs including printer, sailor, reporter, and editor. At some point he procured a "license" as a Baptist minister, but whether or not he was actually ordained is uncertain; he was commonly referred to as both a D.D. and an LL.D., yet the authenticity of these degrees has also never been certified. Griswold was by no means a born sophisticate, but he apparently taught himself to be one, for all who knew him commented on his expensive clothes and debonaire manner.

The year after Griswold met Poe, 1842, was the turning point in Griswold's career, for from then until his death in 1857 he was one of the most prominent men of letters in America, a thoughtful and provocative advocate of national literature. It was through his numerous anthologies that Griswold gained such great power, beginning with *The Poets and Poetry of America* (1842) and going on through such volumes as *The Prose Writers of America* (1847) and *The Female Poets of America* (1848), all of which went through numerous editions. Hordes of writers, from major to minor, sought his attention and tried to curry his favor, since his anthologies, the first of their kind on the American scene, became the standard by which quality was measured among the American literati. At his death Griswold left behind a correspondence so voluminous that it could be consulted as a historical atlas of the nineteenth-century literary landscape. And an intimate one: these letter writers genially addressed him as "Gris" or "Rufe," although it seems clear that most were writing him in order to get something from him that they thought would advance their careers.

Griswold himself was a keen careerist and an opportunist, not shy about putting himself in positions to be rewarded. He was, in short, a man on the make, and James Russell Lowell, for one, thought him parasitic, as is suggested by the image of him in Lowell's "Fable for Critics" (1848). Alluding to the shepherd in Virgil's First *Eclogue*, Lowell wrote, "here comes Tityrus Griswold, and leads on / The flocks whom he first plucks alive, and then feeds on."

When Poe and Griswold met, the latter was compiling *The Poets and Poetry of America* and Poe was working for *Graham's*. In a section of the "Autography" series, December 1841, Poe mentioned Griswold as a person of "fine taste and judgment"; and in the spring of 1842, when Griswold's book appeared, Poe was mentioned in it, as an "eminently distinguished" author. That summer, Poe reviewed Griswold's anthology, pronouncing it "the most important addition which our literature has for many years received," and following up his praise in a letter to Griswold in which he pointed out some faults—as he always did—but concluding that it was "a better book than any other man in the United States could have made of the materials."

Soon thereafter, Poe resigned the editorship of *Graham's*, and Griswold took his place as editor. Whether because of professional jealousy created by this succession or some other reason, very soon thereafter Poe wrote to a correspondent in the South that in the new magazine he was going to launch he would "make war to the knife against the New England assumption of 'All the decency and all the talent' which has been so disgustingly manifested in the Rev. Rufus W. Griswold's 'Poets and Poetry of America.'" In lectures that year, Poe also had withering things to say about the anthologist, and then in 1843, two anonymous articles, at least one of which has been definitively attributed to Poe, held Griswold up to ridicule.

Yet, unabashed, Poe appealed to Griswold that same year (11 June 1843) for a loan. It's not known whether Griswold came forward with any money, but he is said to have circulated some "shocking bad stories" about Poe, ones that presage the scurrilous lies that he printed in his posthumous memoir of the author. Off and on for the next two years, Poe and Griswold exchanged barbs, some of them relatively harmless, others laced with venom, until at some point just before his death, Poe apparently expressed the wish that Griswold should serve as his literary executor.

Although Poe probably recognized that Griswold was not to be trusted (he possessed a "constitutional infirmity which prevents his speaking the simple truth," according to one contemporary), he probably also recognized something of himself in Griswold, a kind of alter ego like that which plagues William Wilson. Like Poe, Griswold was both hypersensitive and caustic. When attacked, he was known for the ferocity with which he lashed back at his accusers. He was also "careless, erratic, dogmatic, pretentious, and vindictive." Like Poe, too, Griswold was not at ease with himself and was insecure about his lowly background. Also like Poe, he was essentially a loner in his youth, and he attached himself to two older male authority figures, in this case surrogate brothers or fathers, as Poe did. One such person was George Foster, a twenty-year-old flute-playing journalist who later became known as "Gaslight" Foster for his sensationalistic *New-York by Gas-Light*. Foster was later jailed for forgery (forging checks by Billy Burton, as it happens), and Griswold secured his release from Sing-Sing. Another friend was Horace Greeley, well-known editor of the *New York Tribune* and originator of the catchphrase of the era, "Go West, young man!" Greeley, however, thought Griswold somewhat pathetic, calling him a "chimney corner man." Griswold later pursued what one biographer calls "an idolatrous relation" to Charles Fenno Hoffman, an editor and poet nine years older—handsome and gentlemanly, but with his own demons as well, having lost a leg in a boyhood accident.

Just as Poe was beset by fears and psychic nightmares, Griswold had been scarred, too. Having been raised under the burden of a harsh

Calvinism, Griswold continually worried that he was too worldly and that an afterlife of torment and damnation awaited him. The losses of those whom he had loved made him speculate, as Poe did, about the nature of death and what came after it, and created in him a desperate desire to hold on to and somehow try to reunite with the dead.

Estranged from his wife, in November 1842—just when relations between Poe and Griswold reached their nadir—Griswold became convinced he was going to die, seeing portents of such all around him. He had "trained" his wife in order to prepare her for this, and he said he had dreams of seeing her bending over his coffin. Like much else in his life, Griswold's relationships with women, like Poe's, seem slightly obtuse. He lived in Philadelphia, and his wife and their children lived in New York. On 6 November, his wife gave birth to their first son. Three days later, in Philadelphia, Griswold was told by messenger that both his wife and newborn child were dead. By night train he rushed to New York, where he sat by her deathbed and embraced her dead body for thirty hours. "I speak to her but she does not hear me," he wrote, like a Poe character, just after midnight. "I kiss her cold lips, but their fervor is gone." Forty days after the funeral, Griswold returned to the cemetery, persuaded the sexton to open the vault and pried loose the lid to the coffin. By his own account he lifted up the shroud from the decomposing corpse and kissed her "cold black forehead."

A few months later, the already tenuous relationship between the two men deteriorated considerably. The 28 January 1843 issue of the Philadelphia *Saturday Museum* carried a negative, and extremely personal, review of *The Poets and Poetry of America*. "Did any one read such nonsense?" the reviewer asked. "We *never* did, and shall hereafter eschew everything that bears Rufus Wilmot Griswold's name." The review ends with a strangely prophetic accusation: "what will be [Mr. Griswold's] fate? Forgotten, save only by those whom he has injured and insulted, he will sink into oblivion, without leaving a landmark to tell that he once existed; or if he is spoken of hereafter, he will be quoted as *the unfaithful servant who abused his trust*." Although the anonymous review is now known to have been written by Poe's friend Henry B. Hirst, Griswold apparently presumed that Poe was behind it. His suspicions were confirmed, in his mind, by Poe's traveling lecture on American poetry. In 1843, 1844, and again in 1845, Poe presented his lecture on a number of occasions, always with special criticism of Griswold and his anthology. Thus began a troubled embroilment that would result in Griswold taking his revenge after Poe's death.

A much different literary figure that Poe associated with at this time was Charles Dickens, the most popular writer in the English-speaking world, and a celebrity to American audiences, as became evident when Dickens came to the United States on a much-publicized tour in the spring of 1842. Everywhere Dickens went, he was lionized. People jammed city street corners to see his cortege pass by, balls and fetes were held in his honor, public readings filled huge lecture halls with crowds of people turned away and chanting "Boz! Boz!" outside the building. He was worn out from such appearances in New York, and, when Dickens arrived in Philadelphia, he specifically requested of his hosts that he not have to see his public, but local politicians, hoping to win votes, had promised some of their constituents that they could meet the novelist. Fearing a riot if he demurred, Dickens reluctantly gave in and stood shaking hands with well-wishers for several hours in the lobby of his hotel.

Poe had two interviews with the novelist during his stay in Philadelphia. Despite his distaste for sentimentality and his objections to the novel as inimical to his ideas of unity of effect, Poe nonetheless lauded Dickens, displaying his ability to appreciate great talent, even if at odds with his conceptions of the aims of literature. Poe had reviewed Dickens's first collection of stories, *Sketches by Boz* (known then as *Watkins Tottle*) several years earlier, in the June 1836 *Southern Literary Messenger*, and Poe commented on the opening chapters of Dickens's serialized mystery novel, *Barnaby Rudge*, in *Graham's Magazine*. In the article, Poe again demonstrated his considerable analytic skills by correctly concluding that the end of the book (published in installments) would show that Barnaby was the murderer's own son. Poe said he had figured this out by page seven of the book.

In this review Poe also established some aesthetic ground rules for the genre of the mystery story, such as not misleading the reader with "undue or inartistical means" in concealing the secret of the plot (233). He also demanded that the characters be kept sufficiently mysterious (a difficulty for the novelist, Poe pointed out, since his task was to develop characterization), and that the reader's interest be directed to particular details in order to disguise the solution to the mystery. Ultimately, Poe concluded that this could best be done with a first-person narrator rather than with an omniscient author, since the narrator could be duped—a device Poe used in his own tales of ratiocination.

As with Griswold, Poe was also frankly trying to curry favor with Dickens—although Poe's admiration seems sincere, since he devoted more critical space in print to the works of Dickens than to those of any other novelist. Poe aimed for the kind of stratospheric literary reputation that Dickens had acquired, hoping to emulate the Englishman in his own career: in the review, Poe stated that critical and popular success are not incompatible, inveighing against the "literary Titmice" who judged "solely by *result*"—that is, by popularity and sales (253). Of Dickens, whom he considered a true genius, Poe said that popularity was not in itself proof of excellence, but neither was it at cross-purposes with excellence. Poe then proceeded to show how if a genius used "certain well-understood critical propositions" in a work of art, the "legitimate and inevitable result" would be "vast popularity," such as that which Dickens had enjoyed (226). As Poe grappled with the conundrum of a low standing despite great talent, he began to sound a new theme in his criticism, one which would culminate in "The Philosophy of Composition," where he would circumspectly state that the writer's goal should be "to suit at once the popular and the critical taste" (15), as he himself tried to do.

Poe had prepared for Dickens's visit in advance. Hoping to get a British publisher for his own work, Poe had sent the novelist copies of some of his books. Dickens apparently read them and was favorably impressed, for he arranged for Poe to see him in Philadelphia. In "two long interviews," according to Poe, the two men discussed the backward state of American poetry, with Poe reading Emerson's poem "The Humble Bee" as an example of the amateurish state of American letters. When Dickens left, Poe asked him to try and secure him an English publisher.

Dickens apparently tried to do so, but was unsuccessful, later writing Poe that the publisher he had spoken to believed that no "collection of detached pieces by an unknown author" would sell in London. Dickens closed the letter with polite words about the nice visit he had had with Poe and wished him luck in his career.

About two years later, in January 1844, there appeared an anonymous article in the London *Foreign Quarterly Review* that surveyed recent American writing and concluded that the national literature was still undeveloped and backward. It was rumored that Dickens was the author. Poe was mentioned as a "capital artist after the manner of Tennyson" who "approaches the spirit of his original more closely than any." Injured by tiny slights and hypersensitive to charges of imitation, Poe took the comment as a rebuke and thought he detected in the sentences echoes (from nearly two years earlier) of his conversation with Dickens about Emerson's "Humble Bee." Dickens was then added to Poe's mental list of writers whose talent was inferior to his own and whose reputations were undeservedly high.

By March 1842, *Graham's Magazine*, under Poe's guidance, had prospered. Circulation had soared and the magazine had acquired a justified reputation as the finest periodical of its class in America. Poe had added considerably to the quality of the content, publishing in *Graham's* some of his most fearless and aesthetically astute literary criticism; his popular cryptography series; his detective fiction; and other tales that are among his best known today, like "The Pit and the Pendulum" and "The Black Cat." Yet his work there left Poe dissatisfied. He cited his reason for resigning as a "disgust with the namby-pamby character of the Magazine" and its "contemptible pictures, fashion-plates, music and love tales." Poe's salary was also neither commensurate with his talents nor an ample reward for the vast profits that he had brought in for his employer. Poe might have been able to negotiate a better salary, but he became unapproachable and abrasive whenever an injustice was done to him. He was correct in telling a correspondent that he had "labored solely for the benefit of others (receiving for myself a miserable pittance)," but his arrogance and snobbery often negated the justness of his claims: Poe added, typically, that he had been "forced to model my thoughts at the will of men whose imbecility was evident to all but themselves." It was usually the case that soon after Poe secured steady work, he left it, citing some irredeemable defect with the magazine or with its owner.

Thus Poe formulated his scheme to launch his own magazine—the constant desire of his life, an ambition that dated back even to his pre-*Messenger* days, when as a hack in Baltimore he had drafted the prospectus of a periodical to be edited jointly with his friend Lambert Wilmer, a project that never materialized. Yet "The Penn" and then "The Stylus," as it was named, would go through several false starts and false hopes, and would sadly end up like much of Poe's life, thwarted and ultimately unfulfilled.

Poe's prospectus for the new magazine appeared in the 6 June 1840 issue of the *Saturday Evening Post*. It read, in part:

> *Prospectus of the Penn Magazine, a monthly literary journal, to be edited and published in the city of Philadelphia, by Edgar A. Poe—Since resigning the conduct of The Southern Literary Messenger, at the commencement of its third year, I have constantly held in view the establishment of a Magazine which should retain some of the chief features of that journal, abandoning the rest. . . . It shall be the first and chief purpose of the Magazine now proposed, to become known as one where may be found, at all times, and upon all subjects, an honest and fearless opinion. This is a purpose of which no man need be ashamed. . . . To the mechanical execution of the work the greatest attention will be given which such a matter can require. . . . The price will be $5 per annum, payable in advance, or upon receipt of the first number, which will be issued on the first of January, 1841.*

However, Poe was unable to raise the necessary support and the first issue of "The Penn" never appeared.

The magazine had little chance of success, for the competition was fierce. But Poe was counting on his name recognition, and his experience as editor or assistant editor on other periodicals, to carry sway, and he was consistently enthusiastic about the magazine's future. Several idealistic pronouncements are found in his letters of this period—theatrical statements that were sometimes typical of Poe when engaged in a lost cause. To Joseph Snodgrass on 17 January 1841 he wrote, "I must now do or die—I mean in a literary sense"; and to Frederick Thomas in February 1842, "*If I live*, I will accomplish it, and in triumph." His illness in late 1841 delayed the magazine's launch, but in April 1842 he was telling friends that "The Penn" was still not dead. Yet he had to bow to economic necessity and go to work for Graham. Graham for a while apparently hinted to Poe that he might subsidize "The Penn," and Poe immediately began writing to the most prominent American authors asking for contributions for a yet-to-be-published periodical.

Poe's reputation for, alternately, viciousness or crankiness was well known by now, so it is likely that when his missives reached the genteel residences of Longfellow, Irving, Cooper, and others, they regarded them as the pesterings of a young talent who had flashes of brilliance but was something of a crank. Poe was also unembarrassed to present Irving with a blank check—anything he might wish to offer, any scrap, would naturally be accepted, and with enthusiasm—despite the fact that he had earlier lambasted him in print. Predictably, nothing came in.

Poe became enthusiastic about his magazine again when on 31 January 1843, he and Thomas Cottrell Clarke signed an agreement to publish. The original name, "The Penn," was thought to sound too local, and so the new magazine was called "The Stylus" (another pen). Clarke was a local publisher, and that February, his weekly newspaper, the *Saturday Museum*, had run a biographical piece on Poe by a local poet, Henry Beck Hirst, with material supplied by Poe himself.

This "biography" reveals much about Poe's habit of spinning lies and half-truths about himself in order to exaggerate background elements that might bring him to more prominent public notice. In this article he appears to be both a decisive man of action and a melancholy man apart. Poe emphasized his fictitious adventures as a soldier in Greece and St. Petersburg and drew out the melodrama of his youth in Richmond by stating that he rushed home from Europe to be there the night of Fanny Allan's funeral. Poe offered a physical description, however, that was more the *poète maudit*: "In person, he is somewhat slender, about five feet, eight inches in height, and well proportioned; his complexion is rather fair; his eyes are grey and restless, exhbiting a marked nervousness; his forehead is extremely broad, displaying prominently the organs of Ideality. . . . His hair is nearly black, and partially curling. Our portrait conveys a tolerably correct idea of the man."

But the biographical article was accompanied by a portrait that was nothing like Poe's self-description. The figure in the woodcut looks more like Washington Irving than anyone else—somewhat plump, thickset, and at peace with the world, the very image of the prosperous, much-loved author. He is seated in a Windsor chair, one large hand resting on its arm and the other atop a pile of books. The facial features are also coarse. Poe found the portrait to be essentially a caricature: "I am ugly enough God knows, but not quite so bad as that," he wrote his friend Frederick Thomas. The following week, the magazine's prospectus appeared, headed:

Prospectus of the Stylus:
A Monthly Journal of General Literature
To Be Edited by
EDGAR A. POE
And Published, in the City of Philadelphia, by
CLARKE & POE

This time, Poe seems to have had a reasonable chance at success, for he managed to sign as an illustrator the eminent artist Felix Darley.

But Poe was always uneasy about the prospects for the magazine. Shortly before Clarke had come on the scene, Poe had tried to enlist the support of a poet from Georgia, Thomas Holley Chivers, who rivaled Poe in terms of theatricality, grandiloquence, and erratic behavior. In fact, they had much in common. Chivers was the scion of a wealthy plantation family who fancied himself a mystic. He had studied for a career in medicine, but refused a chair in physiology at a southern university when, while recovering from an illness, he had a vision of harp-playing angels and a fountain of water, which he interpreted symbolically to mean for him to take up a career as a poet. At the age of nineteen Chivers had married the sixteen-year-old daughter of his father's brother. His young bride deserted him; and when he remarried, it was again to a sixteen-year-old girl. They had a daughter, whose birth Chivers claimed to have foreseen eight years earlier in a vision. Chivers rounded up some southern subscribers for Poe's magazine, but in another twist that reads like a Poe story, on Chivers's thirty-third birthday, 18 October 1842, his daughter died from typhoid. Cradling her body in his arms for hours on end, Chivers wrote a long rhapsody about what had just happened, "The Lost Pleiad."

Despite assistance, however, from Chivers and others, Poe again found it impossible to raise sufficient interest and capital. Then, as always when Poe was most seriously depressed, he began to read heavy significance into casual remarks. One such statement, which Poe immediately saw as a sure thing, came to him in a letter from Frederick W. Thomas, a novelist and poet who had spent his formative years in Charleston, South Carolina. He and Poe became friends in May 1840, when Thomas visited Philadelphia; they thereafter remained close, and Thomas was one of the few permanent friends that Poe ever had. Thomas had a naturally rosy view of almost everything, to the point of being oversanguine in his conversations with Poe. Thomas had obtained a temporary clerkship in the Department of the Treasury and wrote Poe a jaunty letter with the sunny forecast of jobs that were there for the asking: "How would you like to be an office holder here at $1500 per year payable monthly by Uncle Sam who, however slack he may be to his general creditors, pays his officials with due punctuality. How would you like it? You stroll to your office a little after nine in the morning leisurely, and you stroll from it a little after two in the afternoon homeward to dinner, and return no more that day. . . . Come on and apply for a clerkship, you can follow literature here as well as where you are." Poe did not believe in the wisdom that if something sounded too good to be true, then it probably was, and so, full of optimism and already feasting off the rewards of distant profits, Poe got ready to jump on the next train to Washington to make application in person, when Thomas wrote back to say that he had better wait awhile, as there appeared to be little available at present.

There was some basis for Thomas's initial optimism. At the time, it was commonplace for politicians to bestow such patronage on literary figures and scholars—both Hawthorne and Melville held customhouse appointments, as did the historian George Bancroft. Moreover, the president at the time was a Virginian, John Tyler, the vice president who had succeeded William Henry Harrison when the latter caught pneumonia while delivering his inaugural speech outdoors and succumbed within a month. (Tyler was called "His Accidency" or "the do-nothing President"—a title that must have rung true to Poe's ears, since the appointment never came through.) Thomas had spoken with the president's son, Rob, who had published some poetry and had heard of Poe. When Poe later ran across one of Rob Tyler's poems, he came up with the idea that "The Stylus" could at least in part be an organ for the current administration. Tory publications like *Blackwood's*, for example, had served this function all along, so why not "The Stylus"? This plan, however, also came to naught.

Poe's hopes of a government sinecure were raised again when it appeared that an appointment to the Philadelphia Custom House was available. After duly making overtures to the government, and as extra surety, having Thomas intercede on his behalf with the president's son, Poe sat at home complacently expecting to see in the newspaper that he had been called to take up the post. But when the day came on which the recipient was announced, it was not Poe but instead a man named Pogue—which sent the alarm bells clanging throughout Poe's nervous constitution like never before. He immediately called on the local collector (the person in charge of making the appointments), one Thomas S. Smith, alleging that the name must have been a misprint—or perhaps, in a greater flight of fancy, a cruel accident of mistaken identity, as in some play about babies switched at birth. Smith, however, confirmed the accuracy of the name and told Poe politely that no more appointments were forthcoming. Poe protested that this could not be so—the president's very own son, Robert, had assured him that he would be appointed. Smith answered him, roughly, "From *whom* did you say?" Poe repeated, "From *Robert* Tyler!" Smith then said, "Hem! I have received orders from *President* Tyler to make no more appointments and shall make none." Poe could only apply to the president if he wished to press his case.

Undeterred, Poe wrote to Thomas asking him to have Rob Tyler persuade his father to write a letter authorizing Smith to appoint Poe. The lost position struck at Poe's sense of entitlement, or, as he put it, "the station in society which is my due." "If Smith had the feelings of a gentleman, he would have perceived that from the very character of my claim—by which I mean my want of claim—he should have made my appt. an early one." He told Thomas, "You can have no idea of the low ruffians and boobies who have received office over my head," once again letting his arrogance and hauteur cast a pall over his talents. Then, Poe started acting in a truly absurd manner, telling people that Smith was not a Tyler supporter at all, but a covert agent in the employ of the president's enemies.

Poe was a hard man to help, but Thomas did his best. Rob Tyler saw the *Museum* biography of Poe and warmed to Poe's earlier idea of using "The Stylus" as a mouthpiece for his father's administration. He invited Poe to come to Washington and meet the president. The visit was a disaster. To begin with, Thomas, who was supposed to be Poe's minder during the visit, was ill, and so those duties fell to Jesse Dow, a journalist Poe had met in Philadelphia who had a clerkship in the post office department. Dow did not know Poe as well as Thomas did; naturally convivial, Dow let Poe be too reckless in his socializing, with the result that at a party on the evening of his arrival, Poe overindulged and wound up drunk. Poe was probably nervous to begin with, overeager for the visit to be a success and pull him out of his troubles.

Poe had agreed to meet Thomas the next morning, a Sunday, at 9 o'clock in the lobby of the Congress Hall Hotel, but he never appeared, later claiming that he was ill in bed. For the next three days, Poe remained alternately "ill in bed" or tipsy. His old nemesis John Hill Hewitt ran into him on Pennsylvania Avenue in a compromised condition, giving Hewitt the perfect excuse to comment on Poe's pathetic existence: "*Un homme blasé*," Hewitt wrote—"seedy in his appearance and woe-begone. He came boldly up to me, and, offering me his hand, which I willingly took, asked me if I would forget the past. He said he had not had a mouthful of food since the day previous, and begged me to lend him fifty cents."

One might think that things could not have gotten any worse, but they did. Poe's behavior became alternately reckless and pathetically comic. He insisted on wearing his coat inside out; he publicly ridiculed another writer-friend, Thomas Dunn English; and he had a furious argument with an unknown Spanish man over the appearance of the man's moustache. Rob Tyler decided that an interview with the president was inadvisable, Poe continued to drink, and Dow poured him onto the train, home to Philadelphia, sending a diplomatic letter ahead of him to Clarke suggesting he meet the poet at the station: "He exposes himself here to those who may injure him very much," Dow wrote, echoing a theme that had now become an obvious pattern in Poe's interpersonal and professional relationships. Dow seems to have been able to "read" Poe quickly and well, for he wrote that "He does not understand the ways of politicians nor the manner of dealing with them to advantage," but then accurately claimed, "How should he? . . . Mr. Poe has the highest order of intellect, and I cannot bear that he should be the sport of senseless creatures, who, like oysters, keep sober, and gape and swallow everything."

Back home and recovered, Poe quickly wrote some conciliatory letters to those involved (including an apology to the Spaniard) in which he tried to laugh off the whole trip as a comedy of errors. Of his drunkenness, Poe told Thomas and Dow that he had been "a little sick" and added that when Clarke met him at the station, "he said my trip had improved me & that he had never *seen me looking so well!!!*" But it didn't wash. On the bottom of this letter, Thomas later wrote a long note to himself—a sort of biographical gloss on the letter writer, ending with the belief that Poe was in a losing battle with alcoholism: "he fought against the propensity as hard as ever Coleridge fought against it. And moreover there is a great deal of heartache in the jestings of this letter."

What no one in Washington knew was the reason for Poe's erratic behavior, nervousness, and descent into the bottle. About one year earlier, on a January afternoon which was the day after Poe's thirty-third birthday, Virginia had been practicing her singing lessons when quite suddenly she began to bleed from her mouth. Poe at first thought she had ruptured a blood vessel, but when the bleeding recurred, he took her to a physician, who said she was hemorrhaging from the lungs, an early stage of what people then referred to as "death-in-life," or tuberculosis. This disease invaded, plague-like, the lives of many famous artists, including Keats, Chopin, and Chekhov.

For two weeks, Virginia was dangerously ill, and Poe thought that she might die. She lay abed in their cramped quarters—the ceiling so low that her head almost touched it—hardly able to breathe except when she was being fanned. Frantic, Poe searched the entire city for the only known remedy (which was actually just a temporary alleviant)—a potion called "Jew's Beer." He managed to find some, but then an accident destroyed the supply he had laid in; again frantic, he went out to get more. Virginia improved, but then spiralled downward again.

For the most part, Poe kept silent in his letters about the horrid situation (surely the reason that Thomas did not spy this as the cause of Poe's depression). A visitor to their Philadelphia residence noted that Virginia's illness was devastating Poe but that he "was so sensitive and irritable" that "no one dared to speak. . . . And he would not allow a word about the danger of her dying—the mention of it drove him wild." George Graham recalled Poe's "anxious solicitude" for his wife's health and saw in the episode an unfortunate analogue for Poe's overall pessimism regarding the quality of existence and a portent confirming his morbid fears of the unknown. Graham wrote:

His love for his wife was a sort of rapturous worship of the spirit of beauty which he felt was fading before his eyes. I have seen him hovering around her when she was ill, with all the fond fear and tender anxiety of a mother for her first-born, her slightest cough causing in him a shudder, a heart-chill that was visible. I rode out, one summer evening, with them, and the remembrance of his watchful eyes eagerly bent upon the slightest change of hue in that loved face, haunts me yet as the memory of a sad strain. It was the hourly anticipation of her loss that made him a sad and thoughtful man, and lent a mournful melody to his undying song.

Poe's emotional ups and downs during the year leading up to his Washington trip paralleled the rise and fall of Virginia's health. His alternating optimism and pessimism about her chances for recovery was a natural response, for the medical profession at the time had little idea of how to treat tuberculosis and could not track the path of the bacilli at all. Thus news swung one day from a prognosis of full recovery to the next, when the patient was said to be terminal. Two weeks after the initial onslaught, Poe thought that Virginia was out of danger, but by June she had had another dangerous hemorrhage that made Poe feel it was "folly to hope" for improvement. In August she had another bout, and in March 1843, the month he went to Washington, the doctors pronounced her condition even worse than before. Her health was failing and it was clearly only a matter of time before she succumbed. Under these conditions, it is little wonder that Poe despaired and gave in to the melancholic morbidity produced by drink. He must have felt he had little to hope for and little to lose.

Poe retold the episode in fictional form in three stories. In "Eleonora," published in September 1842, he constructed a fantasy in which his wife dies but his grief is magically erased. In the story, the narrator marries a childlike bride only to see "the finger of Death," a common image of tuberculosis at the time, "upon her bosom." He determines that "she had been made perfect in loveliness only to die" (471). To relieve Eleonora's anxiety, the narrator promises her that he will not remarry. The story presages Poe's later life. Eleonora dies in tranquility, but very soon after the narrator gives in to temptation and marries the more worldly (and carnal) Princess Ermengarde. Eleonora then appears to him in a vision and absolves him of his promise to remain chaste. The story reveals something of Poe's guilt over trying to have a fulfilled life in the face of Virginia's certain death, and it looks forward to his dalliances with a number of wealthy women in New York in the coming years.

In "The Oval Portrait" Poe explored the idea that Virginia's release from pain would ensure her immortality, through his own art. In the story, a painter requires his wife to sit preternaturally still for days at a time in an ill-lit turret while he obsessively paints her portrait. Turning his eyes "from the canvas rarely" (483), the painter does not see that the more details that are filled in in the portrait, the more lifelike the painting becomes. Yet at the same time, his wife is slowly dying. Standing "entranced before the work" when it is completed, the painter grows "tremulous and very pallid" and announces, "This is indeed *Life* itself!" He then turns to his beloved and sees that she is dead. He does not see, until it is too late, that the lifelikeness of his painting depends on his wife's death.

Poe did not follow the typical patterns of grief; paradoxically, he moved from acceptance to denial. Both these stories, written in the middle stages of Virginia's illness, were wish-fulfillment fantasies by Poe in denial, useless blends of fairy tale and unrealistic optimism. However, in the third fictional treatment of Virginia's disease, Poe tore down the typical fictional barriers against death that he usually constructed. In "The Masque of the Red Death," Poe accepted the terminality of Virginia's illness, throwing out his earlier, hypothetical posturings about cheating death and reuniting with lost loved ones in another realm.

The story uses the familiar paradigm of a plague ravaging a country, this one characteristically unidentified but recalling in most ways some part of medieval Europe. The setting of this story shows something of Poe's similarities to the English visionary painter John Martin (1789–1854), whose phantasmagoric landscapes often depict ancient cities in the aftermath of some cataclysmic event—or, as in other Poe stories, caverns and castles. Virginia's "drowning in blood" was the emotional impetus for the story, yet Poe likely also drew on his memory of the great cholera epidemic that swept through Baltimore in 1831. In the tale, the youthful Prince Prospero (whose name turns out to have ironic significance) gathers his courtiers around him and takes them to a castellated abbey in the countryside, there presumably to escape the ravages of the "red death" (red obviously signifying blood)—just as people did in fleeing the bubonic plague in the Middle Ages, when it was thought that the uncontaminated air of the countryside could be a safeguard against contracting the disease. Like the revelers in Boccaccio's *Decameron*, the friends of the prince tell stories to while away the time. To Poe, however, one more story meant one more minute, hour, or day in which death was cheated, thus recalling his familiar theme of writing as a way of staving off death.

We might note here how often Poe employs the metaphor of a carnival or masquerade ball in his fiction—earlier in "William Wilson," and here in "The Masque of the Red Death"; later it appears in both "The Cask of Amontillado" and "Hop-Frog." In all these stories the scene is meant in one way to evoke an atmosphere of medieval or Reniaissance-era Europe, that indeterminate setting of time and place in all Poe's work. The masque might also function as a symbol for characters' prevailing tendencies to show a self in public—one diffident or innocuous—that is different from the true self—more cunning and sly—they harbor inside themselves. Appearances can never be trusted in Poe's fictive world.

Knowing what we know about Poe's work as a journalist, however, and how immersed he was in the day-to-day social life of the city, we might also wonder if these settings were inspired by that folk parade and related social movement in Philadelphia, the Mummers and their annual New Year's Day parade. This loose fraternal confederation evolved in the city in the late 1700s and by Poe's time there had grown into a more formal, although still not "organized," working-class guild. Following the medieval tradition of their German and Swedish immigrant ancestors, these groups organized huge pageants that allegorically depicted whims and fancies, comic scenes, and elaborate fantasies that were offshoots of the parade's original purpose, to present the mummer's play, a folk drama. "Mummer" in fact, is the German word for "mask" or "disguise."

The original mummer's play, in broad outline, depicted martial combat between various soldiers or ruffians—performance as braggadocio. In villages these events were accompanied by much yelling, clanging of metal, and sometimes even shooting of guns by the locals. But the most interesting element of the play was that in the end the hero was always miraculously brought back to life by a doctor who boasts of his skill in medicine. Imaginatively linking the cycle of death and rebirth with a masque or carnival must have appealed to Poe, as he hopefully hypothesized about an otherworld of repeated dying and resurrection. One theory about the mummer's play is that it was an echo of the ritual of death and rebirth of nature during winter, in which a fertility god is symbolically killed in his old age in order to be reborn anew in spring. This theory might be applied to the role played by Prospero's nemesis, the Death–Grim Reaper–Father Time figure—and the grave tolling of the clock tower bells.

Poe uses the idea of plague in a commonplace way, too—as a manifestation of psychic illness and social imbalance, just as illness and contagion are used in Camus's *The Plague* and Mann's *Death in Venice*. In the Poe piece, we find a society in which typical functions and the normalities of life have broken down, as in the plight of Thebes that occurred after Oedipus assumed the throne. Physical illnesses result and psychogenic symptoms of every kind appear—all of which must have seemed real to Poe in the wake of Virginia's hemorrhaging. Indeed, the whole first paragraph of the story is awash in blood—with the words "red," "blood," or "bloody" repeated six times in six sentences.

In such situations, efforts to thwart or stifle the contagion result only in bottled-up tensions that, when they explode, cause global catastrophe. And indeed, in Prince Prospero's castle (remembering that houses are strong symbols in Poe), when the masked figure of death appears, he passes through a series of seven elaborately confusing rooms, maze-like, each one differently colored, from blue to black, to represent allegorically the movement from morning to night, from birth to death. Poe's deft, almost rhythmic symbolism encircles the tale. The number seven has also often been significant as a cosmic center: the seven planetary spheres, the seven notes of the scale, the seven days of the Creation. And mortal: the seven deadly sins.

In fact, Christian imagery permeates this tale, signalling the vain hope that Prospero (an anagram of "Poe"), who has fled to a place consecrated by the church, holds out for beating death. There is the theological significance of the number seven, the setting of the castellated abbey, and the numerous references to the book of Revelation: the red avatar of death, the sacrificial lamb, and the stealthy onslaught of death at the end of the story, coming, "like a thief in the night" (490). Even in his hedonistic behavior Prospero hopes that religion will protect him. Yet, maddened, he rushes hurriedly through the first six rooms, draws his dagger and approaches, then utters "a sharp cry" and "instantly afterwards, [falls] prostrate in death." One by one the revellers fall too, "in the blood-bedewed halls of their revel." An ebony clock in the last room dies out, the flames of the candles are extinguished (oblivion), "And Darkness and Decay and the Red Death held illimitable dominion over all" (490).

Death is not fooled by the "masks" of the revellers, nor is it impeded by Prospero's elaborate measures. The story ends in defeat and pessimism, with no translation of its hero to a transcendent realm, no reuniting in death with those lost. Poe rarely acknowledged that death "held illimitable dominion," but the hard reality of Virginia's illness made him realize, painfully, that it did.

By 1843 Poe had still not exhausted his creative energies, wracked as he was by Virginia's illness and the failure of his plan to secure a government sinecure. Some hope for the eventual launch of "The Stylus" was still with him, but there was little promise of that panning out as well. In this context, his creative output is remarkable, for Poe produced three other tales during this period that rank among his masterpieces.

"The Pit and the Pendulum" is one of Poe's most terrifying tales. Its narrator is a prisoner of the Spanish Inquisition who tells his story from the bottom of a high-ceilinged, pitch-dark room. The tale reminds one of the sadism and cruelty of war as depicted in the paintings of Goya, especially *The Third of May* and *The Disasters of War*. The story is also Kafkaesque, the character a victim of indifferent forces that become absurd, agents of some grotesque injustice that, in the Poe universe, seems commonplace. Poe himself must have felt much like this, given his travails. The story is also another inquiry or investigation, a variation of the form of the mystery story. The narrator seeks to answer the question of where he is and how he might escape; the reader seeks to understand why the character is being punished like this—a question to which there is no clear answer.

"The Pit and the Pendulum" is preeminently a tale of sensation—like "Usher," of senses overstimulated and of senses deprived. Held captive, the character can nonetheless hear and feel, as when the rats in the pits, in search of greasy morsels of food, come ever closer: "their cold lips sought my own" (503). He can hear "the tumultuous motion of [his] heart, and, in [his] ears, the sound of its beating" (493). He can taste the sweat on his upper lips and can feel "something damp and hard" (493) when he reaches out his hand to touch. But he cannot see. All that his eyes register is "the blackness of eternal night" (493), its shadows and impressions.

As he eventually feels his way around the walls of the cell, he stumbles and comes perilously close to the edge of a circular opening. He falls asleep, and when he wakes finds that he has been "securely bound by a long strap resembling a surcingle" (498). Looking upward, he sees to his horror a giant scythe-like blade, incongruously decorated with the painted figure of Time, swinging ominously back and forth, while descending ever closer to his body. A terrifying paradox of the story is that the pendulum is ever in motion, pressing him close to torment, pain, and then exinction, while his tight bonds deny him any motion at all.

The main figurative pattern in the tale is that of revolutions and convolutions—cyclical motions of up and down, around and back again. In the center of the room is the pit, with its "outward or upward whirls" (501), recalling the image of a whirlpool or maelstrom, as in *Pym* and other stories. One could speculate that Poe was thinking again in terms of the womb, since the "blackness" in the pit suggests danger, whereas the darkness of the womb suggests security. The pit and the pendulum might also be read as opposite symbols of male and female. As in "Usher," their final unification would be complete, in the death of the victim.

In addition, there are technical aspects to the tale that are virtuosic. The flat, declarative sentences with which the narrator tells his tale are disarming in their objectivity: "I struggled for breath"; "The atmosphere was intolerably close" (493). Yet the writing also retains many poetic effects, as Kenneth Silverman suggests by commenting on the onomotopeia and assonance of the hissing of the blade: "surcingle," "cessation," "crescent," "scimitar." These reinforce the importance of the sense of sound in the story. Only sounds can be distinguished, not sights: the pendulum, the rats, and finally, the voices of the rescuers at the end of the tale.

Poe was a master at reader manipulation, at tweaking the emotional responses of his audience with the most subtle of stimuli. Ultimately, Poe's best stories become all about the reader rather than the character, just as Alfred Hitchcock's films, especially ones like *Psycho* and *Rear Window*, draw the viewer in, voyeur-like, to spy on a private moment. (Even Hitchcock's theory of composition seems indebted to Poe's, with its precisely calibrated movement toward a single, unified effect on the

141

viewer.) In "The Pit and the Pendulum," Poe presses all the buttons needed for readers to be terrified, to consider if only for a millisecond that what they are reading may actually be reality. He confirms for us, in a way, that, as in fairy tales, unspeakable acts of mutilation could actually take place. In "The Pit and the Pendulum," Poe does this by making contact with readers' senses, all of which are played with in the story: being hungry and thirsty, being tied up, rats swarming around one's body, walls of red-hot metal closing in on one, a razor-sharp blade swinging menacingly close, and the threat of oblivion.

Like "The Pit and the Pendulum," "The Tell-Tale Heart" is also a variation on the form of the mystery story. In this confessional tale, a lunatic narrator tells us that he has barbarically murdered an old man whom he took care of, for no reason at all, except that the appearance of one of the man's eyes drove him to get rid of it:

> *True!—nervous—very, very dreadfully nervous I had been and am; but why will you say that I am mad? . . . It is impossible to say how the idea entered my brain; but once conceived, it haunted me day and night. Object there was none. Passion there was none. I loved the old man. He had never wronged me. He had never given me insult. For his gold I had no desire. I think it was his eye! yes, it was this! One of his eyes resembled that of a vulture—a pale blue eye, with a film over it. Whenever it fell upon me, my blood ran cold; and so by degrees—very gradually—I made up my mind to take the life of the old man, and thus rid myself of the eye for ever. (555)*

Little by little, like the narrator of "The Black Cat," this person lifts the veil that he keeps between himself and the world, revealing more and more of his criminous mind and perverse psychology to the audience. In this sense, many of Poe's narrators resemble the speakers of Robert Browning's dramatic monologues, like the Duke of Ferrara in "My Last Duchess," who lets out, bit by bit, why he murdered his wife. (Others are like the pathetic title characters of E. A. Robinson's poems, who look back ruefully at their wasted existences and resign themselves to their fates.) Poe's narrator sneaks into the man's room at night, suffocates him with a pillow, and then dismembers the corpse, hiding the pieces beneath three planks in the floorboards of the bedroom. The narrator then calls the police to investigate but ends up confessing to the three investigating officers because he thinks he hears the beating of the old man's heart, confirming for him that murder will out.

Poe is again addressing a pathological condition—the overacuteness of the senses, as in "Usher," "The Man of the Crowd," and other tales. Here, the connection between the mind and the body is again made clear, as the narrator imagines that he hears the heart still beating. Guilt in Poe's stories is produced not by the need for expiation, as in most tales of murder, or even in acquiescence to being conquered or undone—for the narrator gives himself up to the police—but simply in response to abnormal or irrational conditions. As a mystery story, then, it is, like "The Pit and the Pendulum," not a whodunit or even a how-dunit, but a why-dunit. The answer to this mystery is never revealed in a Poe story. It is a universe devoid of morality; characters act the way they do mostly in response to external or internal stimuli. In terms of detective fiction, the story depicts a crime with an absence of motive.

The "vulture eye" suggests some observing consciousness, seeking to illuminate, to show what the narrator tries to keep dark and hidden. Facing the old man's eye, the narrator perhaps views in some macabre diorama his own life, seeing who or what he really is. The old man is a father archetype, like the mythological Kronos who devours his own children so that he will never be replaced by them. The narrator says that he loves the old man and that he has never been afraid of him, but obviously too he feels that the old man is somehow in a position to destroy him. The spectre of John Allan may hover around the figure of the old man as well, given Poe's deep-seated animosities toward him.

"The Black Cat," another story from this period, is similar to "The Pit and the Pendulum" and "The Tell-Tale Heart." As in "The Tell-Tale Heart" and other first-person narratives like "William Wilson," the speaker confesses to us, raising the question of his reliability and even his sanity. The technical aspects of this tale are also astonishing, particularly the egomaniacal declarations of the narrator, someone who is obviously crazed but who wishes his audience to believe him sane. One way Poe accomplishes this is through twisted or inverted syntax, as when the narrator says, "mad am I not—and very surely do I not dream"—an image of his mental disorder (597). Here too we are treated to the objective understatement, chilling in its flat matter-of-factness, as when the narrator confesses to murdering his wife: "I withdrew my arm from under her grasp and buried the axe in her brain" (603). The madmen in such Poe tales as "The Black Cat" and "The Tell-Tale Heart" are frightening precisely because they are so controlled, and because the author studies them with such precision and reasonableness. They are frightening in their very matter-of-factness, making them similar in spirit to visual works by Goya and particularly to the portraits of the criminally insane by Théodore Géricault (1791–1824).

Whereas in "The Tell-Tale Heart," the narrator is driven to confess by the presumably evil presence of the old man's "vulture eye," in "The Black Cat," it is the domesticated pet of the title, named Pluto for the god of the underworld, whose image haunts him and, again, whose eyes seem to penetrate and goad his conscience into submission. (Marriage is also a putative subject of the story, as the cat is a symbol of the feminine and of the domestic life.) Then Poe again deflects our attention from right and wrong, ethics and morals. As in "The Murders in the Rue Morgue," he compels us to think in terms of the spirit of perverseness in all humankind, an unequivocal faculty in which reason is not a factor in considerations of actions and consequences. When the narrator of "The Black Cat" kills Pluto, he says he acts in order "to do wrong for wrong's sake only": "One morning, in cool blood, I slipped a noose about its neck and hung it to the limb of a tree;—hung it with the tears streaming from my eyes, and with the bitterest remorse at my heart;—hung it *because* I knew that he had loved me, and *because* I felt it had given me no reason of offence" (599). Unlike the scenes laid by his contemporaries Hawthorne and Melville, guilt isn't directly present in Poe's world. As Allen Tate once said, Poe wrote as if Christianity had never existed. The narrator of "The Black Cat" seems conscience-stricken, yet he only uses the world "guilt" or "guilty" three times in the course of the story. Poe's characters do what they do not for moral reasons but for psychological ones. Very often they are simply impelled by some instinctive perversity.

These three stories also bring one to the end of Poe's most productive period. He had produced, by most accounts, his major body of fiction. He had been treating for some time recurring themes and concepts, and using specific techniques, in these works. The disarming narrative openings, spoken by such characters as William Wilson and the passenger in "MS. Found in a Bottle," present creatures driven by imagination and hypersensitivity and possessed of a dubious credibility and vague family history (anticipating the narrative techniques of the Argentinian short story writers Jorge Luis Borges and Julio Cortazar, both of whom acknowledged a debt to Poe). These men very often cannot recall how they ended up in their present condition, and Poe emphasizes their psychological abnormality rather than their moral defects. Such characters also suffer from one or more prominent physical and/or mental debilities, yet, technically speaking, there is very little unveiling of character. Poe would say that that was the task of the novelist rather than the tale writer. His characters do not develop and grow; rather, they remain static for the course of the story.

Poe's fiction also owes much to the Gothic—creaky castles and dungeons, trap doors and secret hiding (or burial) places are everywhere; as in the plays of Strindberg, these settings augment the sense of mystery and suspense, as well as reflect the emotional states of his characters. Poe's plots are gruesome and frightening, but he avoids monotony by subtle variations (a corpse stuffed upwards into a chimney; a pit in a cellar; a masked figure who turns out to be untenanted). A common theme is what Poe termed "the most melancholy of all subjects," the death of a beautiful woman, and his female characters are usually combinations of his wife and mother, yet his male characters reveal marked differences— William Wilson, for example, could not be mistaken for the young man in "The Tell-Tale Heart."

Characters' alienation from society and their intensity of feeling suggest the influence of German mysticism and the English romantic poets. Protagonists are obsessed with death, madness, and disease. They frequently suffer from a dissolution of personality, a wasting away of energy, and an unusual species of psychological disorder. They are often drawn by the lure of some force—either of nature, like the sea, or of abnormal compulsions, like roaming the streets of London in "The Man of the Crowd." In tales of the supernatural, Poe frequently delves in areas of the unknown like sleepwalking, clairvoyance, telepathic communication, extrasensory perception, and nightmares.

In some of his critical writings, Poe admitted that goodness may be a by-product of art, but in general he doesn't touch morality in his own tales. Sin and crime are often absent; what happens happens in terms of perverse psychology, not in terms of nonethical behavior. Remorse is always a compulsion, never an accusation of the moral sense after an irresponsible act.

Poverty, restlessness, and a yearning for change prompted Poe to move his family for a fourth time in Philadelphia, this time to a tiny, narrow cottage on North Seventh Street, in the Spring Garden District, a working-class neighborhood. They took in a lodger to help with expenses. And, as always, Muddy, ever energetic and helpful, pitched in to keep the place neat and orderly. Poe kept up his steady pace of stories, poems, and reviews, but he was still constantly pressed for money and had to borrow from friends, by now an ingrained habit. "The Gold-Bug" won a one-hundred-dollar prize from the Philadelphia *Dollar Newspaper* contest; multiple reprintings of the tale and a dramatized version made Poe somewhat more famous than he had yet been. A local printer also brought out a pamphlet, *The Prose Romances of Edgar A. Poe*, which contained "The Murders in the Rue Morgue" and "The Man That Was Used Up," the first in a projected "uniform series edition" of Poe's work, but sales were low, and the publisher did not issue any more titles.

In search of income, that fall Poe began a career as a lecturer with a talk entitled "Poetry of America." His reputation with *Graham's*—probably his renown as a witheringly severe critic—was large, and the hall in which he spoke was packed. Hundreds of people were unable to gain admission. Poe repeated the lecture a week later in Wilmington, Delaware, and then again a month later in New York.

Lecturing, or as it was broadly known in America, the lyceum movement, was just gaining steam when Poe entered the arena in the 1840s. It originated with the British mechanics' institutes, a form of public service in which educators would bring instruction to the working classes. The first American lyceum was started in Boston in 1826. It grew quickly and expanded throughout the New England area, reaching a peak in the winter of 1837–38 in Boston, when twenty-six different courses of lectures were delivered in that city, attended by some thirteen thousand people. The topics and the instructors were varied. Subjects included chemistry, "moral eloquence," phrenology, and more controversial topics like birth control, divorce, and slavery. Among men of letters, Emerson, Oliver Wendell Holmes, Bayard Taylor, Edward Everett, and later, Melville, gave public lectures and profited handsomely from them.

As a lecturer, Poe had quite a presence. By contemporary accounts, he was a very accomplished orator and a master rhetorician. Newspaper reviews lauded him for his apparent ability to strike a gracious balance between severity and impartiality as a critic. Those who attended could not praise his style of delivery and sonorous, melodic reading voice enough, and urged others to go hear him. In *The Spirit of the Times,* John S. Du Solle commented that Poe's lecture was "not only beautifully written, but commends itself by its good sense and good judgment to the attention of every person of taste." George Lippard asserted in another paper that Poe was "an able and eloquent advocate of the right and caustic censor of the wrong." Still another called one of the lectures "a highly philosophical and eloquent discourse." Poe would continue to give such talks on American poetry for the remainder of his life, although his even manner in the Philadelphia lectures would eventually give way to some pyrotechnics and, ultimately, some mixed results.

In Philadelphia, Poe's imaginative work was prolific and brilliant— thirty-one tales in all, the majority of them now canonized as masterpieces ("The Fall of the House of Usher," "The Murders in the Rue Morgue," "The Pit and the Pendulum," and more). He had also had a relatively successful run at the helm of two important and impressive national magazines. Yet turmoil raged inside him, abetted by the insecurities of his jobs at the magazines and his constant search for better-paying work. Beset by worries over what sort of future he could make for his family, Poe sunk to the lowest depths that could be bearable and yet still survive when Virginia contracted tuberculosis. Struck down, like an animal Poe recoiled and then lashed back, insulting friends and running from debts, losing himself in drink, and looking back imaginatively in his fiction on a past and a present that he could now rue with equal bitterness.

NEW YORK

Triumphs and Troubles—"The Raven" and the Longfellow War [1844–1845]

New-York, Sunday Morning
April 7 [1844] just after breakfast

My dear Muddy,

We have just this minute done breakfast, and I now sit down to write you about everything. . . . we arrived safe at Walnut St wharf. The driver wanted to make me pay a dollar, but I wouldn't. Then I had to pay a boy a levy to put the trunks in the baggage car. In the meantime I took Sis in the Depot Hotel. It was only a quarter past 6, and we had to wait till 7. We saw the Ledger & Times—nothing in either—a few words of no account in the Chronicle.—We started in good spirits, but did not get here until nearly 3 o'clock. We went in the cars to Amboy about 40 miles from N. York, and then took the steamboat the rest of the way.—Sissy coughed none at all. When we got to the wharf it was raining hard. I left her on board the boat, after putting the trunks in the Ladies' Cabin, and set off to buy an umbrella and look for a boarding-house. I met a man selling umbrellas and bought one for 62 cents. Then I went up Greenwich St and soon found a boarding-house. . . . I made a bargain in a few minutes and then got a hack and went for Sis. I was not gone more than 1/2 an hour, and she was quite astonished to see me back so soon. She didn't expect me for an hour. There were 2 other ladies waiting on board—so she was'nt very lonely. . . . Last night, for supper, we had the nicest tea you ever drank,

149

strong & hot—wheat bread & rye bread—cheese—tea-cakes (elegant) a great dish (2 dishes) of elegant ham, and 2 of cold veal piled up like a mountain and large slices—3 dishes of the cakes and, and every thing in the greatest profusion. No fear of starving here. The landlady seemed as if she could'nt press us enough, and we were at home directly. Her husband is living with her—a fat good-natured old soul. There are 8 or 10 boarders—2 or 3 of them ladies—2 servants.—For breakfast we had excellent-flavored coffee, hot & strong—not very clear & no great deal of cream—veal cutlets, elegant ham & eggs & nice bread and butter. I never sat down to a more plentiful or a nicer breakfast. I wish you could have seen the eggs—and the great dishes of meat. I ate the first hearty breakfast I have eaten since I left our little home. Sis is delighted, and we are both in excellent spirits. She has coughed hardly any and had no night sweat. . . . I feel in excellent spirits & have'nt drank a drop—so that I hope so to get out of trouble. The very instant I scrape together enough money I will send it on. You can't imagine how much we both miss you.

A fresh start: the scene of cheerful domesticity that Poe painted for Muddy in this, one of the few upbeat letters he ever wrote, suggests that he was optimistic about his chances for success in New York. Poe had moved there that spring because he had been unable to find enough work in Philadelphia to sustain the family. He had sold a number of stories and reviews, and although these and the lectures brought him some money, it wasn't enough. So, as was his habit when he faced up to exhausted possibilities, Poe moved somewhere new, leaving Philadelphia just as he had left Richmond and Baltimore after he had been "used up" there. The lecturing work had given him a moderately steady income stream, and so he hoped to expand his base of renown by relocating to Gotham, the true epicenter of literary activity in that day.

The city was alive with the arts and writing, and excitement was in the air. There was a sense that the young turks were storming the old citadels of literature, wresting away the mantels of fame from an aging regime. Some of the old guard, in fact, were effectively semiretired. Irving was in Spain; Cooper lived upstate and came to Manhattan only occasionally, to meet with his publishers. Nassau Street, several blocks south of city hall and overlapping with lawyers' row, formed the gravimetric center of the city's newspaper and magazine offices, as well as the shops of its numerous booksellers.

Poe worked the district with great energy, looking for openings. Papers were always being started up and abandoned, sold and merged with others; sometimes this provided a new opportunity. Like everyone else, Poe was constantly dropping in to different offices, finagling reviews and other assignments. Poe spoke not just for himself but for many another "young author struggling with Despair itself in the shape of a ghastly poverty" when he wrote in the aptly named essay "Some Secrets of the Magazine Prison-House" that the pay scale for such work was so low that it would make a common laborer's remuneration look like a windfall (1036–37). He was definitely regarded as a minor talent, probably due more to his personal character than his actual work. His reputation for drinking and quarrelsomeness was widely known, and it is doubtful that most of his contemporaries had read seriously his tales and poems. Also, Poe's abrasive and often bellicose personality made itself felt all the time, and this, of course, was what tended to register the most resoundingly with those he met. When he came to write about literary New York, Poe sounded like (and so must have felt like) an insider, but he was most likely regarded as a journalistic drudge who could sometimes come up with a good angle for a story—old wine in a new bottle.

One source of steady white space for Poe was not in Manhattan at all, but in far-flung Columbia, Pennsylvania, where two youths named Eli Bowen and Jacob L. Gossler, neither of them past the age of twenty, were publishing a weekly newspaper of limited circulation, the *Columbia Spy*. That spring, Poe, "well known to the Literary public as an eminent scholar and a distinguished critic," became a regular correspondent, furnishing the paper's readers with a weekly letter from New York that described his wanderings "far and wide over this island of Mannahatta."

Under the title "Doings of Gotham," Poe contributed a series of seven dispatches that ranged over a variety of topics, all presented in a brisk, journalistic style. What impresses one today about these somewhat quaint, old-fashioned missives is the acuteness of their writer's skills at close observation and analysis. Just as in his fiction, so too in his journalism Poe was eagle-eyed, keen to the point where he seems rarely to have missed anything noteworthy or unusual. His memory for detail was remarkable—coin of the realm for the writer.

In his first piece, for example, dated 14 May 1844, Poe noted the beauty of the fountain in Central Park and the puniness of the one near the bowling green; he commented on the fullness of trees in one spot and the paucity in another; and continuing his habit for juxtaposition and contrast, he gave a grim but powerful description of the Irish shanties ("the door is a barrel on end") beside "picturesque sites for villas":

> The old mansions upon them (principally wooden) are suffered to remain unrepaired, and present a melancholy spectacle of decrepitude. In fact, these magnificent places are doomed. The spirit of Improvement has withered them with its acrid breath. Streets are already "mapped" through them, and they are no longer suburban residences, but "town-lots." In some thirty years every noble cliff will be a pier, and the whole island will be densely desecrated by buildings of brick, with portentous facades of brown-stone, or brown-stonn, as the Gothamites have it. (Letter 1, 14 May 1844)

Poe described the public excitement attending the arrival in the city of the famed Fraunhofer telescope, but got rather caught up in trying to ascertain its exact power and dimensions—the downside of being so detail oriented. "The papers . . . give the merely physical length and breadth, with the length and breadth of the boxes in which it came. . . . What has become of the telescope, an account of which Mr. Paine furnished,—some years ago, to the 'Worcester Palladium'? The tube, of Russia iron, was said to be four feet in diameter, and forty-eight feet long . . ." (Letter 4, 4 June 1844).

And in a delirious slide into fantasy (given his poverty), Poe trillingly ticked off the precious knickknacks on display in Tiffany's windows: "a beautiful assortment of Swiss osier-work; chess-men—some sets costing five hundred dollars; paintings on rice-paper, in books and sheets; tile for fencing ornamental grounds; fine old bronzes and curiosities from the ancient temples; fillogram articles, in great variety; a vast display of bizarre fans; ranging, in price, from sixpence to seventy-five dollars" (Letter 4, 4 June 1844). These "letters," of course, were mere ephemera, and it is unlikely that they generated any substantial income for Poe. His early work in New York, therefore, did not really bode well for future success. Even the euphoria of that first letter in the *Spy* seemed to fade quickly, and gloom began to seep into him again, like rainwater into rotting wood.

Worse, Poe's greatest success upon arriving in New York seems to have created a backlash against him, for his first publication, in the *New York Sun*, was a hoax about a balloon crossing the Atlantic. Poe was ingenious at creating such deceptions—recall *Arthur Gordon Pym* and "Hans Pfaall"—and the paper was equally adept at setting the stage so that the public would all the more readily believe them. The regular morning edition of the *Sun* on 13 April carried an announcement, headed "Postscript," that proclaimed, in banner type:

ASTOUNDING INTELLIGENCE BY PRIVATE EXPRESS FROM CHARLESTON VIA NORFOLK!—THE ATLANTIC OCEAN CROSSED IN THREE DAYS!!—ARRIVAL AT SULLIVAN'S ISLAND OF A STEERING BALLOON INVENTED BY MR. MONCK MASON!!

In smaller type, the notice told readers that "We stop the press at a late hour" to announce that, "by a Private Express from Charleston," the paper had just been "put in possession of full details" of the extraordinary adventures suggested and that an Extra would "be positively ready, and for sale at our counter, by 10 o'clock this morning." And indeed by 10 a.m., as promised, the paper issued Poe's story, unsigned, as a one-page broadside under the masthead "THE EXTRA SUN." The headlines again whipped up the spectacular elements of the story, leaving no hyperbole (or type size) unused:

ASTOUNDING
NEWS!

~~~

BY EXPRESS VIA NORFOLK!

~~~

THE

~~~

ATLANTIC CROSSED

~~~

IN

~~~

THREE DAYS!

~~~

SIGNAL TRIUMPH

~~~

OF

~~~

MR. MONCK MASON'S

~~~

FLYING

~~~

MACHINE!!!

Readers were completely gulled, and the story generated quite a bit of excitement over the next several days. People thrilled to the idea of air travel and the possibility of visiting exotic lands and different climes. Entrepreneurs immediately began to lay plans to cash in on the new technology. Businessmen sought to raise capital for transportation services. But the literary wise men of the city, especially the editors of competing newspapers, were not so easily hoodwinked, and several of them, like James Gordon Bennett of the staid and conservative *New York Herald*, castigated in print the *Sun's* proprietor, one Moses Y. Beach, as a "manufacturer of hoaxes of all kinds, whether in banking or anything else, that offers the prospect of 'turning a penny.'" The *Sun* soberly replied in its next issue: "We by no means think such a project impossible," thus letting open the possibility that the story posited only that—a possibility, and soon it came out that the author of the hoax was Edgar Poe.

The story was a great technical improvement over its approximate predecessor, "Hans Pfaall," especially in the way it consistently maintained the scientific and journalistic tone in which it was written. It was later compared to Richard Adams Locke's famous "Moon-Hoax" of August 1835 (which had also appeared in the *Sun*), and Poe was elated about the perfectness with which his joke had come off, positively gloating in his second dispatch to the *Spy* (21 May 1844) that it made "a far more intense sensation" than Locke's hoax had:

> *On the morning (Saturday) of its announcement, the whole square surrounding the "Sun" building was literally besieged, blocked up—ingress and egress being alike impossible, from a period soon after sunrise until about two o'clock P. M. In Saturday's regular issue, it was stated that the news had been just received, and that an "Extra" was then in preparation, which would be ready at ten. It was not delivered, however, until nearly noon. In the meantime I never witnessed more intense excitement to get possession of a newspaper. As soon as the few first copies made their way into the streets, they were bought up, at almost any price, from the news-boys, who made a profitable speculation beyond doubt. I saw a half-dollar given, in one instance, for a single paper, and a shilling was a frequent price.*

But other papers soon chimed in, adding their notes of feigned injury to those sounded by the *Herald*. The Philadelphia *Saturday Courier*, where Henry Hirst's biographical sketch of Poe had appeared some years earlier, declared that "every intelligent reader will be disposed to regard this attempt to hoax as not even possessing the character of pleasantry." And in fact, the "Balloon Hoax" may have given Poe a thrill for a moment, but its eventual effect was to make people around the city feel that he wasn't really trustworthy. Ignoring his rhetorical skills at deception, they began to see him instead as a sort of devious manipulator, or, at best, a spurious showman, like P. T. Barnum.

Life in New York very quickly turned out to be no more rewarding or profitable than it had been in Philadelphia. Poe had come to Gotham expecting to find luscious fruit ripe for the picking; instead all he had managed to gather were a few dry twigs. Editorial work was next to impossible to find. The few pieces Poe sold brought in only a pittance. And he was badly treated, even by those who thought he was a good writer. He made friends with Sarah Hale, for example, editor of *Godey's Lady's Book* (and author of the song "Mary Had A Little Lamb"), who seems to have liked him and wanted to help him, but, like her colleagues, she offered Poe considerably less than the going rate for fiction, probably because she knew that he lived in poverty. Such exploitation made Poe's rage well up inside him, but to his credit he was often able to confine his displeasure to statements of well-honed reason and effective satire (as in his piece "The Magazine Prison-House") rather than bitter invective. There was also by now the well-known fact that on previous jobs Poe had shown up for work drunk, or not shown up at all.

He may have felt that he was *too* visible in the city, too much present, seemingly everywhere, to be thought of as talented. He worried that his colleagues had begun to think of him as the perpetual hanger-on, like a down-and-outer leaning in doorways waiting for a hopeful look or word from those hard at work inside. Therefore, when Muddy joined them from Philadelphia, Poe moved his family some five miles outside the city to what was then the countryside, an isolated two-story farmhouse at what would now be Eighty-fourth and Broadway. They lodged there with a Mr. and Mrs. Patrick Brennan, surrounded by seemingly endless verdure and color and delighted to have more than a dolls' house space to themselves. Poe and Virginia took a bedroom on the second floor, under the eaves, with a separate study in which Poe could work. Muddy had her own room downstairs. The new arrangements helped lift the gloomy mist that had settled around him, even though Virginia grew more visibly weaker by the day. By one account he had to carry her from room to room. He hoped vainly that the clean air and bucolic views would dispel the disease.

The change of scene moved Poe into an uncharacteristic lethargy, and he produced very little writing during his months at the Brennan farm. The slight pieces he did turn out were dutifully taken down to the city by Muddy, who would make the editorial rounds trying to sell them. No doubt she too was taken advantage of by budget-minded editors, for

156

again the sum total that these works brought in was barely enough for the small family to live on. Poe told one city acquaintance that he was "ill in health and wretchedly depressed in spirits," and when in September his old friend Frederick Thomas's unanswered letters to his Philadelphia address caught up with him, Poe apologized profusely for not keeping in touch any better than he had, telling Thomas that he had "been playing hermit in earnest" and had not seen "a living soul out of my family" for seven or eight months.

The impression one receives of Poe living in this farmhouse, going on long rambles in the countryside and pausing for quiet contemplation of nature, is of someone taking stock of himself, assessing his active accounts, and searching for some nonmaterial, transcendent truth that might release him from anxiety, depression, and a sense of futility. These trends are clearly in evidence in some of the fiction he wrote from this period. Behind the terror of these stories is the particular horror of Virginia's certain death.

In the hapless reality of Poe's life, he continually clung to the belief that there was something after death—something outside the rational that held the promise of another existence. Poe said as much to a correspondent around this time when he declared that in his whole life he had been "deeply conscious of the mutability and evanescence of temporal things"—so much so, he declared, that he thought himself unable "to give any continuous effort to anything—to be consistent in anything." In the spring or early summer of 1844, Poe wrote "Mesmeric Revelation," in which he uses an imaginary experiment in mesmerism (an early form of hypnotism in which the power of suggestion sent people into either agitated or sleeplike states) to propose a theory that one's present life is merely preparation for another existence in some immaterial realm.

"The Facts in the Case of M. Valdemar" (December 1845) was published as straight sensationalistic fiction, but it was taken in some quarters as a scientific pamphlet. It is probably Poe's most gruesome tale. Monsieur Ernest Valdemar, knowing he will die from a specific illness, is mesmerized, and from this state announces, "I am dead" (840). He remains in a state resembling suspended death for some seven months, unable either to live or to die, until he is finally removed from the trance. The words "Dead! dead!" come from his mouth, his eyes display a fluid or "yellowish ichor" (841) and his body eventually dissolves into a mass of "detestable putridity" (842).

The story may have been drawn from an account by a New York physician, Dr. A. Sidney Doane, of a surgical procedure that took place while a patient was in a state of "magnetic sleep" (printed in the New York *Broadway Journal* for 1 February 1845). This semicomatose state of consciousness closely resembles the "mesmerized" state of Poe's character. The tale represents another fantastical attempt to control death, but like "The Masque of the Red Death," it ends in failure. Among other things, the disturbingly objective descriptions of the character's body ("The left lung had been for eighteen months in a semi-osseous or cari-langinous state, and was, of course, entirely useless for all purposes of vitality" [835])—hint at Poe's state of mind. The degree of control that the mesmerist has over Valdemar ("subduing him"; "with the fullest exertion of the will") also seems to have overtones, as Poe raged futilely for a way to subdue Virginia's illness.

Poe cheated himself of the honest necessity to come to terms with Virginia's impending death, continuing to refer to her condition as the result of a "singing accident," a ridiculous self-delusion. This just as surely as he realized that the thought of her inevitable death had made him at first dream away whole months, then "awake, at last, to a sort of mania for composition," scribbling all day and reading all night, "so long as the disease endures." To think of writing as a "mania" and a "disease" was to enact a kind of rage that nothing could be done to retard, much less vanquish, Virginia's illness.

We might also divine Poe's thoughts and mood from the letters he wrote about this time to James Russell Lowell. Poe had been corresponding with Lowell, the handsome and witty descendant of a brilliant colonial family, off and on since 1842, when he was trying to launch "The Penn" and Lowell had been talking to various writers about founding his own periodical for native literature, "The Pioneer." Lowell thought highly of Poe, regarding his imagination and intellect as world-class, good enough to stand up against the minds of England and the Continent. Seeing Poe thus, as something much more than an itinerant hack and erratic talent, placed Lowell in the minority of Poe's circle of acquaintances. Probably for this reason, Poe conveniently overlooked the fact that Lowell represented exactly what he found most displeasurable in writers like Longfellow, Emerson, and others. Lowell had been born in Cambridge, Massachusetts, been privately educated, graduated from Harvard College and Harvard Law School, and was now a prominent poet with a lot of money and a high reputation. Later he would become the editor of the most prestigious literary magazine in the United States, the *Atlantic Monthly*, and would succeed Longfellow in his chair of poetry at Harvard University.

George Graham had asked Lowell to write a profile of Poe for his magazine's ongoing series, "Our Contributors." Hearing of the request, Poe told Lowell that he would be "very proud, indeed," if he wrote it. Poe sent Lowell the *Saturday Museum* sketch of his life and offered further help if Lowell needed it. Lowell replied about a month later that the clipping had provided him with many useful "outward facts," but "I want *your own estimate* of your life. . . . I believe that the opinion a man has of himself (if he be accustomed to self-analysis) is of more worth than that of all the rest of the world." Poe was not much given to self-analysis in print (allowing that there is much self-exploration done allegorically in the fiction), but he responded to Lowell's request, thus providing one of the few candid philosophical remarks about himself that are known to exist.

The letter, dated 2 July 1844, reaffirms Poe's belief in an unknowable otherworld in which death could be either arrested or reversed and humans could live in transcendent, perhaps incorporeal states of being. Like Jonathan Swift before him, who saw man as an animal probably incapable of self-improvement, Poe also struck a decidedly elitist note in a series of statements that confirmed his antidemocratic views and his generally pessimistic perspective on the progress of the human race:

I am not ambitious—unless negatively. I, now and then feel stirred up to excel a fool, merely because I hate to let a fool imagine that he may excel me. Beyond

159

this I feel nothing of ambition. I really perceive that vanity about which most men merely prate—the vanity of the human or temporal life. I live continually in a reverie of the future. I have no faith in human perfectibility. I think that human exertion will have no appreciable effect upon humanity. Man is now only more active—not more happy—nor more wise, than he was 6000 years ago. The result will never vary—and to suppose that it will, is to suppose that the foregone man has lived in vain—that the foregone time is but the rudiment of the future—that the myriads who have perished have not been upon equal footing with ourselves—nor are we with our posterity. I cannot agree to lose sight of man the individual, in man the mass.—I have no belief in spirituality. I think the word a mere word. No one has really a conception of spirit.

These ideas were sharply at odds with Lowell's own philosophy, but the latter seems to have accepted Poe's statements as honest differences of opinion. The letter is also notable for its apparent lack of guile or even of posing. It is as frank and unmanipulative a document as Poe ever wrote. Lastly, the letter reveals that Poe's thoughts had turned to grave questions of the point of man's existence, the identity of God, and the origins of the universe. He spoke of mankind deceiving itself "by the idea of infinitely rarefied matter." He continued:

Matter escapes the senses by degrees—a stone—a metal—a liquid—the atmosphere—a gas—the luminiferous ether. . . . But to all we attach the notion of a constitution of particles—atomic composition. For this reason only, we think spirit different; for spirit, we say is unparticled, and therefore is not matter. But it is clear that if we proceed sufficiently far in our ideas of rarefaction, we shall arrive at a point where the particles coalesce; for, although the particles be infinite, the infinity of littleness in the spaces between them, is an absurdity.— The unparticled matter, permeating & impelling, all things, is God. Its activity is the thought of God—which creates. Man, and other thinking beings, are individualizations of the unparticled matter. Man exists as a "person", by being clothed with matter (the particled matter) which individualizes him. Thus habited, his life is rudimental. What we call "death" is the painful metamorphosis.

These ideas look forward to Poe's 1848 treatise on cosmogony, *Eureka.*

Lowell's biographical essay on Poe appeared in *Graham's* in February 1845. It was wholly laudatory, concluding that Poe had "attained an individual eminence in our literature, which he will keep. He has given proof of power and originality." Yet several months later, in May, the two men had their only face-to-face meeting, and Poe told Thomas Holley Chivers he was "very much disappointed" in Lowell's appearance—"he was not half the noble looking person I expected to see." Poe the southern conservative may have been predisposed to judge Lowell, the New Englander, harshly. For his part, Lowell saw how Poe bristled at him and could not take away a favorable impression of the man whom he had lauded in the essay. Lowell was disappointed in Poe, for the latter was "a little soggy with drink." Lowell also thought Poe mannered and pretentious, his dapper neatness merely a façade and his fine eyes and pellucid complexion off-putting, even ghastly. Poe (somehow feeling that Lowell had "misled" him into a false impression of himself) attacked Lowell in August in the *Broadway Journal*, with a favorite weapon—accusations of plagiarism, this time from Wordsworth.

Once again, Poe showed himself a difficult person to help. He resorted to his habit of asserting his independence, as Hemingway did, by kicking away people who had helped him. Perhaps Poe was embarrassed by having to accept "charity" from someone like Lowell, in the form of a positive profile in print. He may have turned hostile in order to show his independence. But such acts were also obviously part of the self-destructive pattern of Poe's character, what he would later call his "imp of the perverse." Lowell felt stabbed in the back. He went on to parody Poe in his "A Fable for Critics" as "three-fifths genius and two-fifths sheer fudge."

Another person tried to help Poe that spring in New York. Again it was someone whom Poe had earlier dismissed as a "graceful trifler," but again the person felt sorry for Poe, discerned his genius, and offered his assistance. This was Nathaniel Parker Willis, probably the most famous journalist in America at the time. Willis had been educated at Yale after preparation at Andover, and in the 1820s had struck out in journalism in Boston, founding the *American Monthly Magazine*. He quickly attained a reputation as something of a bon vivant—a witty and worldly man of letters who created a public image that was carefully tailored to match the persona of his writings. He was said to write at an antique fruitwood desk, ensconced in a crimson-curtained inner sanctum; he invited his readers to imagine themselves on a *dormeuse* with a bottle of Rudesheimer and a plate of olives before them. Poe had long tracked the career of this boy wonder of the writing world, and it was probably Willis whom Poe was parodying in his early burlesque, "The Duc du l'Omelette." Poe's 1839 review of Willis's drama, *Tortesa, or the Usurer Matched*, however, was unusually positive—Poe judged it "the best play from the pen of an American author" (1129).

After the *American Monthly Magazine* folded, Willis left Boston for New York and became the foreign correspondent, for five years, for George Morris's newspaper, the *Evening Mirror*. The details of his travels may be followed in the letters, collected as *Pencillings by the Way* (1844), which appeared irregularly in the *Mirror* beginning in February 1832. He became quite famous, known for his handsome appearance, his elegant taste in dress, and his ability for meeting and pleasing people of importance—all qualities that Poe had tried hard to affect but ultimately couldn't.

Poe had been writing odd pieces for the *Mirror* for about a year and a half and had insinuated himself into Willis's good graces. In October 1844, Willis offered Poe a position on the paper at $750 a year as an assistant editor and what Willis later apologetically described as a "mechanical paragraphist" (an image that makes one visualize Melville's "used up" copyist-clerk, Bartleby). It was clearly charity, for the most part, but Poe had to accept. "It was rather a step downward," Willis recognized, "after being the chief editor of several monthlies . . . to come into the office of a daily journal and sit at a desk, in a corner of the editorial room, ready to be called upon for any of the miscellaneous work of the moment— announcing news, condensing statements, answering correspondents, noticing amusements—everything but the writing of a 'leader,' or constructing any article upon which his peculiar idiosyncrasy of mind could be impressed." Such demanding and deadening duties as these could not have been good for Poe's spirits, but during his time at the *Mirror* he was a model employee—even-keeled, quiet and polite, and apparently sober.

Poe may have identified with Willis in emotional ways. He wrote a sketch of him for his "Literati" series in *Godey's Lady's Book* for May 1846, noting that Willis's career had "naturally made him enemies among the envious host of dunces whom he has outstripped in the race for fame." He also noted that Willis's "personal manner" was "tinctured" with "reserve, *brusquerie*, or even haughtiness" and that he was "by no means adapted to conciliate. He has innumerable warm friends, however, and is himself a warm friend. He is impulsive, generous, bold, impetuous, vacillating, irregularly energetic—apt to be hurried into error, but incapable of deliberate wrong." Willis became one of Poe's strongest defenders after the author's death, writing a long tribute to him to counter Griswold's unflattering portrait. Willis emphasized Poe's gentlemanly qualities, his "unvarying deportment and ability" and emphasized that he was "invariably punctual and industrious" at the *Mirror*, not at all the monomaniacal and delusional freak that Griswold would make Poe out to be.

Poe continued his itinerant journalistic and critical work, contributing articles around town on the literary marketplace, contemporary authors, and the lack of international copyright law. He also began the series he called "Marginalia" in the *Democratic Review* in November, a gossipy melange of commentary on recent reading and speculations about literary goings-on in the city. These were generally well received, as one anonymous correspondent to the *Mirror* declared, "I am glad to see that Edgar Poe is in your clearings. He is a man of the finest ideal intellect in the land ... let him fire away at the humbugs of our literature."

Within a few weeks of going to work for Willis, Poe had moved the family back to the city, first to a cramped apartment at 85 Amity Street, in Greenwich Village, and then to a larger rooming house at 195 East Broadway. He was still set up in far from ideal circumstances, pathetically writing Lowell on 28 October that "a host of small troubles growing from the *one* trouble of poverty, but which I will not trouble you with in detail, have hitherto prevented me from thanking you for the Biography and all the well-intended flatteries it contains." He also noted, however, that he had not been idle and had been, among other projects, collecting materials for a critical history of American literature, something, alas, he never made much progress on.

About that time Poe also sent a long letter to Charles Anthon, a professor of Greek and Latin at Columbia University and an early supporter of the *Southern Literary Messenger*; Poe was still trying to drum up support for his magazine. Citing his past success with *Graham's*, Poe speculated that if Graham could get fifty thousand subscribers for a three-dollar magazine, "among a class of readers who really read little, why may not 50,000 be procured for a $5 journal among the true and permanent readers of the land?" Poe now envisioned not a mass audience, but a select one, composed only of "well educated men . . . among the innumerable plantations of our vast Southern & Western Countries." Poe asked Anthon to use his influence with his own publishers, Harpers, and see if they would undertake the magazine, but Anthon wrote back and told Poe that Harpers had had "complaints" against him and so were not interested.

Then came, quite unexpectedly, a brief flirtation with fame. Poe had probably been working for at least a year or more on the poem that would make him famous, possibly still when he was living in Philadelphia. But "The Raven" seems to have come together entire in the fall of 1844, as Poe hacked away at his "mechanical" work for Willis on the *Evening Mirror*. Something of the forlorn character of that dogsbody position inhabits the lonely and melancholy lover of the poem who is trapped by utter futility. One can read this as a commentary on the general state of Poe's life and career, or more specifically on what he realized was the inevitable loss of Virginia, just as the speaker of the poem has lost his beloved Lenore but tortures himself that she may somehow be reclaimed. The speaker is locked in a torturous cycle of "mournful and never-ending remembrance." Like a character in an Ibsen play, and like Poe himself, the speaker broods on misfortune, yet something of the fantasized power to control death is part of the poem, too, as Poe seems to control so tightly the memorable rhymes and cadences of the poem—what holds its place today in the annals of famous writing. Finally, the poem provides a gloss on Poe's status with the literary world, for he published it pseudo-nymously, under the poetic and suggestive name Quarles, or "quarrels."

Whatever Poe's motivations, "The Raven" was an instant success and, like Byron, Poe woke up to find himself famous. Apparently Poe offered the poem to Willis first, who rejected it, as well as to his former employer, George Graham, who also turned it down. The honor of being the first publisher to print the poem went instead to George H. Colton, of the *American Review*, which ran it in the 29 January 1845 number. But the poem became known to most New Yorkers when the *Mirror* secured permission to reprint it in its 8 February issue. Poe must have been flattered when the poem was imitated and parodied. It created the kind of buzz that attends a publishing event not seen or heard probably since the appearance of the book that as a young critic in Richmond Poe had so thoroughly "used up," *Norman Leslie*.

Readers everywhere thrilled to "The Raven," as the *New World* noted two weeks after its appearance, for its "originality and power." This paper called it "wild and *shivery*," written in "a Stanza unknown before to gods, men, and booksellers." One New Yorker recorded that the poem "electri-fied by the weird cry of Nevermore," and the *Morning Express* noted that it "may well defy comparison." Its incantatory rhythm made it an ideal choice for school texts on elocution and public speaking. A rash of paro-dies broke out in New York, Philadelphia, and Boston, one by a pseu-donymous "Snarles," author of "THE VETO," who adapted the poem to comment on local politics. Others worked variations on the central symbolic object of the bird—"The Gazelle," "The Turkey," even "The Mammoth Squash." Manufacturers used the famous structure and rhythm of the poem to advertise everything from soap to notions to patent medicines.

Ironically, Poe, the archenemy of plagiarism, took the stanzaic struc-ture, the alliteration, and the internal rhyme from "Lady Geraldine's Courtship," by Elizabeth Barrett Browning, a poet who, along with Tennyson, Poe much admired for the musical properties of her verse. In "Fifty Suggestions," a piece for the May–June 1849 number of *Graham's Magazine*, Poe wrote that "with the exception of Tennyson's 'Locksley

Hall,' I have never read a poem combining so much of the fiercest passion with so much of the most delicate imagination" (1305). Poe even imitated (if that is the right word) the imagery in one line, "With a murmurous stir uncertain, in the air the purple curtain," with "And the silken, sad, uncertain rustling of each purple curtain." The bird itself was suggested by Dickens's *Barnaby Rudge*, which Poe had reviewed for *Graham's*. In that piece, Poe thought that Dickens's presentation of the raven, a bad omen, lacked "an analogical resemblance" to Barnaby (243) and called attention to the fact that Dickens had not made full symbolic use of the bird.

Some sources for the poem may also be found in Poe's previous work. The idea of a dumb and nonreasoning creature whose actions nonetheless cause consternation within a human may have been suggested to Poe by his own "The Murders in the Rue Morgue." He had already named the female character in an early poem "Lenore." And the choice of a refrain, "Nevermore," with its sonorous, long "o" sound may also be found in that poem and in "The Conqueror Worm" (1843). "No more" is the phrase that permeates "The Haunted Palace" as well as "Sonnet to Zante."

"The Raven" is probably the most famous poem in American literature, perhaps in the English language. Is it a great poem? History has filed mixed reviews, many of them negatively highlighting the considerable amount of contrivance in the poem, and the large number of stage properties that seem to provide focus, to the detriment of any ideation. The technicolor allusiveness in the poem, the dazzling displays of prosodic wit, seem a little monotonous, like Vivaldi's concertos or Pachelbel's *Canon*—pure genius, no doubt, but also an untiring skill at perpetuating a theme with variations.

What sticks most in the reader's mind are the sounds of the poem, especially the internal rhyme ("rapping, tapping") and the harmony of the long lines, which, like another "musical" poem by Poe, "The Bells," seems almost a song lyric. For this reason, "The Raven" is often derided for being all style and no substance, a bit of deft but ultimately not very meaningful verbal legerdemain. This is what Yeats felt when he called the poem "insincere," and what other artists after Poe suggested when they remarked on the adolescent qualities of "The Raven," and of some of Poe's other writings. T. S. Eliot put it the most glancingly in *From Poe to Valéry* when he called Poe's intellect that of "a highly gifted young person before puberty."

Poe was certainly enamored of the musical properties of verse writing, and had an enormous talent in that regard. The artist Gabriel Harrison recalled his first acquaintance with Poe in the fall of 1844 when he was president of a local Democratic organization and used to run a tea shop in the newspaper district. One evening he "observed a person looking intently through my windows at a display of some Virginia leaf tobacco." Poe entered, commented on the quality of the leaf, and sampled some. He later called in again, at a moment when Harrison was trying to compose a campaign song for his club. "I acquainted him with the fact," Harrison recalled, "and while I was waiting upon a customer, he had composed a song to the measure and time of the 'Star Spangled Banner.' It was used by the club successfully through the campaign of 1844." In critical writings, Poe tended to overpraise poets like Tennyson, of whom Poe said, "he seems to *see with his ear*" (1332). More practically speaking, Poe the literary businessman must have known that poems suitable for recitation exercises could not fail to be profitable financially.

"The Raven," like many of Poe's tales, is spoken by a monomaniacal character who has suffered a grievous loss. Not willing to accept that reality, he occupies himself, vainly, in a search for some way that death might be reversed. The raven reminds him, through its sombre and sonorous litany, "Nevermore," that this will never be so. We meet this self-destructive speaker in his study, having fallen asleep, while "pondering, weak and weary, / Over many a quaint and curious volume of forgotten lore." This character, a student, is a Faust archetype, based on that famous character in English literature who is so assiduous a seeker after forbidden knowledge that he sells his soul to the devil. The "forgotten lore" suggests forbidden knowledge, the occult, or any ancient books that may contain clues to the great mysteries of the universe.

Working again, as he often does in his tales, by dichotomies or dualisms, Poe sets up a contrast between the student and the symbolic object which defines his "chamber," the bust of Pallas, and the raven which perches on it. This incident jars him, breaking in on his temporary peace, through sleep, and producing agitated emotionalism upon awakening. Pallas Athena was the virgin goddess of wisdom, Zeus's child, who sprang full grown from the mighty god's forehead. (Her temple was the Parthenon, whose name comes from "Parthenos," "the maiden.") The contrast is therefore between knowledge or wisdom and what the Raven represents, nonreason, or intuitive truth. In different terms, this is the mind-body dichotomy that Poe explores in numerous other works.

Another contrast is presented through setting and time. The poem takes place "upon a midnight dreary" in "bleak December," both the time of night and the time of the year representing the end of something, and simultaneously the beginning of something else. Some have speculated that the poem takes place on New Year's Eve, others that Poe was imaginatively re-creating the night when his mother died, in December. The tomb-like silence and claustrophobia inside is also contrasted with the tempestuous outside, and "the Night's Plutonian shore."

But surely the most haunting aspect of "The Raven" is the effect of the bird's mournful dirge on the speaker, emotionally rent from his self-torturing sorrow and denied consolation, only the promise of "never-ending remembrance." The marvellous ambiguity of the poem's famous refrain is of a piece with Poe's abiding theme of trying to journey to the core of death and still live to tell the tale. The speaker hopes for consolation and gets from the bird only a monodic reply, telling him both that he will "nevermore" regain his lost Lenore and that he is cursed to "nevermore" forget the fact that he has lost her.

Fifteen months after the publication of the poem, Poe followed up on its success with a fascinating, although highly disingenuous account of its origin, "The Philosophy of Composition." This essay, published in *Graham's Magazine* for April 1846, shows Poe at his most craftsmanlike. Like one of his tales of ratiocination, it is a window on his considerable analytic skills as well.

In the essay, Poe tells us that he wrote the poem backwards, beginning with the denouement, which gave the plot its "indispensable air of consequence," or causation. The denouement was predicated upon the effect to be produced in the reader. Keeping originality "always in view," Poe wrote that he asked himself of all the possible effects, "which one shall I select? Which one is most susceptible to producing a lasting impression" on the intellect and soul of the reader? Poe says he made his choice based on both necessity and circumstance, the requirement that he must earn money and the inability to suppress whatever poetic idea his soul had to utter.

Wanting to please, then, "at once the popular and the critical taste" (15) (something that may account for the poem's contrivances), Poe next determined an ideal length of one hundred lines (he ended up with one hundred and eight). The poem could not be too short, since it needed unity of impression, nor too long, since it needed to be read at one sitting. Poe believed that there was really no such thing as a long poem, but that a long poem was merely "a succession of brief . . . poetical effects" (15). The brevity of the poem, he wrote, must be in "direct ratio of the intensity of the intended effect" (15). Next, the subject, which would be Beauty— according to Poe, "the sole legitimate province of the poem" (16) (a rein-forcement of his "Letter to B—," in which he declared that a poem had "for its *immediate* object pleasure, not truth" [11]). After that, the pivot, something on which the construction of the poem would turn. This was the refrain, varied a bit from stanza to stanza, soothing the ear with repe-tition and surprising the mind with the altered significance of the similar sounds. Poe's last desideratum was "what will the Raven say?" His answer, "of all melancholy topics," the most melancholy would be death and espe-cially "the death of a beautiful woman" (18–19). This topic, it should be noted, was certainly not original to Poe: the newspapers and magazines of the period were filled with stories and poems that took up this subject.

Poe's idealized account of the composition of the poem is more inter-esting biographically than as anything else. Its exaggerated air of dispas-sionate objectivity and methodical control over the manic energy of creativity suggests a man who raged above all else for control—for order, unity, and harmony, those very things that his volatile, capricious, and insensibly irrational world would not give him. In other words, "The

169

Philosophy of Composition" ("The" in its title suggesting that there is only one) is as much a cover-up as anything else for Poe's own lack of control. At one point he writes that he set out "to render it manifest that no one point in [the poem's] composition" would be "referrible either to accident or intuition . . . the work proceeded, step by step, to its completion with the precision and rigid consequence of a mathematical problem" (14–15). And later, speaking of the necessity of originality, Poe notes that it "is by no means a matter . . . of impulse or intuition" (20). One could not imagine a stronger hedge against the irrationality and disorder of one's life than this hyperanalytic essay, with its almost supernatural claims of prescience and precision.

In terms of Poe's aesthetic, it is interesting to note that his two major critical statements (both written around this time) convey completely opposite notions of creativity. On the one hand, there is the ratiocinative "Philosophy of Composition," with its obsession with order, symmetry, and control. Balanced against that is the later "The Poetic Principle," which gushingly pays tribute to poetry writing as a fount of inspiration, spontaneity, and emotional abandon. Here again Poe seems to have been a creature of dual impulses that pulled and tugged at him without end. One might also note the obvious: that Poe's tales are not just about obsessive-compulsives, but about manic-depressives, as well. His fictive universe, perhaps best imaged in *The Narrative of Arthur Gordon Pym*, is a precarious cosmos of catastrophic rises and falls, mood swings that well fit the rhythms of his own bipolar personality.

Both "The Raven" and "The Philosophy of Composition" also reveal Poe's pride and his inflated sense of mastery at writing. One story goes that shortly after finishing the poem, but before it appeared, Poe ran into William Ross Wallace on the street. He told the Kentucky novelist of his great achievement, saying, "Wallace, I have just written the greatest poem that was ever written." "Have you?" Wallace replied. "Would you like to hear it?" Poe asked, and getting an affirmative answer began to recite it. He finished, turned to Wallace for his opinion, and Wallace said, "Poe—they are fine; uncommonly fine." "Fine?" said Poe, contemptuously. "Is that all you can say for this poem? I tell you it's the greatest poem that was ever written." To counterbalance these claims we might recall Poe's apparently confidential quip to his friend Frederick Thomas (one of the few people Poe ever spoke to in a completely candid manner): "'The Raven' has had a great 'run'—but I wrote it for the express purpose of running—just as I did the 'Gold-Bug,' you know. The bird beat the bug, though, all hollow."

Although he earned very little from "The Raven" (the lack of a copyright law enabled publishers to reprint the poem as many times as they wanted for free), the poem did succeed in renewing New York's interest in Poe as a writer. It effectively paid his cover price for admission to New York literary society, and he met scores of influential people who seemed willing to promote him through their networks.

The most important such person Poe met was Evert A. Duyckinck, an anthologist of American writing and editor of the New York *Literary World*, who at the time had taken under his wing another fledgling literary find, Herman Melville. Duyckinck was also the informal founder of Young America, a loose confederation of writers—most of whose members, like Cornelius Matthews, Poe thought were third-rate. These authors propagandized, through editorials and critical writings, for a national literature that would be democratic in nature, championing homespun American values and featuring the common man as its main character. Poe, of course, must have been revolted by that idea, with his aristocratic manner and apposite notions of literary form, but as usual he willingly accepted the charity that was offered him and bonded with Duyckinck quickly. Duyckinck urged Wiley and Putnam to publish Poe's *Tales*. The volume was well received, and the publishers later brought out *The Raven and Other Poems* in November. For the first time Poe received a decently favorable royalty rate.

The most important result of the success of "The Raven" was a revitalization of Poe's lecturing work. On 28 February Poe gave a well-publicized and well-attended talk on the poets and poetry of America, his standard topic, to an audience of about three hundred at the Society Library in New York. As a lecturer, Poe was compelling, ranging freely across the boundaries of a variety of topics, expanding his audience's horizons of

171

knowledge, like an intrepid explorer. This time Poe removed his caustic remarks about Griswold from the speech, since the two had reached a détente a little earlier when Griswold wrote Poe saying he would include him in his new anthology of American prose writers. Griswold took issue with Poe's oft-repeated charge that he allowed his "private grief" to color his critical conclusions. Poe replied in a conciliatory manner, saying in effect that he hoped they two could forget the past.

In these lectures, Poe cut a dramatic figure, dressed in characteristic raven black. Reports confirm that he was a soft-spoken, eloquent reciter of verse, well attuned to rhythm—so much so that he "almost sang the more musical versifications." There was substantial money to be earned from these engagements, about one hundred dollars per lecture. But as princely as that sum was, it was not enough to make up for years of near-zero income, and for deficits created by borrowing money from friends.

What happened next is baffling and pathetic. Poe had resurrected his career and was riding high on a new wave of creative energy that crested with his New York fame as author of "The Raven." Anyone other than Poe would have turned his recent fame to advantage. What did Poe do? He used his celebrity status to begin, in the *Mirror*, another plagiarism campaign—this time, an all-out firestorm—directed at Longfellow, the alleged "plagiarist." The success of "The Raven" melted away like butter in a fire, and Poe entangled himself in a petty war of words with the literati, ruining his prospects for creative renewal, as well as personal happiness.

Poe had been firing shots across Longfellow's bow since a review in February 1840 had accused the professor of "purloining" the central image for one of his poems from Tennyson. Poe, no doubt feeling over-worked and underpaid, resented Longfellow for his cushy position as both a poet of eminence in America and an academic, the holder of an endowed chair at Harvard, and he was also the husband of an heiress. According to N. P. Willis, Poe made the attack in part because he felt that "Longfellow is asleep on velvet; it will do him good to rouse him. His friends will come out and fight his battle." When Poe went to work for the *Evening Mirror,* he took the opportunity to needle Longfellow when on 13 and 14 January 1845 he reviewed the collection *The Waif.* Poe praised Longfellow's "Proem" as the best in this anthology, but he also charged that Hood's "The Death-Bed" was similar to an unspecified poem in Griswold's *Poets and Poetry of America* and accused Longfellow of including only those poets whom he could "continuously *imitate* (is that the right word?) and yet never even incidentally commend" (702). Poe now also widened the attack to charge that Longfellow's play, *The Spanish Student,* showed many similarities to his own unpublished play fragment, *Politian,* "to establish at least the *imitation* beyond all doubt" (755). He also suggested that Longfellow had plagiarized Bryant, so that now Poe was using one poet he mildly disliked in order to berate another that he severely disliked.

This article touched off a series of attacks and counterattacks between Poe and the Boston literary coterie that quickly escalated into an all-out war. An unknown writer, calling himself "Outis," printed an attack on Poe in retaliation, charging that "The Raven" had been plagiarized from a sentimental poem, "The Bird of the Dream," as well as from Coleridge's "The Rime of the Ancient Mariner." Poe then responded with five swift, successive, but fairly feeble articles. Yet to none of them did Longfellow respond, maintaining instead a dignified silence.

It is entirely possible that "Outis" (Greek for "no man," from the blinded Cyclops in *The Odyssey*) was Poe himself, who wrote the attack in order to stoke the fires of controversy. Poe was known to be quarrelsome and paranoid, as many writers are. Like Frost, Hemingway, Norman Mailer, and many other twentieth-century authors, Poe deployed his character flaws in his art, and made great professional use of them in the management of his public personality. Like Sinclair Lewis, who once publicly challenged God to strike him dead while he spoke from a church pulpit, Poe could be disingenuous, crafty, and manipulative. Unfortunately for Poe—unlike these other writers—his attempts usually backfired and brought him too much negative publicity. But it is worth considering that in these public feuds Poe probably knew what he was doing but simply managed it poorly.

Nevertheless, Poe's "relationship" with Longfellow ran true to form for Poe—a destructive pattern of beginning with mutual praise, followed up by his request for material for his magazines; then, when resentment built up, there inevitably followed vicious attacks and recriminations. The "Longfellow War," as it came to be called, consumed Poe for three-quarters of the year 1845. It brought down notoriety on him and made him him lose the friendship of such notables as James Russell Lowell and Evert Duyckinck. Yet the ironies are what is most striking about the episode. After Poe died, Longfellow bought five copies of Griswold's edition of Poe's works in order to help the destitute Maria Clemm. Longfellow astutely perceived that Poe's obsession with plagiarism was rooted in a deep-seated sense of injustice and an unbalanced view of his own achievements, forgivable, however, in someone of such genius. "The harshness of his criticisms," Longfellow wrote, "I have never attributed to anything but the irritation of a sensitive nature, chafed by some indefinite sense of wrong."

Poe's obsession with plagiarism was in part a defense mechanism, to convince himself that his own rather liberal borrowings from other people's writings were excusable, another example of his self-destructive tendencies. It was also, as George Graham discerned, part and parcel of the peculiarities of his temperament: "It was an occupation peculiarily suited to his captious, scrutinizing, analytical mind, to his doubting and suspicious temper, to his peculiar notions concerning evidence, ratiocination, and to his wide and discursive reading, to his fine poetic memory, and to his peculiar habits of finding proofs in trifles light as air, and of seeking for them in the most improbable places and manners."

Poe's preoccupation with plagiarism had begun early in his career. In a footnote to the 1829 *Al Aaraaf, Tamerlane, and Minor Poems*, Poe even sought to reveal, for the reader's benefit, his own literary indebtedness: "Plagiarism—see the works of Thomas Moore—passim—." Yet a year or two later, Poe saw a volume of Thomas Campbell's verse lying on a West Point classmate's desk. He picked it up, tossed it contemptuously aside, and said, "Campbell is a plagiarist." One critic has chronicled the pervasive atmosphere of plagiary and accusations about it in the British quarterlies of the time, concluding that Poe probably felt himself a member of a cosy club that he wanted to belong to when he levelled his own accusations at Longfellow and others.

Complicating the matter is the inconsistency with which Poe used the term "plagiarism." He often simultaneously and interchangeably used their opposites—"originality," "novelty," and "strangeness." He attached so much importance to originality because he used it as the benchmark with which to judge true genius in art. Yet Poe was not blindly pursuing some unattainable requirement, since he at least once observed that plagiarism can become, even with a great writer, inevitable. He even declared that "of one hundred [possible] plagiarisms" in any work of art, "seventy-five would be, not accidental, but unintentional." The crucial point that Poe could never determine with precision was when plagiary passed from the subconscious, or unintentional, into the realm of the deliberate.

It is clear, however, that Poe's concept of originality had little to do with photographic realism. As he said in a review of Bulwer-Lytton's *Night and Morning* in 1839, it transcended gross reality and appertained "to the loftier regions of the *Ideal*" (155). Poe's charges against Longfellow, therefore, were not isolated and capricious. They were the culmination of a significant phase of Poe's career in which he had devoted part of himself to the study of originality, the cornerstone of his aesthetic. He had pondered long and deeply what originality was to the true artist.

Despite these lofty aesthetic ideals, however, Poe nonetheless was in part beset by paranoia and neuroses, bordering sometimes on psychosis. His sad insecurity is revealed in a letter to a minor critic, Jedediah Hunt, who had published in the *Broadway Journal* a brief commentary on Poe's charges against Longfellow. "I recognize in you an educated, an honest, a chivalrous, but, I fear, a somewhat over-hasty man," Poe wrote in reply.

There are points at which you do me in justice. . . . For example, you say that I am sensitive (peculiarly so) to the strictures of others. There is no instance on record in which I have ever replied, directly or indirectly, to any strictures, personal or literary, with the single exception of my answer to Outis. You say, too, that I use a quarter of the paper in smoothing over his charges—but four-fifths of

*the whole space occupied is by the letter of Outis itself, to which I wish to give all
the publicity in my power, with a view of giving it the more thorough refutation.
The charges of which you speak—the charge of plagiarism &c—are not made
at all. These are mistakes into which you have fallen, through want of time to
peruse the whole of what I said, and by happening upon unlucky passages.*

Such statements present a picture of a petty and defensive man, respond-
ing overemphatically to minor slights as strongly as to well-founded
criticisms.

In early 1845 Poe had begun contributing to the *Broadway Journal*,
then edited by Charles F. Briggs, a Nantucket-born writer who had served
as a sailor and had published a very successful novel, *The Adventures of
Harry Franco*, in 1839. James Russell Lowell had given Poe's name to
Briggs, his friend, in December 1844, and in January Briggs took Poe on
as assistant editor. On 21 February Poe became the coeditor with Briggs
and assumed his by-now familiar tasks of supervising production, corresponding with contributors, and editing the copy that came in for each
issue. It was a good position: Poe was paid a reasonable salary, plus one
third of the profits (divided among him, Briggs, and the publisher) each
month. In July Poe became sole editor of the magazine, buying out his
partners, on money borrowed from Horace Greeley, Chivers, and even
from some enemies—Fitz-Greene Halleck lent him one hundred dollars
and Griswold, by his own account, lent him twenty-five. Poe was back
to his old habits of begging, but they accomplished what he wanted:
"*Will* you aid me at a pinch—as one of the greatest pinches conceivable?
If you will, I will be indebted to you, for life?" In this somewhat indirect
way, Poe realized his lifelong dream of owning and publishing a literary
monthly.

The *Broadway Journal* was definitely more serious and intellectually
oriented than earlier periodicals Poe had managed. Poe reviewed books
and also published art, theatre, and music criticism, poetry, and political
articles. Although he reprinted much of his earlier work, he also wrote
many appreciative reviews of major figures such as Milton, Tennyson,

Burns, and Shelley; moreover, he branched out into theoretical writings about American drama and later reviewed actual plays.

Observing live theatre gave new dimensions to Poe's characteristic concern with the technical skill, structure, and design of a literary work. Poe wrote two notices of Anna Cora Mowatt's *Fashion; or Life in New York*, generally regarded as the first American comedy of manners. His first notice concentrated on the merits and defects of the play; the second was a more general discussion of the "prospects of the drama." In the first piece (29 March 1845), Poe reiterated his belief that dramatic action should give an illusion of reality to the audience, and he demanded verisimilitude in all aspects of its presentation. Consequently, Poe deplored Mowatt's reliance on convention and hackneyed stage tricks such as soliloquies, reading letters in loud stage whispers, and "preposterous asides."

In the second notice (5 April 1845), Poe expressed much hope for a revival of the drama in America but felt that it could only be accomplished if playwrights would stop slavishly depending on past conventions. The lack of originality remained for Poe the great enemy of progress in art. Poe was also eminently practical in his views. His concern with getting art to reach the public without sacrificing purity for popularity dates back to his earliest "tomahawk" reviews of mediocre writers with undeservedly high reputations, and it pervades the "honest and fearless opinion[s]" expressed in many of his reviews for *Graham's Magazine*.

As if perversely to compensate, however, for the reasonableness of his dramatic reviews, his time at the *Broadway Journal* also saw flare-ups of his irrational and unpredictable behavior. One particularly unsavory episode involved Richard Henry Stoddard, a nineteen-year-old would-be poet who that summer had submitted his "Ode on a Grecian Flute" to Poe's magazine. Not hearing anything for several weeks, Stoddard screwed up his courage and went to the *Journal* offices to inquire about the status of his submission. Being told that Poe had left for the day, Stoddard called on him in his apartments and was received most graciously by the editor. Poe told Stoddard that he had read his poem with great appreciation and intended to run it the following week. As he was leaving, Stoddard spied

Virginia lying on a bed, apparently asleep. "She was dressed in black," he recalled, "and was pale and wasted. 'Poor lady,' I thought; 'she is dying of consumption.'"

The following week Stoddard opened a copy of the issue in which his poem was to appear and found instead a printed notice apologizing for its omission and saying that it had been lost. Confronting Poe about the omission in his office, Stoddard found Poe surly and irascible. Poe responded to Stoddard's inquiry with an allegation that the poem had been plagiarized from someone else—Poe couldn't say who. Stoddard assured him that the poem was genuine, but Poe would not relent. He cursed and threatened to throw Stoddard out of the office, with force if necessary. Stoddard "could not understand why [he] had been subjected to such an indignity" and got his revenge by circulating this story, in successively more negative versions, for many years after Poe's death. He even composed a poem about Poe, entitled "Miserrimus" (most miserable) which repeated the most egregious of Griswold's lies about the author.

With poverty nagging at him and with Virginia's illness worsening daily, there is no question but that Poe was coming apart little by little, like a slow-ripping seam in threadbare clothes. He had tried to maintain his sobriety for a year or more, but that summer he was drinking hard and heavy, creating states of illness that left him, as he told Duyckinck, "dreadfully unwell." He intended to retire again to the country and get into better shape, but this plan dissolved in a bitter cocktail of sloth and self-loathing.

One poignant glimpse of him at these emotional lows is afforded by his friend Chivers, who was in New York that summer and encountered Poe weaving from side to side down Nassau Street, "drunk as an Indian." Chivers took his friend by the arm and steered him home, but on the way they encountered one of Poe's nemeses, Lewis Gaylord Clark. Chivers thought that Poe was going to attack Clark, but instead he rushed forward and shook hands with him, and the following conversation took place:

CLARK: *Why, Poe! Is that you?*
POE: *Yes, by God! This is Poe. Here is my friend Dr. Chivers from the South.*

178

CLARK: *What! Dr. Chivers, the author of so many beautiful poems?*
POE: *Yes, by God. Not only the author of some of the beautifullest poems ever written any where, but my friend, too, by God!*
CHIVERS: *I was very much pleased with Willis Gaylord Clark's poems [Clark's brother].*
POE: *What business had you to abuse me in the last number of your magazine?*
CLARK: *Why, by God, Poe, how did I know the article referred to was yours? You had always attached your name to all your articles before, and how in Hell did I know it was yours?*

"A damn coward," Poe apparently said to Chivers as they made their way past Clark, homewards for Poe to recuperate.

This recklessness can also be observed in the circle of literary women—so-called "bluestockings"—in which Poe moved during the summer and fall of 1845. As the author of "The Raven," Poe was in great demand at the most fashionable of the salons that these wealthy society ladies held in their exquisitely furnished homes in Manhattan's toniest neighborhoods. Most of these women were hangers-on, educated and literate people who had a taste for the arts but who were for the most part superficial and interested in literature only because it was fashionable to be. Their wealthy husbands, lawyers and bankers, subsidized the gatherings with their considerable bank accounts. In effect, Poe was taking charity from the titans of commerce, a pathetic fact that would be satirized by Poe's colleague at the *Broadway Journal*, Charles F. Briggs, in his novel *The Trippings of Tom Pepper*: here, Poe is depicted as "Austin Wicks," a sycophantic critic who is the guest of honor at a local soiree.

At such literary parties, Poe consorted with many women writers, among them Frances Sargent Osgood, Elizabeth F. Ellett, Anne Charlotte Lynch, Sarah Anna Lewis ("Stella"), Anna Mowatt, and Jane Ermina Locke. After Virginia's death he formed a romantic attachment to one of the more gifted of them, Sarah Helen Whitman, and later still he befriended similar female patrons of literature, among them Annie Richmond, Louise Shew, and Susan Archer Talley Weiss. Poe formed friendships with women more easily than he did with men. Doubtless this was because such women as moved in these circles were starry-eyed when it came to catching glimpses of famous poets, particularly a *poète maudit*, such as Poe styled himself. Possessed of no critical strictures, little formal education, and not motivated by any professional rivalry (what female writer in the nineteenth century could hope to compete with a man?), these women happily sat at Poe's feet and luxuriated in the pride of knowing a famous writer on a first-name basis.

Poe did not so much talk to them as fall "into a sort of eloquent monologue, half dream, half poetry." Indeed, Poe was noted for the soft-spoken manner in which he would recite his famous poem. Adjusting the atmosphere of the drawing room in which he took center stage, one listener recalled that he would "turn down the lamps till the room was almost dark, then standing in the center of the apartment he would recite those wonderful lines in the most melodious of voices. . . . So marvelous was his power as a reader that the auditors would be afraid to draw breath lest the enchanted spell be broken."

At one of these gatherings, at the home of Anne Lynch, Poe met Fanny Osgood, a thirtyish poetaster whose verse had in the past been praised by Poe for its "true imagination as distinguished from its subordinate, fancy." Her husband was Samuel Stillman Osgood, a portrait painter of considerable reputation; Poe sat for him, in fact, later that year. Fanny (whose first name was the same as that of Poe's adoptive mother, Fanny Allan) was a cheery, impressionable person who willingly sought Poe out and conducted something of a flirtation with him that in a short while became the talk of literary New York. They wrote poems addressed to each other that were then printed in various New York papers. Poe was not the only object of her pursuits (another was Rufus Griswold), and she eventually separated from her husband. Fanny and Poe were often together, although there is no evidence that anything improper occurred between them. In fact, Virginia was present at some of Mrs. Lynch's soirees, glimpsed one time in a homemade gown, "sitting pale and smiling beside the fire while her husband recited 'The Raven.'"

Poe obviously enjoyed the devoted attention he received from these worshipful women, and Virginia seems to have voiced no objections, certain as it is that she knew of his dalliances, especially with Fanny Osgood. In fact, she apparently sanctioned them. Osgood later told Rufus Griswold that she "maintained a correspondence with Mr. Poe in accordance with the strict entreaties of his wife, who imagined that my influence over him had a restraining and beneficial effect." Such passionate but platonic encounters occurred because women attracted to artistic genius wanted to coddle and mother the writer, protect him from himself, encourage him with their (or their husband's) money, food, and drink. Like so many of Poe's women, Fanny too would die of consumption, six months before his own death.

The general picture that most scholars have presented of Poe's relationships with these minor women writers has been neutral to negative. Poe is seen as somewhat callous, insensitive to their obviously deep feelings for him and merely using them whenever they were convenient outlets—for money, for living amenities, for contacts and references, as well as for sex. While most of these alliances seem to have been mainly platonic, it seems unlikely Poe would have been uninterested in physical pleasure, and he was certainly crafty enough to be able to use elements of what attracted these women to him to advantage. Poe is often also typically portrayed as condescending to these women's literary efforts.

Yet Poe was actually quite interested in their writings and saw himself in part as a mentor to them, someone who could foster their talents and help promote them in the public sphere. He was a patron of women writers in an age when most male writers were patronizing. This view was best summed up when Hawthorne derisively referred to "that damned mob of scribbling women"—a reference to the popular set of female authors who, in his view, clogged the thin and not very substantial publishing pipeline for native works with their scores of sentimental novels and delicate, lachrymose poetry. Poe, however, appreciated these women's work, reviewed their books favorably, and puffed them whenever he could. Some of the female authors whom Poe promoted were Caroline Kirkland, Maria Jane McIntosh, Elizabeth Oakes Smith, Amelia Welby, and Sarah Josepha Hale. He also reviewed a great many British women writers, and accorded Elizabeth Barrett Browning his highest praise. In America, Poe was well ahead of his male colleagues at the time in foreseeing that writing could become an available profession for people other than white gentlemen, and in fact it was just after his death, in the 1850s, that new professional doors opened up for female authors. Most of the best-sellers before the Civil War were written by women.

Two disasters rounded out what had initially promised to be Poe's most successful year: the unsurprising demise of the *Broadway Journal* and a lecture in Boston that turned into a public relations fiasco. Still enjoying popularity as the author of "The Raven," Poe was in demand as a speaker. James Russell Lowell, at this point still admiring of Poe, had arranged for him to read some of his poems before the venerable Boston Lyceum on 16 October 1845.

Lyceum activity had never really caught in Poe's homeland, the South—at least not with the same fervor as it had in New England (where it originated), primarily because southern aristocrats feared that education of poor whites and slaves would damage the economy. The South also lacked a large middle class, the main patronage of lyceums, which were originally founded on a kind of egalitarian philosophy that Poe might have found distasteful: that education should continue all through life, regardless of age and gender, and in particular that learning helped stave off the temptation of alcohol (something Poe might ironically have related to). As the lyceum movement grew, lecturing became a popular activity for Poe's peers—famous writers, historians, explorers, and religious philosophers, including Ralph Waldo Emerson, Henry David Thoreau, Oliver Wendell Holmes, Wendell Phillips, and Horace Greeley were always on the circuit.

What thoughts must have crossed Poe's mind as he stood before this audience at the Odeon Theatre in Boston? Poe's feelings about Boston were, at best, mixed. It was the place of his birth and was therefore associated lovingly in his memory with Eliza; he had also lived there when he was in the army, and he had published his first book of poems there, identifying himself on the title page as a "Bostonian." But Poe despised the literary coteries in Boston and believed that American literature suffered from a New England bias. This view was of a piece with Poe's southern-ness. He opposed the currents that threatened to sweep society toward total Jacksonian democracy, just as when a student at the University of Virginia he had sided more with John Marshall's urbane, conservative thought and opposed Jefferson's push for democracy and reform. Poe also unequivocally associated Boston with the transcendentalists (the Frogpondians, as he derisively called them), Emerson, Thoreau, Alcott, and others.

The event was given full coverage in the press, with one Boston news-paper predicting a standing-room-only crowd. But given Poe's public image as a "characterless character," the organizers of the event were nerv-ous, and to make sure he showed up on time, they went to his hotel room beforehand to collect him. They may have taken as an ill omen the fact that Poe looked decidedly surprised to see them, been a bit flustered when he invited them into his room, and been downright flummoxed when he got down on his knees and began emptying a steamer trunk, rummaging around in it to extract piecemeal pages of what appeared to be the poems he was to read that evening.

When he arrived at the hall, Poe found out that he was actually the second bill of an engagement headlined by Caleb Cushing, a native Bostonian who had recently been appointed American commissioner to China. Cushing delivered a two-and-a-half-hour-long address, guaranteed to glaze the attention of any audience, especially one there primarily to see the infamous poet Poe. When Poe finally arose to be introduced and to speak, he began with a repetitious and wandering fifteen-minute apology for the "indefiniteness" and "general imbecility" of the poem he was about to recite, noting that he had mislaid the manuscript of the poem he intended to present. Thomas Wentworth Higginson, then a young Harvard student and later one of the "discoverers" of Emily Dickinson, was in the audience and recorded a curious sycophancy in Poe's manner: "a sort of persistent, querulous [and] nauseous flattery" of his Boston audience. Perversely, Poe then seems to have traded in his obeisance for another fifteen minutes of insulting jibes at Boston literary culture. The centerpiece of this part of his presentation was, not surprisingly, some inflammatory remarks about didacticism in poetry—a trademark of Longfellow's verse.

The lyceum lecture can be seen as emblematic of the significant sectionalist element of Poe's aesthetic. It's very likely that the theory of poetry writing that Poe was now developing, "The Poetic Principle," had its roots in his antagonism toward northern politics and social attitudes. Poe tenaciously argued that "Beauty" and "Truth" were like oil and water, obstinately keeping apart from each other. His elevation of "Beauty"— the poem for the poem's sake—and his dislike of the didactic element in art may have existed because Poe equated "Truth" with the approaching tide of progress and democracy. Poe thus advocated a beauty no truth could invade. One should recall his statement to James Russell Lowell about the spurious notion of human progress, and one should note how the vast majority of his stories and poems exist in a kind of fairyland rather than the day-to-day reality of life in the United States.

But the program was not over yet. Next, instead of presenting a "new poem," as advertised, Poe read a long, almost unintelligible poem (the early, mystical "Al Aaraaf"), and the audience grew weary and restless. His sponsors were confused and disappointed, but they treated him to a nice reception afterwards and tried to put the best face on the evening. Late in the program Poe finally did consent to read "The Raven," but by then most of the audience had left, insulted by his remarks about New England writing. The episode, of course, further damaged Poe's already eroding reputation.

The fallout continued even as Poe returned to New York, for the Boston papers abused him mightily. A reporter for the Boston *Evening Transcript*, Cornelia Wells Walter, pursued Poe in print, calling his appearance a childish effort, and other writers followed suit. Poe replied to his detractors in the *Broadway Journal*, unwisely and unreasonably. He claimed that although he had been born in Boston, he was now "heartily ashamed" to admit it. Boston's hotels were "bad" and their poetry was "not so good," but their pumpkins pies were "delicious." Any good qualities the Bostonians may possess were erased by the fact that they had "no soul." The evidence for this last assertion was the fact that they had always evinced toward Poe nothing but "the basest ingratitude for the services we rendered them in enlightening them about the originality of Mr. Longfellow." Poe was not finished, however: enraged by what he perceived as indifference on the part of his hosts, he insulted them by claiming that the poem he had read was a hoax—something written when he was only ten years old.

By replying to Wells, Poe seems to have been trying to launch another literary war of words, like the Longfellow episode. The lack of restraint, perhaps calculated, inspired Lewis Gaylord Clark to enter the fray in his *Knickerbocker Magazine* and berate Poe for any circumstances so distressing that they "would cause a poet . . . to read a rhapsody composed and published in his tenth year, and afterward bring forward, as a proof of the stupidity of his audience, that they listened to him with civil attention." Never one to let a slight go unremarked, Poe took Clark's bait and promptly started tangling with him in the 22 November issue of the *Journal*, this time taking up nearly four columns. By anyone's standards, what Poe said was downright embarrassing. This time he claimed that there was a cabal against him, a secret knot of conspirators who had invited him to Boston only to entrap him.

In the long run, it probably made matters worse that southern newspapers, like William Gilmore Simms's *Southern Patriot*, stood up for Poe in print. They saw him as a fellow southerner who had been abused by the North and tried to present his ludicrous defense as a sane and reasonable reply to a group of unjust accusers. All that did was polarize the issue even more, and Poe emerged from the episode permanently tarred as a rabid, unenlightened southerner out to malign New England and all that American literature stood for.

To add to these problems, Poe's magazine was foundering. The *Broadway Journal* had never made the money it was supposed to, and upon his return from Boston Poe probably could foresee its inevitable demise. In part it was not Poe's fault, for he had no business sense to speak of, and by becoming the proprietor of the *Journal* he was overreaching. At previous magazines, Poe had been successful, but only in the editorial department, not the accounting one. When he first took over, Poe executed his duties faithfully and reliably, but he soon grew overworked, doing all the editing and reviewing virtually by himself. He told Chivers that it was "utterly impossible to conceive how busy I have been, editing the paper, without aid from any one, all the time."

To compensate, Poe curtailed much of what the magazine had been famous for—coverage of the arts and culture scene in New York—and instead filled the columns with much of his own work and that of his friends. The result was a botched effort. As the issues went to press, more and more empty space appeared in the magazine, space he simply did not have material to fill. He resorted to his old habit from the *Messenger* days of padding out his critical reviews with unusually long excerpts from the books being discussed, but even then he often had to descend to printing apologies for not offering readers more material. The issues got thinner and thinner as the months wore on.

Much of the time, too, Poe wasn't even careful. More and more typographical slips and printer's errors pockmarked the pages—things Poe should have caught and corrected before the issues were sent to the newsstands. Now more issues were printed with errata pages that detailed, like a schoolboy's report card, the demerits he brought on himself as the sloppy editor of a shoddy broadside. Poe had fallen far from his impeccable image as the meticulous editor of *Graham's*.

Then there were the persisting problems of money. Even as Poe's fame (and notoriety) went up, his income went down. In November, Wiley and Putnam had issued *The Raven and Other Poems*, but the royalty arrangement was still less than what other writers would have received. "The Gold-Bug" (another reappropriation of a popular narrative form, the buried treasure/pirate narrative) continued to sell stratospherically—more than three hundred thousand copies, but Poe received nothing in return, only the original one hundred dollars of prize money. Throughout his career, Poe wrote steadily and at times prolifically, but, as one scholar has determined, his total literary income—for life—amounted to only sixty-two hundred dollars. To offset the deficits, Poe fell back on his imperfect technique of asking friends for loans. Kennedy, Duyckinck, Chivers, Neilson Poe, and others were touched for ten or twenty dollars each.

Some responded; others were silent—understandably, for anyone could smell desperation in a request for money that cited as its reason an unnamed cabal that was moving against an author whose only literary sin was integrity and commitment to truth telling.

Ironically, Poe's paranoiac statement to a peer that there was "a deliberate attempt now being made to involve me in ruin" might have applied more accurately to Briggs than to him: another reason the *Broadway Journal* was declining was because Briggs, something of a self-styled publicity hound, had been using the periodical to initiate ideological clashes between North and South. Briggs was a New Englander but he despised the sanctimonious piety of the abolitionists. Having Poe on the masthead gave him an excuse to mount splenetic attacks on Poe's "Frogpondian" enemies. This naturally put off many subscribers and gave the magazine a reputation as a fringe publication, something run by cranks.

When Briggs pulled out, Poe sold a half-interest in the magazine to a customs inspector with some literary skill, one Thomas Lane, essentially on the hopes that the buyer would pay off a group of long-standing debts. Instead, however, Poe and Lane limped along, like two pensioners trying to keep up with the young turks, and the quality of the paper became even worse. To this we must add Poe's depressed state of mind, for Virginia's illness was pulling him down even as he tried to keep his literary and financial affairs afloat. The stress of all these responsibilities made Poe unstable; he told Duyckinck that he seemed "to have just awakened from some horrible dream, in which all was confusion, and suffering. . . . I really believe that I have been mad—but indeed I have had abundant reason to be so."

As was the pattern, Poe began to drink heavily and to renege on his obligations. New York University had honored him by commissioning a poem for a literary event, but Poe apparently could not come up with one, so he drank, became ill, and went to bed for a week. The ever-faithful Maria Clemm was virtually alone among Poe's allies in discerning that the root of all his problems was his love for Virginia. In a letter to Thomas Holley Chivers, she said: "I do believe that the poor boy is deranged! his wife is now at the point of death . . . and cannot bear to see

187

him! Oh! my poor Virginia! She cannot live long! She is wasting away, day by day—for the Doctors can do her no good. But if they could, seeing this continually in poor Eddy, would kill her—for she dotes upon him! . . . would to God that she had died before she had ever seen him."

In late December, Poe went on a drinking binge and disappeared from the *Journal* offices for several days. The 27 December issue went to press incomplete, with many pages blank. Lane tried to cover for Poe, but in the end he sensibly decided to bail out of his investment. By January 1846, the *Journal* ceased publication. Poe printed a valedictory note in the last issue that cited "unexpected engagements demanding my whole attention" as the reason for its shutting down: "I now, as its editor, bid farewell—as cordially to foes as to friends." A more candid assessment, a self-justification and defense for its failure, was offered to George W. Eveleth: Poe simply said it was the fault of Thomas Lane, "to whom I transferred the Journal, and in whose hands it perished."

Now in debt more than ever, and without steady work, Poe degenerated into drink, just as Virginia's illness was becoming acute. The year 1845 had begun with the promise of being Poe's annus mirabilis. Yet its end was sad. Poe would write less and less and would wander, as George Graham remarked, "from publisher to publisher, with his fine, print-like manuscript, scrupulously clean and neatly rolled, [finding] no market for his brain." For the rest of his life, Poe was to drift aimlessly through a series of low-grade writing assignments; improvident schemes to make money quickly; petty, internecine quarrels with other writers that sapped his already low supply of creative energy; and after Virginia's death, desperate attempts to win the affections of nurturing women, efforts that culminated not in happiness at all, but in depression, delusion, and even an attempt at suicide.

CHAPTER 8

QUARRELS, LOVES, AND LOSSES

[1846–1848]

The years 1846–47 were Poe's least-productive period. Embittered by the loss of the *Broadway Journal* and his never-abating poverty, he slid further into drink, depression, and illness. As he often did, instead of pursuing means that might reverse his losses, he instead plunged recklessly into two ill-advised affairs, one romantic and the other literary, that further damaged his already sinking reputation. One was an affair with one of the bluestockings, a querulous and bitter poet named Elizabeth Ellet. The other was a war of words with the New York literati. By the time of the worst event in his diminishing life, the death of Virginia, he had effectively destroyed whatever fame or admiration he had garnered. He became ill, painfully poor, and deeply depressed.

The first of the bitter quarrels that was eventually to unman him psychologically was a dalliance with Ellet, a minor southern poet who fell in love with him. Unlike his "affair" with Fanny Osgood, in this case it appears that he was the pursued rather than the pursuer. Again doubtless flattered by an attractive woman's attention, Poe encouraged her, and Ellet wrote him love letters. Poe was apparently more bemused by these letters than touched by them. By some accounts he was even haughty in his treatment of Ellet, seeing her tortured protestations of love in the letters as fodder for mockery and snide humor. According to one account, Ellet one day came to the Poe house on Amity Street and found Virginia and Fanny Osgood (of whom she was jealous) reading her letters to Poe aloud and laughing hysterically. (Virginia apparently approved of Poe's closeness to Osgood and confided in her greatly.) By another account, Ellet visited Virginia and found an Osgood letter in the house; she then persuaded Osgood to ask Poe to return all of her letters to Poe lest Osgood be found out.

Apparently, Ellet next sent two literary women friends, the journalist Margaret Fuller and the literary salon hostess Anne Lynch, to the Poe house to demand Osgood's letters. Poe handed them over truculently, and in a beligerent spirit said that *Ellet* should ask for *her* letters returned as well, as there might be compromising material in *them*, too. Poe then apparently gathered up the Ellet letters and took them to her house, leaving them there in her hands.

The exact truthfulness of these various accounts is in dispute, but one certain fact was that Ellet sent her brother, a physically imposing man named Colonel William Lummis, to confront Poe about the return of *her* letters. Poe protested that he had already returned the letters, but the brother, who knew something of Poe's low reputation, presumed that Poe was a lying blackguard who was trying to weasel out of his obligations. Lummis threatened to kill Poe if he did not return them. Poe, enraged, went to the house of a friend, Thomas Dunn English, and asked to borrow a pistol to defend himself. English refused, and enraged Poe further by doubting that he had ever possessed any letters from Ellet. Poe then punched English in the face. English got the better of him, but Poe, in telling of the incident later, denied reality and said that he "gave E. a flogging which he will remember to the day of his death."

This story appears to be a complete fabrication, for Thomas Lane, his short-lived partner on the *Broadway Journal*, was present at English's house at the time and reported that Poe "was drunk and getting the worst of it, and was finally forced under the sofa, only his face being visible. English was punching Poe's face, and at every blow a seal ring on his finger cut Poe." Lane tried to separate them, when Poe cried out, "Let him alone. I've got him just where I want him." In this embarrassing episode Poe resorted, as he had in the past, to physical violence and then distorted the truth in the name of pride.

Poe took to his bed to nurse his wounds and to evade the public spotlight. Somewhat pathetically, he instructed the physician who attended him to convey an apology to Ellet. Poe denied that he had ever said that there was anything improper in the letters Ellet wrote him, and that if he had, he must have been temporarily insane. This ill-conceived apology was soon retailed around the different magazine offices on Nassau Street, and Poe's enemies gleefully appropriated it to prove that the author had gone off the deep end for sure. More to Poe's worse luck, his old friend Joseph Snodgrass believed the reports to be true, as he commented in the 18 April 1846 Baltimore *Saturday Visiter* that "EDGAR A. POE, according to a New York letter writer, labors under mental derangement, to such a degree that it has been determined to consign him to the Insane Retreat at Utica.—This will be a painful piece of intelligence to thousands."

The episode ruined Poe's reputation as a chivalrous southern gentleman and ostracized him from the New York bluestockings. Anne Lynch permanently crossed his name off her list of salon invitees. Poe became vindictive toward Ellet, in the fall of 1848 characterizing her to Sarah Helen Whitman, with whom he was in love at the time and whom he was forewarning of any possible treachery by Ellet, as "a woman whose loathsome love I could do nothing but repel with scorn. . . . Her whole study, throughout life, has been the gratification of her malignity by such means as any other human being would rather die than adopt."

The incident took its toll on Poe physically, as well. He lay abed often, telling people he was too ill to do any writing. He also did no lecturing, lucrative as that platform had proven to be, probably for fear of being jeered at onstage, given his recent public debacles with the Longfellow War, the lyceum incident, and now l'affaire Ellet. He still worked the old angles of publicity, as when he asked Duyckinck to plant a story about him in his magazine citing "continued ill health, with a pressure of engagements" as the cause of his absence from public view. But when invited to speak by literary societies at Dickinson College and at the University of Vermont, he quickly declined. With no publications and no lecture engagements, one wonders what the ragged family did for money, for Poe had realized virtually no income these past months. How they stayed together is a wonder, too: it must have been the pressing reality that all they had was each other and that that, at least, was a bulwark against madness.

To economize, as well as to distance himself from the public arena, in February 1846 Poe moved the family yet again, this time to a cottage thirteen miles outside the city in the little village of Fordham, at what is now 192nd Street and Kingsbridge Road. The house was a standard frame-built workman's home, common to nineteenth-century America: austere and rudimentary. However, the modest residence was clean, as always, owing to Muddy's ministrations, and although there was little furniture, it was comfortable. There was a sitting room in front with a kitchen and small bedroom in back. A few copies of Poe's own books sat on the shelves, with special places of honor reserved for volumes by Robert and Elizabeth Browning. His personal book collection appears always to have been a small one; most likely, he moved residences so much that he was not able to maintain a large collection. In difficult times, too, Poe had sold off much of his library. Upstairs was Muddy's bedroom and a small study for Poe. The house was situated at the top of a hill with much surrounding green space, well tended, and several large cherry trees that swathed the yard in shade. On the front porch Poe kept caged songbirds, perhaps a symbolic tribute to his mother, which he talked to and studied intently in the late afternoons. Although distant from the city, Poe had easy access to it, since a station on the Harlem railroad line a mile and a half away could take him to Manhattan in very little time.

As it had before, the countryside worked as a salve on Poe's psychic wounds. When people came to visit, Poe would often propose a ramble in the woods and along the way a game of leaping, or long-jumping, in which Poe excelled. Like the indulgent mother of a schoolboy, Maria would urge that they be careful, and she would then stay behind to watch over Virginia. One member of such an expedition recalled that when they returned, Muddy noticed that Poe had rips in his gaiter-shoes and cried out, bemoaning that such carelessness would cost him money he didn't have. If only an editor would buy one of Poe's poems, she held forth, then Eddy could have some new shoes.

Mary Gove Nichols, a health reformer, homeopathist, and sometime writer, was a frequent visitor to the Fordham cottage; she left behind a picture of life there. Muddy, tall and stooped, seemed to her "a sort of universal Providence for her strange children." Virginia was by now an invalid, and her illness was eroding Poe's wherewithal with each passing day. In the only letter Poe is known to have written to his wife, apparently during a brief stay in the city for an unspecified interview, perhaps for an editorial position, Poe told Virginia, "You are my *greatest* and *only* stimulus now, to battle with this uncongenial, unsatisfactory, and ungrateful life." The only writing she is ever known to have done for Poe is a Valentine's Day acrostic-poem in which she vainly promised him that "Love alone shall guide us" and "shall heal my weakened lungs." Nothing of the sort, it was obvious, would ever take place, and even Gove, whose faith in such spiritual practices as mesmerism and phrenology would seem to hold out for miracles, was realistic. She described Virginia as possessed of "an unearthly look. One felt that she was almost a disrobed spirit, and when she coughed it was made certain that she was rapidly passing away."

Gove was assisted in her support for the Poes by a kindly neighbor, Marie Louise Shew, who raised two subscriptions for the family, keeping them from starvation. She also spread the word that the Poes were essentially charity cases now, and notices to that effect began to appear in the newspapers. One stated that Poe and his wife "are both dangerously ill with the consumption," and that "they are so far reduced as to be able barely to obtain the necessaries of life." Willis saw the paragraph and undertook to help Poe by writing a testimonial to him, publishing it in the *Mirror*. Willis's words were well meant, but his admission that one day Poe had come into his office and "with no symptoms of ordinary intoxication" had nonetheless "talked like a man insane," could not have done Poe's reputation any good. During these travails, Poe put on a brave front, however, writing Willis that "Even in the city of New York I could have no difficulty in naming a hundred persons, to each of whom—when the hour for speaking had arrived—I could and would have applied for aid, and with unbounded confidence, and with absolutely no sense of humiliation."

Seeking escape from his troubles, for the first time in his life Poe showed a moderate interest in formal religion. Spiritualism in one form or another, of course, is everywhere present in his writings, but religious faith is notably absent. There is rarely an acknowledgment of the existence of God (or any kind of divine agency), and in the overall atmosphere of deliberate amoralness and the emphasis on abnormal psychology, sin and morality are rarely suggested as character motivations. Yet Poe could not have been untouched by the great religious fervor that seized the United States during his lifetime. Fanny Allan, his foster mother, was very pious, and John Allan was a strict churchman. When the Monumental Episcopal Church was erected in Richmond in 1814, Allan purchased a pew. Although Allan had at least one illegitimate child, he subscribed to a view of life based on the Puritan-American pieties.

In England, at the school of the Misses DuBourg, Poe was taught the catechism of the Anglican Church, and received further religious instruction at the school of the Reverend Dr. Bransby. Although the University of Virginia was notable for its nonsectarian character, Jefferson certainly advocated a philosophy of reason, peace, and morality. At West Point and in the army, chapel attendance was compulsory.

Most likely Poe reacted against the Judeo-Christian tradition by maintaining a silence and by imputing to his characters (usually) psychological and physiological causes for their actions. To break with the church, particularly the church in the South, meant a total break with society itself. It was to become, in essence, an outcast (like William Wilson) from what was the accepted mode of conduct and belief in the first half of the nineteenth century. As one critic puts it, "The church was . . . the final sanctification of the whole southern code of morals, slavery, politics, love, oratory, war, daily living, even of a pseudo-Greek revival in architecture." Poe's creation of his outré situations and half-crazed characters might be the result of a loss of a connection to a once-strong religious temper.

The persisting stance Poe adopted, too, that of a man apart, may perversely explain his attraction to the group of Jesuit priests who staffed a college, St. John's, located next to the cottage. Poe visited the campus of this college (now Fordham University) quite frequently, and befriended Father Edward Doucet, who allowed Poe to use the college's library. Poe liked the priests at the college because they were "highly cultivated gentlemen and scholars [who] smoked, drank, and played cards like gentlemen, and never said a word about religion." Father Doucet, in turn, admired Poe's courtly demeanor: "I always thought he was a gentleman by nature and instinct," he later said.

This attitude is more an embracing of secular cosmology than a religious faith. In some ways Poe answered the question of what form God took in his cosmological treatise, *Eureka* (he felt that God was material, and thus all matter was "God"). But a compelling oddity in the nexus between Poe's life and his works was why he did not embrace more fully the Christian notion of an afterlife. The persistent question of his fiction was how to die and yet live, how to reunite with lost loved ones in an otherworld beyond the material one. In the nineteenth century particularly, the answer to that would have lain with the doctrine of salvation through the sacrifice of Jesus Christ. Poe's small Bible, given to him by Mrs. Clemm in 1846, was reported to have been one of the books in his trunk when he died. Yet C. F. Briggs (if he can be trusted as a source) wrote James Russell Lowell in 1845 that Poe thought the Bible was "all rigamarole." Piety and morality based on Christian doctrine must have permeated his daily existence as a youth in Richmond, and especially the lives and philosophical outlooks of the African American community which served the Allans and families like them. Poe surely was exposed to this point of view.

More to the point, the type of fervid evangelical Christianity that particularly permeated the South in Poe's youth was pitched perfectly to appeal to those beset by misfortune (like the slaves). In his adult life, through Poe's continual poverty, his sense of gloom and helplessness, of being ensnared by dark forces that tortured him, he became precisely the sort of person apt to snatch at the lifeline traditional religion would have offered. Most likely, Poe, with his powerful intelligence, recognized the simplicity of such an outlook. His mind required a doctrine or philosophy more complex than that in order to convince himself that there was still hope.

In the spring, Poe returned to writing, but perversely, in this environment of peace and harmony, he chose a pen dipped in acid. From May to October, Poe published in the Philadelphia-based *Godey's Lady's Book* a series of controversial profiles of American writers called "The Literati of New York City—SOME HONEST OPINIONS AT RANDOM RESPECTING THEIR AUTORIAL MERITS, WITH OCCASIONAL WORDS OF PERSONALITY." The series very nearly ended Poe's career as a writer and compounded the problems he had already created by his amours with the literary women and his attacks on Longfellow.

In these mostly vitriolic attacks, Poe held nothing back and very often resorted to outright lies in order to (he felt) provide a correction to the upward curve of these figures' popularity. The result was a plunge into further self-destruction, seemingly inexplicable since at this point Poe was completely without money, essentially without allies, and was coming seriously close to tarnishing what honor he had left. Nonetheless, by tilting with his fellow writers in a series of silly, lengthy, and deeply damaging quarrels, Poe lost the few remaining friends he had and acquired more enemies than most people could battle in one lifetime.

Poe said his intention was to give "my own unbiased opinion of the *literati* (male and female) of New York," and also to give "very closely if not with absolute accuracy" an impression of them based on his interactions with "conversational society in literary circles" (1120). A total of thirty-eight sketches appeared over time, ranging in length from five hundred to five thousand words. The first installment began gently, offering praise to the obscure (George Bush, a professor of Hebrew at the University of New York), the moderately known (George Colton, the editor who had first published "The Raven"), and the famous (N. P. Willis, one of Poe's few remaining allies). But with the fourth sketch, that of Charles F. Briggs, Poe launched into an extended diatribe on an "envious host of dunces" (1130) that he felt were then at the height of their popularity. The first issue of *Godey's* that carried the series was in such demand that the publisher ordered another printing and published a notice in the *Evening Mirror* offering "to repurchase copies of the . . . number at '25 CTS.' each."

Actually, many of the writers had only a local reputation, and Poe vented his spleen most vociferously on third-tier figures. Poe's profiles of them, in fact, may have been the most attention ever paid to them in print.

196

In this sense, one must read Poe's articles as the work of someone worse than irrational and more so, petty and mean-spirited. Poe called Briggs "profoundly ignorant" (1134) and sneered that he had "never composed in his life three consecutive sentences of grammatical English." Not satisfied with assailing Briggs's intellect, Poe next made fun of his looks: a "not prepossessing" appearance, graced by a low forehead and small gray eyes which were "not so good" (1133). Physical descriptions concluded the succeeding sketches, very few of them complimentary.

The group of writers profiled reads like a manifest of all the people whom Poe had worked with, written for, or competed against: Clark, Colton, Briggs, Duyckinck, Hoffman, Willis. Included also were sketches of many of the bluestockings—Stella Lewis, Anne Lynch, Fanny Osgood, and Anna Mowatt. Most of these people were the same ones who, a short year and a half ago, had welcomed Poe and embraced his talent when "The Raven" had appeared to such widespread praise. Now he levelled against them slanderous statements, unsparingly. Poe naturally drew the ire of these well-respected authors; they weren't afraid to challenge his acidulous opinions in print. Thus began another war between Poe and the rest of the literary world. It gave grist to the newspaper gossip mills and, worse, siphoned off whatever creative energy Poe might have been able to direct toward quality fiction and poetry writing.

Briggs was the first to retort, immediately firing back with a scathing attack (unsigned, in the *Evening Mirror*, but known to be his work) that said Poe had been confined to an insane asylum. The piece created an uproar; it compelled the students in Charles Anthon's grammar class to make a "pilgrimage to Bloomingdale to gaze upon the asylum where [Poe] was reported to be confined." Mimicking Poe's formula, Briggs closed his rebuttal with a physical description of Poe that was hardly flattering and wounded Poe on a point in which he prided himself, the suggestion that his broad forehead denoted intelligence: "forehead rather . . . low, and in that part where phrenology places conscientiousness and the group of moral sentiments it is quite flat; chin narrow and pointed, which gives his head, upon the whole, a baloonish appearance, and which may account for his supposed light-headedness."

The literary power brokers of Gotham quickly closed ranks and banded together to topple Poe. Briggs lined up his allies, thanking them for their "generous offer to hammer Poe on my account." Clark, of the *Knickerbocker*, and Hiram Fuller, of the *Evening Mirror*, quickly did a headcount of their troops and extracted promises to aid the cause in print. But it was Poe's attack on Thomas Dunn English, the former friend who enraged Poe by not supporting him against Elizabeth Ellet's allegations, that was the most inflammatory. In the June *Godey's*, Poe took a cheap shot at English: he charged that the author didn't know proper grammar and usage. "No spectacle," he wrote, "can be more pitiable than that of a man without the commonest school education busying himself in attempts to instruct mankind on topics of polite literature." Then, with tongue in cheek, Poe wrote, "I do not personally know Mr. English."

This last statement sent the alarm bells clanging up and down Nassau Street like never before. Hiram Fuller rushed to English's aid by printing his "Reply" to Poe for 27 June. The *Mirror* carried English's "Reply," prefaced by a note from Fuller:

THE WAR OF THE LITERATI.—We publish the following terrific rejoinder of one of Mr. Poe's abused literati, with a twinge of pity for the object of its severity. But as Mr. Godey, 'for a consideration,' lends the use of his battery for an attack on the one side, it is but fair that we allow our friends an opportunity to exercise a little 'self-defence' on the other.

Sensing a no-holds-barred battle, area papers in New York, Philadelphia, and even some in the provinces stropped and lathered the story from every angle, seeing it as an opportunity to boost circulation figures from the tried-and-true precinct of controversy. The *Public Ledger* reported that "The New York Literati are by the ears again, and are saying all sorts of complimentary things of each other in the tartest possible manner." In the *Spirit of the Times*, the editor reported that Poe had made "an ungenerous attack" on English and that the latter was now "back upon the literary meat-axe in a style which shows pretty conclusively that he knows Mr. Poe pretty well." In his *National Press*, George P. Morris high-handedly "condemn[ed] all literary squabbles" as being in bad taste, but quickly added that "when attacks are made, rejoinders will follow."

Poe did not sit idle. He drummed up support from sympathetic editors in the South, among them Joseph Field, in the St. Louis *Daily Reveille,* Simms in the *Southern Patriot,* and an unknown writer in the New Orleans *Daily Picayune.* Once again, Poe showed his iron connection to the South and displayed his conviction that much of the injustice borne against him stemmed from his Richmond upbringing and his southern political sympathies.

Poe's reply appeared in the 10 July *Spirit of the Times* and English's rejoinder in the 13 July *Mirror.* English attacked Poe's morality and sanity and dared Poe "to a legal battle," threatening "to prove all the assertions made in his first official dispatch." As caustic as the war of words had become, some papers, like the *Public Ledger,* urged a truce: "Bringing authors 'before the public in relations exclusively private' violates the precepts of a gentleman." But no one would listen, especially not Poe. His wrath next came down on Godey himself, who instead of publishing Poe's reply in his own magazine paid ten dollars to have it printed in the *Spirit of the Times,* then debited Poe's account for the amount. Poe testily wrote him that "I am rather ashamed that, knowing me to be as poor as I am, you should have thought [that] advisable" and that he had "put this matter in the hands of a competent attorney, who would of course bring the ten dollars before the court, as an item."

For once the gods must have been smiling on him, for Poe won the libel suit and was awarded $225.06 for damages and $101.42 for costs. Despite the intense animosity against him, Poe was able to produce several character witnesses at his trial and, perhaps because none of his antagonists were willing to step out from behind the protective veil of print, the defense could produce none. Poe did not, however, use the money to pay off old debts or shore up his eroding finances. Instead, he bought a new black suit, some "sumptuous delicacies," and a number of decorative items for the cottage at Fordham.

Both English and Fuller, however, got their revenge. The former published a pseudonymous novel entitled *1844, or The Power of the*

"*S.F.*", into which he inserted passages caricaturing Poe as "Marmaduke Hammerhead," someone who "never gets drunk more than five days out of the seven; tells the truth sometimes by mistake; [and] has moral courage sufficient to flog his wife." And that summer in the pages of the *Mirror*, Fuller depicted Poe as a degenerate without actually naming him, but most everyone knew to whom Fuller referred when he recounted a day when "A poor creature . . . called at our office . . . in a condition of sad, wretched imbecility, bearing in his feeble body the evidences of evil living, and betraying by his talk, such radical obliquity of sense, that every spark of harsh feeling towards him was extinguished, and we could not even entertain a feeling of contempt for one who was evidently committing a suicide upon his body, as he had already done upon his character."

At least two of Poe's friends tried to talk sense into him in the wake of "the war of the literati." Southern novelist William Gilmore Simms (who, ironically, had been treated harshly by Poe in his *Messenger* reviews) advised Poe to stop wasting his energy on petty disputes, especially since Poe was really just swatting at gnats—writers so minor that today they would not even exist in footnotes were it not for Poe's attacks on them. But Poe did not heed Simms's advice any more than he did the counsel offered him by Thomas Holley Chivers, exclaiming to him that "flocks of little birds of prey" were massing against him, ones who "always take the opportunity of illness to peck at a sick fowl of larger dimensions." All along, Poe claimed, this cabal had been "endeavoring with all their power to effect my ruin." Poe felt that his enemies were closing in on him, like dogs on a fox, and his self-destructive tendencies accelerated unchecked, for even as he was buttressing himself against this unidentified onslaught, he was planning a book called "Literary America," a longer and (if possible) harsher version of "The Literati."

Some of Poe's tales during this time give glimpses into his perverse psychology; others reveal attempts to gain the upper hand (over enemies, perceived or real, and/or fate) and attempts to impose order on chaos. In July 1846 Poe published a little-known but quite revealing piece that is partly an essay on the nature of human impulse and partly the fictional monologue of a condemned poisoner speaking from his jail cell. "The Imp of the Perverse," written in the wake of the Longfellow War and Poe's other troubles, illustrates how his jealousies and sense of betrayal amounted to outright mania. In the piece, Poe seeks to explain how emotional entanglements and estrangements may be explained by the human need to act in a contrary manner—to "persist in acts because we feel we should not persist in them" (827).

As examples of such behavior, Poe drew from his personal experiences and from his fiction. The varyingly "perverse" wishes of a speaker to tantalize his audience by circumlocution and thus provoke their anger seems a justification for his appearance at the Boston Lyceum. The compulsion to procrastinate, even though one knows that delay will amount to ruin, suggests Poe's recent lassitude in work habits. And the suggestion that human nature would, if only for a millisecond, compel anyone standing on a precipice into the temptation to leap over the edge is a gloss on the perverse-acting, monomaniacal characters of much of his fiction, as well as the pattern of perverse behavior among the supporting characters of *Arthur Gordon Pym*, like the Tsalalians and others who turn from friendly to dangerous or vice-versa. ("Pym" is approximately "Imp" spelled backwards.) Characters in Poe's fiction often propel themselves forward against their own unconscious actions. (Even in such a minor piece as this, Poe's infuence on other writers is obvious: Andre Gide's character Michel in *The Immoralist* seems almost modeled on Poe's narrator. Both characters pursue a path of calculated self-destruction.)

And what of Poe controlling his own "imp"? At a time when Poe was drunk, paranoid about plagiarism, and confined in bed for days on end (a self-imposed measure in order to renege on speaking engagements), he presented a public face and, in his writing, a voice, that was so bound up in scholarly rigor and precise analysis that it presented him as the champion of order—an out-of-control personality raging for control of his fictive world, a Prospero-like figure who creates and then masters his own universe. Yet Poe may also have expected failure and feared it most at the height of his brief successes. There was a sense in him always that the ground he walked on was slippery, or unstable; it might drop from beneath him at any moment, and he would fall and fall forever.

As a counterbalance to these impulses, Poe renewed his commitment toward the mind and the faculty of reason, staples of his attitudes and his fiction all along—in the Dupin stories, in his interest in cryptography, in his mathematically inclined thinking, and in his almost mechanical, craftsmanlike approach to writing. At this time he seems to have notched up this hyperanalytic self even more than before. In a January review he claimed, "This is the age of *thinking*. Indeed it may well be questioned whether mankind ever substantially thought before." Once a believer in pseudosciences like mesmerism and phrenology (827), Poe now dismissed them as unfounded on reason. Earlier an admirer of German literature, he now evidenced a new disdain for it as "one indistinguishable *chaos* of froth" (1414) and preferred Voltaire, spokesperson for the Age of Reason, to Goethe. His critical pieces all adjured critics to construct their work on philosophical principles and to make clear "the machinery of [their] own thoughts."

Poe's acquaintances at this time even commented that in person he seemed overcontrolled. Lowell found him rather formal; Briggs said he gave the impression of being under restraint. Such is the persona behind "The Philosophy of Composition," published in May 1846. Its rigorous, template-like strictures for how "The Raven" was written read like someone desperately trying to impose order on an increasingly chaotic existence. So too with "The Domain of Arnheim," like "Imp" partly a story and partly an essay, in which Poe fantasized about removing himself from the imperfect world of a commercial republic, with its philistinism and anti-intellectualism, and fleeing to an Arcadia, a perfect world of art where prosperity was assured and one could live the life of the mind without distraction. How often, in his lowest emotional moments, Poe must have wondered whether he had made the right decision in choosing this effete, cerebral life over others. Like Nietzsche, who identified with Poe and commented sympathetically on him in such works as *Beyond Good and Evil* (1886), Poe was a tormented and tortured individual. And like two other authors whom he closely resembles, Kafka and the German poet Rilke, Poe often took as his theme how the extraordinary artist can never fit into mundane or intolerable reality. He must therefore seek escape through his imagination. Thus, the central character of "Arnheim" is an architect who creates the perfect garden—artful, but giving the appearance of artlessness, a landscape where formal perfection can only be viewed macroscopically. Symmetry and order are the twin columns that frame and support this ideal world of art.

Poe's other theme, predictably, was revenge—a direct offshoot of his professional quarrels and rivalries at this time. "The Cask of Amontillado" is a taut, chilling tale that presents another overcontrolled narrator bent on gaining the final upper hand in a bitter rivalry. Long-standing animosities have simmered between Montresor's family and that of his enemy, Fortunato, until one evening at a masquerade ball during Carnival (a scene reminiscent of "The Masque of the Red Death"), Montresor lures his rival away from the party and down into the musty catacombs deep underground, where the wine is stored. He does so with the promise of letting Fortunato taste an exceptional bottle of amontillado. Although today this type of sherry is regarded as a medium variety, rather sweet (compared to fino or amoroso), according to Poe's information, it was considered the driest of the varieties available. Poe thus ingeniously plays on the contrast between the dryness of the sherry and the sweetness of revenge, just as other elements of the story balance out the alternate indulging or depriving of the senses, one of his trademark techniques. The nitre in the walls of the caves makes Fortunato cough incessantly (a macabre reminder of the coughing fits to which the tubercular Virginia was subject). And ironically, Fortunato dies not only not being able to taste the sherry but also being deprived of the senses of sight and of hearing, as Montresor walls him in, with brick and mortar, to his crypt-like fate—buried alive, like so many Poe characters.

As in "The Pit and the Pendulum," the story brilliantly evokes a sense of claustrophobia and its feared result, total deprivation of the senses, or oblivion. (In a much different work, *The Professor's House*, Willa Cather showed the reverence she held for Poe's technical virtuosity— acknowledged earlier in her college graduation essay—by modelling the

203

various edifices in that novel on Poe's claustrophic interiors and on the malleable architecture of some of his famous houses, metonyms for the house of the soul.) The tale also shares elements of stories like "William Wilson," especially in its confessional form. "The thousand injuries of Fortunato I had borne as I best could," the narrator tells us, "but when he ventured upon insult I vowed revenge. You, who so well know the nature of my soul, will not suppose, however, that I gave utterance to a threat. . . . A wrong is unredressed when retribution overtakes its redresser" (848). Who is the narrator speaking to? Following his fondness for masquerade balls as metaphors, Poe suggests that this carnival is the celebration leading up to Lent. Thus perhaps the audience is a priest and the narrator a penitent. Throughout, the story has a sense of last-rites confession to it, culminating in the macabre twist in the final sentence: "For the half of a century no mortal has disturbed them. *In pace requiescat!*" (854)

Poe always delighted in wordplay, and here he puns on various concepts: "cask" and casket; Fortunato being most unfortunate; the "silencing words" and the "mocking echo" of the caves; and the mason's trowel which Montresor holds up jokingly to his victim: the eleven tiers of the wall that imprisons Fortunato correspond to the eleven heiratic levels of Freemasonry, that secret fraternity which, in Poe's America, had come under increasing suspicion as cabalistic and subversive. Poe may also be using the fraternal order in a bitter way, to suggest that he is taking revenge on those members of the literary clique that had blackballed him. Freemasonry had its strongest foothold in New England, that region of the country that usually most incited Poe's ire. When he was in Boston arranging for the publication of *Tamerlane and Other Poems* in 1827, there was a much-publicized kidnapping of an author who had been about to publish an expose of the organization, a Captain William Morgan. This incident could not have escaped Poe's notice, since it was widely reported in the papers. In the 1820s and 1830s, in Baltimore as well—where Poe next stationed himself—anti-Masonic forces were in full retaliatory mode against the Masons, who had seized a good measure of political power. Poe's family friend in Baltimore, the lawyer and man of letters William Wirt, was a fierce anti-Mason who in 1832 had even been nominated as the presidential candidate on the Anti-Masonic Party ticket.

A final personal element of the story in its revenge aspect may lie in the numerous allusions to John Allan. "*Nemo me impune lacessit,*" the Montresor family coat of arms, is Latin for "No one injures (attacks) me with impunity," a reference to the depiction of the heel of Christ bruising the serpent's head in *Paradise Lost.* But it is also, as Kenneth Silverman points out, the national motto of Scotland and of the revered Order of the Thistle, to which John Allan's family, of Scottish ancestry, belonged. In addition, Allan much resembles Fortunato—he was admired and respected, interested in wines, and a member of the Masons. One biographer has even detected in the word "amontillado" an anagram of the name "Allan." For Poe, old animosities still shuddered and rattled in his dark subconconscious, like the unquiet dead that roam through his fiction.

Shortly before the libel suit was settled, in February 1847, Virginia's health began to fail noticeably. That fall, she had taken a serious turn for the worse, being much weaker and more pallid than in the past. Poe continued to refer to her illness as resulting from a burst blood vessel while singing, nearly five years earlier, but he must have known that the cause of her wasting away was tuberculosis. She displayed the classic symptoms of the consumptive—a wracking cough, chest pain, shortness of breath and loss of appetite, weight loss, fever and chills.

Muddy was as troubled as Poe, for some twenty-five years ago, she had lost another child named Virginia, barely two years old. Muddy had then lost Henry, fewer than ten years ago—possibly to the same disease. Now Virginia Eliza lay on her deathbed, looking almost ghostly and suffering great misery, constantly struggling for breath. Mary Gove, who visited the cottage frequently, commented on the psychic bond between mother and daughter and was struck by the contrast between Virginia and Muddy, whom she described as "a tall, dignified old lady, with a most ladylike manner, and [a] black dress, though old and much worn, [that] looked really elegant on her. She wore a widow's cap of the genuine pattern, and it suited exquisitely with her snow-white hair."

Her features were large, and corresponded with her stature, and it seemed strange how such a stalwart and queenly woman could be the mother of her almost petite daughter. Mrs. Poe looked very young; she had large black eyes, and a pearly whiteness of complexion, which was a perfect pallor. Her pale face, her brilliant eyes, and her raven hair gave her an unearthly look. One felt that she was almost a disrobed spirit, and when she coughed it was made certain that she was rapidly passing away.

Gove recalled that the cottage was always wax-neat, but so "purely clean" that it also looked "scant" and obviously "poverty-stricken." There were no linens on the bed, which was made only of straw. Virginia lay wrapped in Poe's old military cloak, for lack of a bedspread, with the large tortoise-shell cat resting on her stomach, "conscious of her great usefulness" as the only real source of warmth. Poe held Virginia's hands, and Muddy her feet.

As Virginia sank rapidly, she could barely speak, but she begged Muddy to take care of her husband after she passed away: "Darling, darling Muddy, you will console and take care of my poor Eddie—you will *never, never* leave him? Promise me, my dear Muddy, and then I can die in peace." On 29 January, the day before Virginia died, Loui Shew and Mary Starr were at the cottage. Poe took Loui aside and said: "My poor Virginia still lives, although failing fast and now suffering much pain." Shew was struck by the unrelieved pathos of the scene. She later wrote that some days before Virginia's death, with Poe in the room, the author's wife had shown her the few keepsakes she had been able to keep with her in their nomadic life—a picture of Poe from much earlier, and also a worn letter written to Poe by the second Mrs. Allan. "It expressed a desire to see him, [and] acknowledged that she alone had been the cause of his adopted Father's neglect." Poe read it, weeping.

Virginia Eliza Poe died on a Saturday, 30 January 1847, almost exactly five years to the day she had first been diagnosed with tuberculosis.

She was the same age as Poe's other Eliza, his mother, when she had died, and to make the comparisons even more macabre, Poe may have realized that consumption was likely the disease that had also claimed his mother. When Virginia stopped breathing, Poe crumpled, as if shot through the heart with a bullet.

Loui Shew helped with the funeral arrangements, spraying cologne in the room in which Virginia died and bringing suitable burial garments. Muddy was grateful for the cerements, later saying that "my darling Virginia would have laid in her grave in cotton" if not for Loui's kindness. Loui also painted a watercolor portrait of Virginia on her deathbed, draped in the fine linen sheets in which she was laid to rest. The portrait shows the young woman propped up on pillows, her face turned to one side, her large eyes closed. Her face shows none of the emaciation typical of consumptives, so the image is somewhat idealized, as fitting as that would be for Poe, who had described Virginia's death in several tales long before she had passed, and who mourned her in much the manner of his fictional protagonists.

Virginia was buried on the afternoon of 2 February, in the family vault of the owners of the cottage, in the cemetery of a Dutch Reformed Church about a half mile away. Mary Starr was at the cottage that very cold day and stayed at the house while many assembled mourners went to the gravesite—Loui Shew, Willis, his partner George Morris, Evert Duyckinck, Mary Gove, Cornelius Matthews, and others. Loui had given Poe suitable mourning garments but was dismayed to find that he went to the gravesite draped in the old cloak that had served Sissy as a blanket.

Virginia's death left Poe adrift. Muddy became his only secure mooring, and he began to refer to her more often as "mother." (The 1849 poem "To My Mother" hails Muddy for filling the emotional breach in his life that was created by the deaths of Eliza and Virginia.) Muddy alone, however, could not care for Poe and nurse him back to health, so she in turn depended heavily on Loui Shew, who responded with kindness and largesse. Muddy made Loui promise to come to the cottage "every *other* day, for a long time," or until Poe was able to return to work. "I hope and believe *you will not fail him*," she wrote.

Shew, the daughter of a physician, had had a long time to observe Poe in his erratic health. Whereas the homeopathist Mary Gove had counseled him to eat raw vegetables and fish for "brain power" and had prescribed other folk remedies, Shew noticed from close physical contact with Poe that he had an irregular heartbeat; after ten beats there would be a pause and then a fluttering resumption. One day she took him into the city to be examined by Dr. Valentine Mott, one the most eminent physicians of the day and the founder of the medical college at New York University. He confirmed Loui's informal diagnosis and concluded that, even when in good health, Poe was suffering from a lesion on one side of his brain. This was what had produced the "brain fever" Poe so often spoke of and was why he could not bear any stimulants or intoxicants. They brought about "insanity," as did sedatives, which had to be administered mildly.

In the months following Virginia's death, Poe fell gravely ill, deeply depressed and hovering near the brink of madness. It was really due only to Shew's ministrations that he pulled himself out of such depths, as he acknowledged in the fragmentary poem of 1847 "The Beloved Physician," writing that "The pulse beats ten and intermits. / God nerve the soul that ne'er forgets / In calm or storm, by night or day, / Its steady toil, its loyalty." Nonetheless, Poe often felt that all was hopeless and many a day did not care whether he lived or died. He rebelliously slipped out from under Muddy's watchful eyes to go out and drink on the binge, desperate to forget the ghastly death of his beloved Virginia.

He was far from rational, and most of the year 1847 was lost. Chivers wrote him often, at one point urging him to come back to the South and live with him. On days when Poe lay abed in Fordham, drunk and sometimes delirious, he retailed for Loui Shew all the old fictitious stories of his uneven life—how a scar on his shoulder, for example, was the result of a knife fight over a girl in a foreign port, or how a novel attributed to Eugene Sue was actually written by him. Seeking some comfort on Christmas Eve, Shew, a devout Episcopalian, took him to midnight mass at the Church of the Holy Communion in the city. He was fine for the first part of the service, looking straight into the chancel, reciting the psalms, holding the prayer book "like a 'churchman,'" and surprising Loui when he "struck up a tenor to our sopranos." However, when the priest several times repeated part of the text, "He was a man of sorrows and acquainted with grief," Poe grew jittery and anxious. Finally, he whispered to Loui to "remain quiet" and that he would wait for her outside. With that, Shew said, "he rushed out, *too excited to stay.*"

The entire year Poe battled drink and depression, unleashing inside him a "terrible evil" which he spoke of to his friends. Looking back on his *annus terribilis* in a letter of January 1848 to George Eveleth, Poe analyzed his feelings in terrifying detail:

> *You say—"Can you* hint *to me what was the terrible evil which caused the irregularities so profoundly lamented?" Yes; I can do more than hint. This "evil" was the greatest which can befall a man. Six years ago, a wife, whom I loved as no man ever loved before, ruptured a blood-vessel in singing. Her life was despaired of. I took leave of her forever & underwent all the agonies of her death. She recovered partially and I again hoped. At the end of a year the vessel broke again—I went through precisely the same scene. Again in about a year afterward. Then again—again—again & even once again at varying intervals. Each time I felt all the agonies of her death—and at each accession of the disorder I loved her more dearly & clung to her life with more desperate pertinacity. But I am constitutionally sensitive—nervous in a very unusual degree. I became insane, with long intervals of horrible sanity. During these fits of absolute unconsciousness I drank, God only knows how often or how much. As a matter of course, my enemies referred the insanity to the drink rather than the drink to the insanity. I had indeed, nearly abandoned all hope of a permanent cure when I found one in the* death *of my wife. This I can & do endure as becomes a man—it was the horrible never-ending oscillation between hope & despair which I could* not *longer have endured without the total loss of reason. In the death of what was my life, then, I receive a new but—oh God! how melancholy an existence.*

From the experience of Virginia's death came some new poems. One of the most haunting of these is "Ulalume," whose title suggests ululation,

209

or a mournful wailing sound. In the poem, a lover is urged by Psyche, or his soul, to remain faithful to his departed love, and they are reunited at poem's end "To bar up our way . . . From the secret that lies in hidden in these wolds . . . Have drawn up the spectre of a planet / from the limbo of lunary souls— / This sinfully scintillant planet / From the Hell of the planetary souls." "Annabel Lee," another poem from somewhat later, posits a nonsexual, childlike attachment between two persons, one of whom is claimed by Death ("her high-born kinsmen") who "shut her up in a sepulchre / In [a] kingdom by the sea." But their love withstands such shackles, or entombment:

> But our love it was stronger by far than the love
>> Of those who were older than we—
>> Of many far wiser than we—
> And neither the angels in Heaven above
>> Nor the demons down under the sea
> Can ever dissever my soul from the soul
>> Of the beautiful Annabel Lee:—

> For the moon never beams without bringing me dreams
>> Of the beautiful Annabel Lee;
> And the stars never rise but I see the bright eyes
>> Of the beautiful Annabel Lee;
> And so, all the night-tide, I lie down by the side
> Of my darling, my darling, my life and my bride
>> In her sepulchre there by the sea—
>> In her tomb by the side of the sea.

In this image lies Poe's abiding faith in the transcendence of the soul. And Annabel Lee, like all the women in Poe's life, lives forever in his imagination in terms of her girlish beauty—a "mournful and never-ending remembrance."

Poe's technique in the poems is worth noting, too. Many of the poems, especially "Annabel Lee" and the quietly savage "For Annie," follow the lyric or ballad stanza form. This was a popular, melodious mode of poetic expression in nineteenth-century America that owed much to the African American spirituals and work songs of the South. Both "Annabel Lee" and "For Annie" might be seen as influenced by these types of songs, as well as "The Raven," with its regularly changing refrain, suggesting a change in the mood of the speaker. Like Poe's poems, the spirituals also used choric repetition as a means of emphasis. These poems, like the slave songs, also frequently refer to the redemptive and protective power of water—an idea not usually found in Poe's fiction.

As a youth in Richmond, Poe must have had strong exposure to African American art forms. Perhaps if his break with observed religion was simmering in his youth and teenage years, he may even have recognized that there existed another religious universe, beyond the limits of the pious middle class of Monument Episcopal Church. This other religious world lay in the camp meetings and prayer-songs of the black field workers—the torch-lit revivals that were punctuated by painful wails and mournful dirges, then capped by unrepressed ecstasy—like the alternating ululations and exclamations of peace in Poe's own "Ulalume." The spirituals were the expression in art of the inarticulate—the marginalized and the desolate who felt separated and lost, precisely Poe's condition when John Allan sent him packing for Richmond, and when Poe lit out for the North.

The late poems are interesting for other elements as well. "For Annie" evokes powerful images as Poe recalls the end of a "lingering illness" in which "the fever called 'Living' / Is conquered at last." As the speaker recovers, he rests "so composedly" in his bed "That any beholder / Might fancy me dead— / Might start at beholding me, / Thinking me dead." He goes on to speak of "the fever called 'Living' / That burned in my brain" and sees death as a return to infantile bliss:

I have drank of a water
  That quenches all thirst:—

Of a water that flows,
  With a lullaby sound,

From a spring but a very few
  Feet under ground—
From a cavern not very far
  Down under ground.

In these lines the speaker creates an amalgam of mother's milk and some sedative or narcotic, inducing serene sleep. The final image of maternal tenderness is arresting, as it depicts both an infant's slumber and the peaceful repose of a corpse:

She tenderly kissed me—
  She fondly caressed—
And then I fell gently
  To sleep on her breast—
Deeply to sleep from the
  Heaven of her breast.

When the light was extinguished,
  She covered me warm,
And she prayed to the angels
  To keep me from harm—
To the queen of the angels
  To shield me from harm.

And I lie so composedly
  Now, in my bed,
(Knowing her love)
  That you fancy me dead—
And I rest so contentedly
  Now in my bed,
(With her love at my breast)
  That you fancy me dead—
That you shudder to look at me,
  Thinking me dead:—

But my heart it is brighter
  Than all of the many
Stars of the Heaven—
  Sparkles with Annie—
It glows with the thought
  Of the love of my Annie—
With the thought of the light
  Of the eyes of my Annie.

Poe's poetry from this period presents images of a kind of placid horror. Even the melodious "The Bells" (which sounds much like the spiritual song "Mary and Martha Jes' Gone 'Long") deceives and disarms the reader, moving from an unassailable lightheartedness at the beginning, with its evocation of Christmas sleigh bells to "mellow wedding bells." It segues into "loud alarum bells," foretelling horror and catastrophe and ends with the tolling of the "iron bells" of a funeral: "What a world of solemn thought their monody compels." The poem chronicles the faith-destroying horror of the transformation from youthful gaiety to death. The final stanza exhibits a pessimism about existence, in which man is "the plaything of a lying, sadistic Overlord of Life, the banquet of a ghoul-God":

From the rust within their throats
  Is a groan.
And the people—ah, the people—
They that dwell up in the steeple,
  All alone,
And who, tolling, tolling, tolling,
  In that muffled monotone,
Feel a glory in so rolling
  On the human heart a stone—
They are neither man nor woman—
They are neither brute nor human—
  They are Ghouls:—

213

And their king it is who tolls:—
And he rolls, rolls, rolls,
    Rolls
A pæan from the bells!
And his merry bosom swells
    With the pæan of the bells!

Animating Poe's poetry at this time is a rage for extinction, an anger with mere existence, and a turbulent undercurrent of hatred that several times surfaced in his dealings with even the most solicitous of his friends, like Loui Shew.

As thoughtful as these poems appear to us today, they were all rejected more than once before Poe was finally able to sell them, for the usual pittance. He had to take charity money from Shew, which was bad enough—but eventually he had to accept one hundred dollars from a minor poet, Sarah Anna (Stella) Lewis, to write a favorable review of a recent book by her. Shew and Poe argued harshly over this incident, and Poe, the critic who had so uncompromisingly championed high standards, was ashamed. Whenever Stella Lewis came to visit, he would rush out the back of the house to escape her, fleeing either to the "fields and forest" or to the grounds of the Catholic school nearby. Shew, who was repelled by Lewis, a fat, gaudily dressed woman with only a mediocre talent, was once sent after Poe by Muddy: "I found him sitting on a favorite rock muttering his desire to die, and get rid of *Literary bores.*"

He turned again to Fanny Osgood for comfort. He knew that, before her death, Virginia had approved of his liasion with Fanny, as she apparently had regarding other women Poe had attached himself to. Visiting Virginia the day before she died, Mary Starr reported that Virginia had told her to "be a friend to Eddie, and don't forsake him; he always loved you—didn't he, Eddie?" Poe seems to have been drawn more to Fanny than to anyone else and now, free to marry, his passion for her intensified. Fanny, however, was still married, and as a respectable society woman she could not possibly listen to Poe's suggestive discussions. She found his theatricality frankly embarrassing, as her brother-in-law, the Reverend

Henry Harrington, indicated in recalling a visit by Poe to the Osgood house: "in passionate terms [he] had besought her to elope with him. . . . he went down on his knee and clasped his hands, and pleaded for her consent . . . she met him with mingled ridicule and reproof, appealing to his better nature, and striving to stimulate a resolution to abandon his vicious courses . . . finally he took his leave, baffled and humiliated, if not ashamed."

Fanny rebuffed him, as he surely knew she must, and in a bitter twist, Poe's nemesis Rufus Griswold, who had succeeded him as editor of *Graham's*, now appeared on the scene to succeed him as the object of Fanny's affections. Griswold had remarried after the death of his first wife, but the marriage had failed, and he had obtained a divorce. He now fell under Fanny's spell, much as Poe had earlier, and Griswold somewhat recklessly used his influence in literary circles to court her, taking her to the most fashionable salons, critiquing her work in progress, and sponsoring her among publishers and editors. Fanny repaid Griswold's gratitude, however, not by leaving her husband and marrying him, but by dedicating her 1848 *Poems* to the anthologizer, "as a souvenir of admiration for his genius, of regard for his generous character, and of gratitude for his valuable literary counsels." Ironically, it may have been Fanny's regard for Griswold that persuaded Poe to make Griswold his literary executor.

Thrashed about by Fanny's pique and flightiness, Poe managed to complete very little work during the rest of 1847—a revised version of his Hawthorne review, which appeared in the November *Godey's Lady's Book*, and some minor pieces. During these months he was occasionally spotted in the city, in a somewhat improved mood. Griswold recalled meeting him in the street and finding him "extremely civil." Poe sometimes called at the Washington Square home of Loui Shew, who was trying to awaken his religious faith. She succeeded in some respects, at one point extracting from Poe the conviction that at that time he had "renewed my hopes and faith in God," but this may have been the statement of someone who felt that, all else having failed, religious faith certainly could bring him no harm. On the other hand, a daguerreotype of him taken about this time suggests good health, even jauntiness.

He looks thin, but not hungry. He is well dressed and for the first time is wearing a small waxed moustache, its ends neatly twirled.

At about this time, Poe began to hear rumors of his nascent fame in France, where a translation of his *Tales* had just appeared. Although they never met, the symbolist poet Charles Baudelaire became Poe's champion in Europe, encouraging his reputation there. Although Baudelaire mistakenly assumed that Poe's characters were all one hundred percent projections of himself, he nonetheless discerned the terrifying power and startling originality of Poe's thinking. As the final months of 1847 drew to a close, Poe once more sought support for his dream magazine, giving lectures and readings in order to raise money for its launch, but in the end nothing seemed to be coming together for him. He wrote an admirer about his still-to-be-realized magazine project: "As regards the Stylus—that is the grand purpose of my life, from which I have never swerved for a moment."

Thus the new year, 1848, brought about in Poe a resolution to rebuild his life. He did so by doggedly seeking a rational explanation for the chaos of his existence. The previous fall, he had begun writing a philosophical treatise, *Eureka*, which he came to regard as his magnum opus, the culmination of his life's work. Written out of the tragedy of his young wife's death after an oppressive five years of suffering, *Eureka* was Poe's inspired view of life and the universe—a huge subject that he described, with great seriousness, as a work that "will (in good time) revolutionize the world of Physical & Metaphysical Science." "I say this calmly," he told a friend, "but I say it."

The book derived from a February lecture entitled "The Universe" that Poe presented at the venerable Society Library in New York. Owing to a terrible storm, the lecture was sparsely attended, but among those present Poe's ideas got mixed reviews. In a slight southern accent, with his coat tightly buttoned across his slender chest, Poe presented a lecture that was, according to some enthusiastic attendees, a rhapsody of brilliance. One listener claimed that the lecture was "the most elaborate and profound" he had ever heard. But Poe's friend Duyckinck disparaged the effort, calling it "a mountainous piece of absurdity."

216

Feeling that his lecture was misunderstood, Poe seems to have set to the task of producing the book version with great care, writing both inside the cottage and even outdoors throughout early 1848. Maria Clemm recalled that Poe did not want to be alone when writing, so she would sit up with him until sometimes as late as four o'clock in the morning, dozing in her chair while he worked at his desk. At other times, they "used to walk up and down the garden, his arm around me, mine around him, until I was so tired I could not walk. He would stop every few minutes and explain his ideas to me, and ask if I understood him." By May, Poe had finished the work, and it was brought out in June by George Putnam, whose recollections indicate that he should have heeded some warning signs before countersigning the contracts, for Poe suggested to him that "Newton's discovery of gravitation was a mere incident compared with the discoveries revealed in this book"; Poe asked for a first printing of no fewer than fifty thousand copies. Putnam wisely brought out an edition of five hundred copies, advanced Poe fourteen dollars against royalties, and made him sign an agreement saying that he would repay the advance if the book failed to make it back. The book failed to sell out its first printing and had few reviews, most of them indifferent.

T. S. Eliot's later blunt judgment of the book seems of a piece with that of Poe's contemporaries: "it makes no deep impression . . . because we are aware of Poe's lack of qualification in philosophy, theology, or natural science." Certainly the work is a melange of Poe's various interests and beliefs, including traditional pantheism, popularized versions of nineteenth-century astronomical thought, and some of the current pseudosciences like mesmerism and phrenology. On the other hand, Poe seemed amazingly to anticipate some of the theories of modern science: the time/space continuum, the view of an expanding and contracting universe, a general proposition akin to chaos theory, and an explanation (still a valid theory) for why the sky is dark at night.

Eureka was based on the "nebular hypothesis" of the Marquis Pierre-Simon de Laplace, a French mathematician, who in a 1796 work had explained the creation of the heavenly bodies by the gradual coalescence of a thin, luminous substance diffused through space. His theory held that the infant solar system resembled a hot, slowly rotating nebula. The sun's atmosphere, in condensing, left equatorial rings which in turn condensed to form the planets. Of great consequence in this theory was the idea that the universe had not been completely forged by a single divine stroke but *was still being created.*

Poe's understanding of Laplace came to him through the works of John Nichol, a professor of astronomy at the University of Glasgow. One book in particular, *Views of the Architecture of the Heavens* (1837), had gone through seven editions in seven years and was one of the most widely read books of popular science in Poe's day. Only a week or so before Poe presented his lecture at the Society Library, across town at the New York Mercantile Library Nichol had begun a series of well-attended lectures on astronomy; the New York newspapers praised them and printed large extracts from them. Nichol endorsed Laplace's theories and extended them to suggest that one day these single entities could be merged into a cluster of clusters and then into a single sun, an idea that accorded with Poe's long-held belief in an Original Unity. In *Eureka* he commented on an abnormality in the physical universe and saw it as analogous to human civilization, an affirmation of his antidemocratic views:

> *This constitution has been effected by* forcing *the originally and therefore normally* One *into the abnormal condition of* Many. *An action of this character implies reaction. A diffusion from Unity, under the conditions, involves a tendency to return into Unity—a tendency ineradicable until satisfied. (1278)*

Such ideas were very much in the air in Poe's time, because between 1800 and 1850 America experienced a huge shift from Baconian science—science as generalization and classification—to dynamic theories of electromagnetism, thermodynamism, and atomic hypothesis; in the words of one historian, this signalled "the beginning of the great era of the unification of force."

In many ways, *Eureka* holds the key to unlocking the mysteries of many of Poe's writings. Arguing by analogy (at the time a widely used mode of philosophic and scientific thought), Poe saw in the theory a confirmation, through scientific demonstration, of his belief in an otherworld of repeated dyings and rebirths. In this sense, *Eureka* most closely parallels William Butler Yeats's book-length summation of his spiritual philosophy, *A Vision* (1925), and Poe's belief in a cycle of plural existences resembles Yeats's ideas about the cycles of human history and of revolution (literally, a turning around again) as depicted in his image of the gyre. (*Eureka* also resembles the visionary writings of William Blake.) Some seven years earlier, Poe had remarked in a review: "the only irrefutable argument in support of the soul's immortality—or, rather, the only conclusive proof of man's alternate dissolution and re-juvenescence ad infinitum— is to be found in analogies deduced from the modern established theory of the nebular cosmogyny" (323–24).

In *Eureka* Poe also depicts the universe as an aesthetic object. He sees the cosmos as controlled by physical laws corresponding to his deeply held Aristotelian views of Unity of Effect and Unity of Action. As the universe gradually expands by radiation and then by gravitation and attraction, all matter will return to Unity or Nothingness, at which point, by another act of creative will, the whole process will repeat itself. Thus, the original unity, or the desire to return to the original Oneness, an abiding theme in Poe's fiction. Using the ideas of Laplace and Nichol, Poe saw the cosmos as confirmation of the concept of the perfect plot, just like the one Poe had been developing for years in his criticism. Just as in his seminal, defining essay on Hawthorne's tales, in which he likened the unified plot to a building "so dependently constructed, that to change the position of a single brick is to overthrow the entire fabric," in *Eureka* he likened the universal reciprocity of adaptation to a plot so arranged that one cannot tell whether one incident "depends from any one other or upholds this."

"The plots of God are perfect," Poe writes. "The Universe is a plot of God." Therefore, to Poe's eminently logical but at this time also emotional makeup, desperate to find a rational explanation for the irrationalities and imperfectnesses of his life, the cosmos was a supremely perfect tale or poem, thus validating his existence, confirming his philosophical and aesthetic views, and perhaps giving him hope for his future. *Eureka* is unmistakably the work of someone who needed to feel he was in control. It has often been asked why Poe would suddenly turn from fiction of the most unrealistic kind to a scientific treatise. This is not so surprising considering the pattern of his writings after "The Raven." Most of these texts reveal a man raging for control. We see this in the hyperanalytic lucidity of "The Philosophy of Composition" just as we note that a story like "The Facts in the Case of M. Valdemar" circles back, continually, to its emphasis on "facts"—on data, verifiable and constant.

At the same time, Poe was more desperate for love than ever before. The death of Virginia had left him shocked and incredulous; more than that, he came to feel that the affection and attention that a woman could pay to him would keep his demons in check, possibly even allow him to lay his sad past to rest. To that end, he became intent on remarrying as soon as possible. Once again, Poe was interested in a platonic relationship, a nonsexual union with a woman who would act more as mother or sister than lover. This seems to be the reason why the women he pursued and was pursued by were, for the most part, not very attractive. Lambert Wilmer, his old Baltimore friend, once remarked that of all the men he had known, Poe "was the most *passionless*," and W. H. Auden, oddly for someone who was not heterosexual himself, averred that Poe's love life was the sort that was largely confined to "crying in laps and playing house." Like Virginia, these women were also not intellectual. They resembled Muddy more than anyone else—large-hearted, kind, and unquestioning, more like docile fawns than alluring does.

How Poe went about courting these women, however, suggests how reckless, impetuous, and unrealistic he was in his aims and expectations. For a while, it looked as if it did not seem to matter who he ended up with, so long as it was someone who fit the general profile—wealthy or not, bookish or not, northerner or southerner. Poe's analytic mind did not, it seems, extend to matters of the heart, for during most of the year 1848, he pursued at least four women, more or less at the same time: Jane Locke; Nancy Richmond; Helen Whitman; and, for a brief time that summer, his former Richmond sweetheart, Elmira Shelton nee Royster. Poe seems to have wanted it this way. He was nothing if not theatrical, and he liked the intense, dangerous allure of anonymous love letters, of endearments whispered in the hushed secrecy of hiding places—the garden of some grand country house or a dark alcove in a spacious drawing room. It may also suggest a fundamental inability to commit to a single relationship, for ego, too, must have played a role. But at bottom, Poe's personal embroilments and entanglements throughout the year, like those earlier ones with Fanny Osgood and Elizabeth Ellet, were pathetically comic, the stuff of French farce.

The first woman Poe turned to after Virginia's death was Loui Shew. Shew, who described herself plainly as "a mere countrywoman," was unsophisticated and unworldly. After her divorce from a physician, the deeply religious Shew had devoted her life to volunteer work helping the poor and needy. She obviously saw Poe as a case for a social worker, and in nursing him back to health felt that she had performed a valuable good deed. Once Poe seemed to have moved past the worst of his illness, however, Shew looked to other people who might benefit from her ministrations and did not regard Poe as a love interest. She was apparently little flattered by Poe's poetic endearments, in the poems "To a Physician" and "To M. L. S.—," and in the essay/tale "The Domain of Arnheim," in which Loui appears as a woman "not unwomanly, whose loveliness and love enveloped [the hero's] existence in the purple atmosphere of Paradise" (864).

Poe used other means to woo her as well. While visiting her home in May 1847, he suggested to Loui that they try to write a poem together—an outrageous suggestion, since Poe had grand ideas about the literary vocation and high standards for the creation of art. It may be that he had already been formulating the resultant poem, "The Bells," in his mind before broaching the idea to her. She recalled that he came to her one day and said, "I have to write a poem. I have no feeling no sentiment, no inspiration." After tea, she "playfully said, here is paper. A Bell (very jolly and sharp) rang at the corner of the street. He said 'I so dislike the noise of bells tonight. I cannot write. I have no subject. I am exhausted.'

So I took his pen and wrote 'The Bells. By E. A. Poe.'" The melodious poem, however, did not help Poe convince Loui that they should be married.

Undaunted, Poe pressed on, and the more bold he grew the more Loui cringed and stepped back in alarm. She sympathized with Poe and obviously felt deep affection for him, but she did not want to marry him. In June 1848 she finally had to tell him to stop pursuing her. When she did so, Poe was the one who cringed, recoiling like a wounded animal and then withdrawing into the most nauseous type of self-pity. His letters, pleas for sympathy and reconciliation, use the calculated strategy of ennobling Loui, characterizing her as the virtuous woman who will save him, the debased reprobate, from a life of debauchery and drink. Rebuffed, Poe journeyed south that summer, ostensibly to drum up support for his magazine by giving a series of readings and lectures, but also to flee the scene of an emotional injury.

Early in 1847, just after Virginia's death, another woman, Jane Ermina Locke, had begun corresponding with Poe when she sent him some poems to critique. After Virginia died, Poe pursued the relationship through the mails but was dismayed to find, when Jane visited him in Fordham in June 1848 (the same month that Loui Shew had told Poe to stop pursuing her), that she was a middle-aged housewife with five children—Poe had thought her a young, comely lady who was part of the art world. Jane did, however, arrange for Poe to lecture in her hometown, Lowell, Massachusetts, on 10 July, and while there Poe stayed in her home. He apparently did not reject the idea of an affair, however, for he returned for a second visit in October. But on this occasion he infuriated Locke by wooing one of her neighbors, Mrs. Nancy L. Richmond.

Mrs. Richmond, known as Annie to her friends, was no more attractive than these other women, but a photograph from the period conveys an image of steady reliability, of plain sensibleness, without glamour, that may have attracted Poe to her. Annie was kindhearted and simpleminded. Her letters are written in the most gushing, sentimental language of the time. As with Loui Shew and other women, Poe promptly put his literary talents to work in wooing Annie. She figured first in the story "Landor's

Cottage," in which a "slender" figure of a woman "about twenty-eight years of age" steps toward the narrator and compels him to say to himself, " 'Surely here I have found the perfection of natural, in contradistinction from artificial *grace*.'" Poe was also enchanted by the spell that Annie's "spiritual gray" eyes and light chestnut hair cast upon him, an "intense . . . expression of *romance* . . . or unworldliness" unlike, he said, any feeling he had yet experienced (896). Mrs. Richmond was also the "Annie" of the taut, tragic poem "For Annie." Annie was married and thus unattainable, but this was a reality that Poe refused to recognize; he continued to pursue her throughout the year, even as he became involved, more deeply than with any of his other lady friends, with Helen Whitman.

Sarah Helen Whitman, of Providence, Rhode Island, was a poet well known in the circles of New York bluestockings. The widowed Helen was initially more the pursuer than the pursued; she had had her eye on Poe for some time, beginning at Anne Lynch's February 1848 Valentine's Day party, when Helen submitted a poem, "To Edgar A. Poe," which was read aloud at the gathering. This was the first of sixteen poems that Helen addressed to, or wrote about, Poe. For his part, Poe seems to have remained somewhat aloof from Helen, for reasons that are unclear—perhaps it was the intensity of his interest in Loui Shew or Annie Richmond. Helen had done her homework on the poet, for she knew many details of his personal life, through her friendships with Lynch and other literary women, namely Fanny Osgood.

When "To Edgar A. Poe" appeared in the *Home Journal*, it attracted Fanny's notice; she had apparently recovered from her earlier "affair" with Poe, for she sent Helen a "friendly warning," noting that "the Raven in his eyrie . . . has *swooped* upon your little *dove cote* in Providence. May Providence protect you if he has!—for his croak [is] the most eloquent imaginable. He is in truth 'A glorious devil, with large heart & brain.'" This missive seems to have been playfully intended to encourage Helen to pursue Poe in his "eyrie" in Fordham, rather than to warn her away from him and bid her to stay sequestered in Providence.

Poe responded to Helen's poem with a poem of his own, a second "To Helen," in which he recalled an evening in Providence in July 1845 when he had been visiting there with Fanny Osgood and saw (but did not meet) Helen from afar. In a later love letter, Poe explained,

You may remember that once, when I passed through Providence with Mrs. Osgood, I positively refused to accompany her to your house, and even provoked her into a quarrel by the obstinacy and seeming unreasonableness of my refusal. I dared neither go nor say why I could not. I dared not speak of you—much less see you. For years your name never passed my lips, while my soul drank in, with a delirious thirst, all that was uttered in my presence respecting you. The merest whisper that concerned you awoke in me a shuddering sixth sense, vaguely compounded of fear, ecstatic happiness, and a wild, inexplicable sentiment that resembled nothing so nearly as the consciousness of guilt.

Helen was more physically attractive than the other bluestockings, but equally compelling was her sad personal history, which may have engaged Poe's romantic imagination. When Helen was twelve years old, her father, Nicholas Power, was a businessman on the verge of financial failure. He took to sea to visit some of his interests in the South and was not heard from again, until nineteen years later, when he suddenly reappeared. At age twenty-five, Helen had married a Boston lawyer, but he died soon thereafter, leaving her a childless widow. She had lived in that state for the past fifteen years, in the same plain, clapboard house on Benefit Street with her eccentric younger sister and her domineering mother, Anna Power. Helen had over the years developed interests in some of the same pseudosciences that Poe sometimes put faith in, like mesmerism and phrenology. Like Poe, she was drawn to spiritualism and believed in psychic connections and coincidences—her birthday, January 19, was the same as Poe's. Her poetry, while not masterful, far surpassed that of Poe's other lady friends in quality of technique and in ideation. In short, they seemed to be a good match.

That summer when Poe went south, he stayed for a while in his boyhood stamping grounds of Richmond, Virginia, and while there learned that the woman to whom he had been lightheartedly "engaged" when he was fifteen, Elmira Royster, had become widowed. He called on her, to her surprise. Elmira was happy to see Poe and welcomed him. He began

to consider her a potential wife, as well, until his thoughts were interrupted by the arrival by mail of two stanzas of love poetry from Helen.
Upon reading them, Poe left Richmond immediately and headed back
by steamer to New York.

Helen was apparently serious and had started on a path that would lead
to an engagement, for she had been vetting Poe's qualifications for marriage.
In turn, friends of Poe's confirmed the seriousness of his interest in her,
among them Rufus Griswold, who visited Helen in Providence in mid-July.

Griswold's emotional state was no better than Poe's had been the previous year. After the tragic death of his wife and son, Griswold had gotten
married again, to a Jewish woman from Charleston, South Carolina, but
they became estranged, and he had just obtained a divorce. He had secured
a position lecturing at New York University, but the figure he cut around
campus was grim and unnerving. He often could not leave his rooms at the
university because of uncontrollable crying jags. He drank and took opium
to quiet his nerves. He still looked young, however, and his literary energies had not flagged. Griswold told Helen that Poe had praised her work
highly in his lecture at Lowell. When she asked him why so many people
disliked Poe, Griswold replied that Poe had done nothing "exceptionably
wrong" and that his enemies were more to fault for the quarrels than he.
Helen also sought and received reassurances about Poe's character from
the English poet Anna Blackwell, a friend of Whitman's, to whom Poe had
confidentially written for information about Helen. She revealed to Helen
that Poe had asked about her, as he also had to Maria Jane McIntosh, a
Georgia-born novelist who had met Poe once at Fordham and reported that
during the visit, he had spoken of little else except Helen.

On 21 September, Poe arrived in Providence to meet Helen and profess his love for her. The courting began swiftly, and in earnest, with Poe
writing several long, effusive love letters to Helen after his visit. The first
of them, dated 1 October, in part describes his initial attraction to her at
Anne Lynch's Valentine's Day party:

> *Judge, then, with what wondering, unbelieving joy I received in your well-
> known MS., the Valentine which first gave me to see that you knew me to exist.*

The idea of what men call Fate lost then for the first time, in my eyes, its char-
acter of futility. I felt that nothing hereafter was to be doubted, and lost myself,
for many weeks, in one continuous, delicious dream, where all was a vivid yet
indistinct bliss. . . . And now, in the most simple words at my command, let me
paint to you the impression made upon me by your personal presence.—As you
entered the room, pale, timid, hesitating, and evidently oppressed at heart; as
your eyes rested appealingly, for one brief moment, upon mine, I felt, for the
first time in my life, and tremblingly acknowledged, the existence of spiritual
influences altogether out of the reach of the reason. I saw that you were
Helen—my Helen—the Helen of a thousand dreams—she whose visionary lips
had so often lingered upon my own in the divine trance of passion—she whom
the great Giver of all Good had preordained to be mine—mine only—if not
now, alas! then at least hereafter and forever, in the Heavens.

During the Providence visit, Poe and Helen were seen about town frequently, in various bold embraces. At one soiree, a friend recalled that the
two of them had been behaving strangely, as if they were suppressing
emotions, when "Simultaneously both arose from their chairs and walked
toward the center of the room. Meeting, [Poe] held [Helen] in his arms,
kissed her; they stood for a moment, then he led her to his seat. There was
a dead silence through all this strange meeting."

The following day, they walked out to Swan Point Cemetery; such
secluded places were popular spots for lovers' trysts in the nineteenth
century. Poe asked Helen to save him from himself, and he told her of
Jane Stanard and her kindness to him after the death of Fanny Allan. He
went so far as to compare Helen to Jane. Poe revealed that Jane had been
the first "Helen" of his poem, "the first, purely ideal love of my soul."
Helen in turn told Poe of some early losses of her own; they thus seemed
joined in mutual psychic empathy, their destinies conjoined.

Poe proposed marriage on the spot, but Helen would not consent, she
said, right away. One reason, Helen said, was ill health and age. She was
old to be marrying, for the time. Her sister and mother were not wealthy
and depended on her to a degree for their financial well-being. Poe, it
must be said, did not exactly hold out the prospect of riches. Helen also

had a very weak heart and a nervous temperament that she feared might not survive the physical elements of marriage. She also frankly needed time to consider the offer in light of Poe's erratic life and in light of the still-circulating rumors about his moral character.

Another of the letters Poe wrote Helen upon returning to Fordham attempts to answer the charges, so often brought against him, of unprincipled behavior:

I must now speak to you the truth or nothing. It was in mere indulgence, then, of the sense to which I refer, that, at one dark epoch of my late life, for the sake of one who, deceiving and betraying, still loved me much, I sacrificed what seemed in the eyes of men my honor, rather than abandon what was honor in hers and in my own.—But, alas! for nearly three years I have been ill, poor, living out of the world; and thus, as I now painfully see, have afforded opportunity to my enemies—and especially to one, the most malignant and pertinacious of all fiends—[a woman whose loathsome love I could do nothing but repel with scorn—] to slander me, in private society, without my knowledge and thus with impunity.

These hyperbolic letters sound a lot like those that the younger Poe had written to John Allan from Charlottesville, when he was defending himself against what he believed to be similarly unfair assessments of his character.

Helen continued to consider Poe's offer, wavering between acceptance and rejection. Poe's emotional state was worse than ever before. Afraid that Helen would turn him away, he continued to pursue the already-married Annie Richmond, calling her "my own sweet *sister* Annie, my *pure* beautiful angel—*wife* of my soul—to be mine hereafter & *forever in the Heavens.*" Annie's response no longer surives, but one wonders what she thought of Poe, knowing that at the same time he was making such rapturous claims about her effect on his "soul," he was professing undying love for her next-door neighbor.

Poe was close to a complete breakdown, and he returned to Providence on 4 November to see Helen. But instead of seeing her, he told Annie in a letter of 16 November, he bought two ounces of laudanum and took a

227

train to Boston, where in a hotel room he ingested half of the drug in a suicide attempt.

I remember nothing distinctly, from that moment until I found myself in Providence—I went to bed & wept through a long, long, hideous night of despair—When the day broke, I arose & endeavored to quiet my mind by a rapid walk in the cold, keen air—but all would not do*—the demon tormented me still. Finally I procured two ounces of laudanum & without returning to my Hotel, took the cars back to Boston. When I arrived, I wrote you a letter, in which I opened my whole heart to you—to you—my Annie, whom I so madly, so distractedly love—I told you how my struggles were more than I could bear— how my soul revolted from saying the words which were to be said—and that not even for your dear sake, could I bring myself to say them. I then reminded you of that holy promise, which was the last I exacted from you in parting—the promise that, under all circumstances, you would come to me on my bed of death—I implored you to come* then*—mentioning the place where I should be found in Boston—Having written this letter, I swallowed about half the laudanum & hurried to the Post-Office—intending not to take the rest until I saw you—for, I did not doubt for one moment, that* my own *Annie would keep her sacred promise—But I had not calculated on the strength of the laudanum, for, before I reached the Post Office my reason was entirely gone, & the letter was never put in. Let me pass over, my darling* Sister, *the awful horrors which succeeded—A friend was at hand, who aided & (if it can be called saving) saved me—but it is only within the last three days that I have been able to remember what occurred in that dreary interval—It appears that, after the laudanum was rejected from the stomach, I became calm, & to a casual observer, sane—so that I was suffered to go back to Providence—Here I saw her, & spoke, for your sake, the words which you urged me to speak—Ah Annie Annie! my Annie!—is your heart so strong?—is there no hope!—is there none?—I feel that I must die if I persist, & yet, how can I now retract with honor?*

This hysterical letter suggests desperation and, more than that, insecurity. After recovering in Boston, Poe returned to Providence to try to see Helen.

In addition to his letters, Poe's condition can be adduced from a daguerreotype portrait taken of him in a downtown Providence studio on a Thursday morning, the ninth of November, four days after his failed suicide attempt. This picture is one of the most haunting images in American literature. It is dark, taken against a dimly lit background, and shows a person who might very well be crazed. The gaze is at once penetrating and vacant, the darkness of the irises blacker than oblivion, the rings around the eye sockets just as deep. Rather than being an image of despair, the picture suggests complete disconnection with the material world, and in fact was eventually named the "Ultima Thule" daguerreotype (a Latin phrase used to suggest the extreme limits of travel and discovery), after the lines in Poe's poem "Dream-Land":

I have reached these lands but newly
From an ultimate dim Thule—
From a wild weird clime that lieth, sublime
Out of SPACE—out of TIME.

Most telling about the image is the fact that everything is slightly out of kilter. The nose is askew, the eyes asymmetrical, the mouth turned precipitously down at one corner and up at the other. Even the moustache, usually so delicately waxed and combed, is bushy and unevenly trimmed.

It is clear from the image that drink had also taken its toll physically on Poe, who was just thirty-nine years old. No one looking at the picture would have said that it was of a person who had once swum six miles against the current of the James River on a hot summer day. The skin is puffy and pasty and one eyelid appears to be drooping. It bears an uncanny resemblance to the famous photograph of Baudelaire by Nadar. In fact, Baudelaire wrote of the "Ultima Thule" daguerreotype that in it Poe looked "very French" and noted that despite the immense masculinity of the high foreheard, it was "all in all, a very feminine face. The eyes are vast, very beautiful and abstracted." Baudelaire might have been describing a Poe heroine.

Later that day, Poe got wildly drunk and appeared at Helen's home on Benefit Street, begging her this time not for her hand in marriage, but for her help in restoring his sanity. Perversely, Helen then told him that she would marry him and took him at once to see a famous local physician, Dr. Abraham H. Okie. After spending an hour with Poe, Okie diagnosed him as suffering from "cerebral congestion," essentially the same diagnosis as that given by Loui Shew's physician, Valentine Mott. Okie recommended rest, but had no cure or even treatment to offer. In another bizarre twist, Poe was taken into care in the home of William Pabodie, a neighbor of Helen's who wanted to marry her himself. Poe apparently stayed in Pabodie's home for several weeks, through the rest of November and for most of December, writing Helen passionate love letters while doing the same to Annie Richmond. To Helen, he claimed, "The terrible excitement under which I suffered, has subsided, and I am as calm as I well could be, remembering what has past. *Still* the Shadow of Evil *haunts* me, and, although tranquil, I am unhappy. I dread the Future.—and you alone can reassure me." Then two days later:

You allude to your having been "tortured by reports which have all since been explained to your entire satisfaction". On this point my mind is fully made up. I will rest neither by night nor day until I bring those who have slandered me into the light of day—until I expose them, and their motives, to the public eye. I have the means and I will ruthlessly employ them. On one point let me caution you, dear Helen. No sooner will Mrs E. hear of my proposals to yourself, than she will set in operation every conceivable chicanery to frustrate me:— and, if you are not prepared for her arts, she will infallibly succeed—for her whole study, throughout life, has been the gratification of her malignity by such means as any other human being would die rather than adopt. . . . Helen, beware of this woman! She did not cease her persecutions here. My poor Virginia was continually tortured (although not deceived) by her anonymous letters, and on her death-bed declared that Mrs. E. had been her murderer. Have I not a right to hate this fiend & to caution you against her? You will now comprehend what I mean in saying that the only thing for which I found it impossible to forgive Mrs O. was her reception of Mrs E.

Neighbors, friends, and relatives of Helen were constantly stepping in to advise her against marrying Poe, but this seems only to have galvanized her resolve to go through with it.

Perhaps seeing the inevitable, on 15 December Helen's mother had a lawyer draw up what was in effect a prenuptial agreement in which she obtained full control of the family estate, putting it out of Poe's reach. Poe agreed to the arrangement, signing the document willingly and apparently without regret. By 20 December he had recovered sufficiently to give a lecture entitled "The Poetic Principle" to the Franklin Lyceum in Providence. Helen sat in the front row attentively, fully committed to marrying him.

Two nights later, Helen and her family gave an engagement party at Benefit Street. When Poe appeared, he was drunk. Probably nervous over having to perform under the stressful scrutiny of Helen's family, he may have steeled himself with a few pre-party libations. His extreme susceptibility to the effects of alcohol undid him again, and the event was disastrous. The next morning, not learning from his mistakes the night before, Poe apparently took another glass of wine and then went to apologize in person to Helen. He proposed to atone for his mistakes and wrote a note to the rector of the local Episcopal church asking him to publish the banns for their marriage. He gave the note to William Pabodie, who, hoping still to prevent the marriage, did not deliver it. Unknowing, Poe wrote to Muddy on Saturday 23 December that he and Helen would be married on Monday, Christmas Day, and would leave for Fordham "on Tuesday on the first train."

But the marriage never took place. The same afternoon that Poe wrote to tell Muddy his good news, he and Helen were sitting, as they often did, in an alcove in the local library, when a private communication was handed to Helen "cautioning me against this *imprudent marriage* & informing me of many things in Mr. Poe's recent career with which I was previously unacquainted. I was at the same time informed that he had *already* violated the solemn promises that he had made to me & my friends on the preceding evening." Shocked, Helen cancelled preparations for the wedding.

It was a good while before Poe accepted the fact that he and Helen were not to be husband and wife. He kept writing her, imploring her to

231

reconsider. She sympathized with his feelings and agreed that much injustice had been brought down on him, but she would not relent. Poe's last letter to Helen from Fordham, dated 25 January 1849, addresses her not as "my *dearest* Helen," but as "Dear Madam" and closes with the equally formal "E. A. Poe."

> *In commencing this letter, need I say to you, after what has passed between us, that no amount of provocation on your part, or on the part of your friends, shall induce me to speak ill of you even in my own defence? . . .*

> *Alas! I bitterly lament my own weaknesses, & nothing is farther from my heart than to blame you for yours—May Heaven shield you from all ill! So far I have assigned no reason for my declining to fulfil our engagement—I had none but the suspicious & grossly insulting parsimony of the arrangements into which you suffered yourself to be forced by your Mother—Let my letters & acts speak for themselves—It has been my intention to say simply, that our marriage was postponed on account of your ill health—Have you really said or done anything which can preclude our placing the rupture on such footing? If not, I shall persist in the statement & thus this unhappy matter will die quietly away—*

Despite the fact that she would not marry Poe, Helen nevertheless always thought fondly of him and was adamant in her belief in his literary genius. She became one of the most vocal of Poe's defenders after Griswold published his slanderous memoir of the author. In 1860 Whitman published a book-length defense of her one-time love, *Edgar Poe and His Critics*. Lest anyone doubt the depth of her awe, she wrote, "We confess to a half-faith in the ordinary superstition of the significance of anagrams when we find, in the transposed letters of Edgar Poe's name, the words 'a God-peer.'"

CHAPTER 9

THE JOURNEY AND
THE LIGHTHOUSE

(1849)

Devastated by his failed romance with Helen Whitman, Poe began the year 1849 in not much better shape than he had begun the previous year. In the first months, he foundered emotionally, reaching out desperately to whoever of his lady friends he felt could give him consolation. He turned first to Annie Richmond, making the best of a hopeless situation when he wrote her that he felt unburdened now that Helen had called off their engagement. But Annie was a perceptive woman, and she could see that Poe was merely putting a positive face on what was for him a personal tragedy almost equal to the death of Virginia. To Annie he made an offering of his spiritual love, as opposed to the physical love he said he had felt for Helen, telling her that "there is *nothing* in this world worth living for except love—love not such as I once thought I felt for [Helen], but such as burns in my very soul for *you*—so pure—so unworldly—a love which would make *all* sacrifices for your sake."

In February, however, Jane Locke, who felt insulted by Poe's rejection of her, turned vindictive and started a campaign to convince Charles Richmond, Annie's husband, that his wife and Poe had more than just a platonic relationship. The viciousness of Jane Locke's attack on Poe recalls Elizabeth Ellet's attempts to disrupt the courtship between Poe and Fanny Osgood. Like Ellet, Jane Locke was successful. Poe was devastated that he had lost Annie, just as he had lost Helen, Loui, Fanny, and

Virginia. But surprisingly, this time Poe lay down in defeat and took the pain inflicted on him without lashing back. He told Annie that it now only remained "to consult *your* happiness—which under all circumstances, will be & must be mine." Probably Poe was tired of the stress of his embroilments and entanglements and decided to accept this new fate with docility. He did not want to sacrifice Annie's friendship, but felt he had to.

Poe had experienced a new, uncharacteristic surge of creative energy. For the first six months of the year, he was active as a writer and a lecturer. He published with some regularity, often in the Boston *Flag of Our Union*, a popular weekly. He paid tribute to Annie in "Landor's Cottage," a sentimental, idealized sketch in which the faithful love is living in seclusion and serenity, untouchable by those other than Poe. Poe also wrote a bizarre tale of the future, a dystopian fantasy called "Mellonta Tauta," which airs his strong antidemocratic views. Set in 2848, one thousand years in the future, "Mellonta Tauta" is, like other Poe works, a blend of parody, social criticism, and science fiction, with some political satire and mysticism thrown in for good measure. Poe's brushes in life with the rabble-rousing mob are much in evidence in these late tales. They appear variously as friends, editors, and authority figures—but all are offensive and presented as beneath the aristocratic Poe, who firmly disbelieved, as he had told Lowell some years ago, in the innate goodness of man and in the idea of human perfectibility. In "Mellonta Tauta," Poe coarsely describes democracy as a "very admirable form of government—for dogs" (880).

The credulous mind of the masses is also criticized in "Von Kempelen and His Discovery," a tale in which a character asserts that he can turn lead into gold. Poe wrote "Von Kempelen" as an outright hoax, playing on the California gold rush of 1848; he hoped that, like "M. Valdemar," it would fool people into believing it true and produce another sensation like the earlier story had. However, Poe had trouble placing the tale, despite the topicality of its subject; although he offered it to Duyckinck for a pitiful ten dollars, that editor turned it down, even though he had helped Poe in the past.

Another story is a revenge tale, "Hop-Frog," that shows Poe's bilious mood following his failed courtship of Helen Whitman. "Only think of your Eddy writing a story with *such* a name as 'Hop-Frog,'" Poe wrote Annie Richmond. "You would never guess the subject (which is a terrible one) from the title, I am sure." The story is indeed one of Poe's weaker efforts, but biographically it is fascinating, for it allegorizes what Poe felt was his shabby treatment at the hands of editors, publishers, and fellow writers. In the story, a sadistic king orders about his court jester, "a dwarf and a cripple" (899), forcing him to bend to the most horrid humiliations in order to survive. One of these is forcing him to drink wine because he knows that one sip will turn the jester mad. Hop-Frog gains his revenge by persuading the king and his seven ministers to dress up as orangutans soaked in tar and covered with flax. The dwarf effects the release of his love, the servant girl Trippetta, at the masquerade at which the king and his courtiers will show off their practical joke. A thrill seeker, the king agrees to be chained together with his ministers in a circle and hung from the chandelier in the center of the ballroom. Thus enchained, they are held captive while Hop-Frog, "pretending to scrutinize the king more closely," holds the flambeau to the flaxed coat and watches it instantly burst into flames (907).

"I now see distinctly," he said, "what manner of people these maskers are. They are a great king and his seven privy-councillors,—a king who does not scruple to strike a defenceless girl and his seven councillors who abet him in the outrage. As for myself, I am simply Hop-Frog, the jester—and this is my last jest."

Owing to the high combustibility of both the flax and the tar to which it adhered, the dwarf had scarcely made an end of his brief speech before the work of vengeance was complete. The eight corpses swung in their chains, a fetid, blackened, hideous, and indistinguishable mass. The cripple hurled his torch at them, clambered leisurely to the ceiling, and disappeared through the sky-light.

It is supposed that Trippetta, stationed on the roof of the saloon, had been the accomplice of her friend in his fiery revenge, and that, together, they effected their escape to their own country: for neither was seen again. (908)

"For neither was seen again": prophetically, for Poe, this would come true, but in his revenge fantasy, Poe escaped, with Virginia; and as in the earlier tale "Eleonora," he escaped to an otherworld of happiness and peace.

235

"Hop-Frog" is full of self-commentary. The character's name is not his real name, since like Poe he was not given one at baptism (900). The jester's excessive susceptibility to wine is another obvious self-reference, as are his "large eyes [which] *gleamed* rather than shone"; Trippetta, whose name echoes that of Virginia, is described as thin and "pale as a corpse" (904). And Hop-Frog's agility may be a reflection of Poe's own youthful athletic prowess. The despicable king and his "electors" are reminiscent of John Allan, who was called "the Elector of Moldavia." More important, "Hop-Frog" may also be a parody by Poe of much of his earlier work, a self-mockery that shows the bitter depths to which he felt he had descended. The king and his court ("large, corpulent, oily men" [899]) may suggest Poe's various editors, especially those like Billy Burton, who grew fat while Poe grew poor. In contrast, Hop-Frog is "inventive in the way of getting up pageant, suggesting novel characters, and arranging costume," as a creative writer is, and he works at the beck and call of the king, who orders him to "let us have the benefit of your invention. We want characters—characters, man—something novel—out of the way. We are wearied with this excessive sameness" (901).

Yet a jester is only good for entertainment, which is probably what Poe felt at his lowest moments. More and more Poe came to believe that these people were contemptuous of him, or, at best, indifferent, like the king in a fairy tale throwing coppers at the feet of his impoverished subjects. More revealing is the narrator's emphasis on the "chaining arrangement," in which the actions of each person enchained depend on those of the other seven; this image recalls Poe's theory of unity of effect and his strictures against the disarrangement of parts. The protagonist's name, Hop-Frog, suggests Poe, as "Hop" is "Poh" spelled backwards—the nasty slight commonly inflicted on David Poe, the author's father. "Frog" recalls Poe's derisive name for the literary clique he despised more than all, the Frogpondians, or New England intellectuals.

Even specific stories seem to hover in the background of "Hop-Frog": the orangutans from "The Murders in the Rue Morgue," the conflagration from "Metzengerstein," the carnival scene from "William Wilson," the masquerades from "The Masque of the Red Death" and "The Cask

236

of Amontillado"; the dwarfishness recalls Morella the child, the perverseness most all of Poe's obsessive narrators. Even the devolution of the
House of Usher, with twin sufferers Roderick and Madeleine, seems
mirrored in the ascension, to angels and the heavens, of Hop-Frog
and Trippetta at the end of the story.

Such fantasies suggest Poe's disgust with the literary world and with
his stagnant career. Both now seemed unbearably bitter, like a wine too
soon decanted. However, at least to his acquaintances, Poe put a positive
face on his work, and he still had great aspirations. In February, he boldly
told his steadfast friend Frederick Thomas: "Literature is the most noble
of professions. In fact, it is about the only one fit for a man." Nonetheless,
when given the occasion to do so, Poe vented his rage. At this time, about
his only reliable outlet for writing was the *Southern Literary Messenger*,
for he was good friends with its current editor, John Reuben Thompson.
Thompson was only too happy to print Poe's anonymous critique of
James Russell Lowell's "A Fable for Critics," which was attacked as a tract
penned by a rabid abolitionist, full of blind bigotry. Poe's pretext for the
remark was Lowell's omission of southern writers (and, of course, his slap
at Poe for being "two-fifths genius and three-fifths sheer fudge"), but it
was still a cheap shot that was delivered in a venomous, injured tone.

Poe still held out hope for "The Stylus," and wrote cheery, optimistic
letters to his friends Frederick Thomas and George Eveleth, prophesy-
ing momentous events in his future. But like his concessionary letter to
Annie Richmond earlier in the year, these statements do not have the ring
of sincerity about them. They suggest instead a tired and defeated
warrior, relieved to be able to lay down his arms.

Then, in late April, an act of providence—or so it seemed to Poe, for
all at once "The Stylus" was revived, his reputation was poised on the
brink of a huge growth curve, and it looked like fame and wealth would
soon be his. The divine agency came through a letter from one Edward
H. N. Patterson of Oquawka, Illinois, who wrote Poe of his honest
admiration for his talents and his desire to underwrite his dream magazine. Patterson, though only twenty-one, had inherited the local newspaper from his father. He was well set financially, and thus the ideal

backer for Poe's magazine. He seemed serious, for he asked Poe for detailed figures on the number of subscribers that would be needed, printing costs, and so on. Patterson wanted the literary contents to be exclusively under Poe's aegis, "not doubting that even a cheap Magazine, under your editorial control, could be made to pay well, and at the same time exert a beneficial influence upon American Literature." Poe must have felt that he was dreaming.

An added layer of the fantastic was the fact that Patterson had written the letter on the eighteenth of December of the previous year; the letter had been incorrectly forwarded to a post office near Fordham, where Poe rarely called for his mail. Poe must therefore have been worried that Patterson's offer might have expired, so he quickly replied with the details Patterson asked for, in the process getting in his own requirements: "We must aim high—address the intellect—the higher classes—of the country (with reference, also, to a certain amount of foreign circulation) and put the work at $5." He continued: "Such a Mag. would begin to pay after 1000 subscribers; end with 5000 would be a fortune worth talking about:— but there is no earthly reason why, under proper management, and with energy and talent, the work might not be made to circulate, at the end of a few years—(say 5) 20,000 copies—in which case it would give a clear income of 70 or 80,000 dollars—even if conducted in the most expensive manner, paying the highest European prices for contributions & designs. I need not add that such a Mag. would exercise a literary and other influence never yet exercised in America." For added effect, Poe then flashed his most impressive credentials: "I presume you know that during the second year of its existence, the 'S. L. Messenger' rose from less than 1000 to 5000 subs., and that 'Graham', in 18 months after my joining it, went up from 5000 to 52,000. I do not imagine that a $5 Mag. could ever be forced into so great a circulation as this latter; but, under certain circumstances, I would answer for 20,000. The whole income from Graham's 52,000 never went beyond 15,000 $:—the proportional expenses of the $3 Mags. being so very much greater than those of the $5 ones."

In further correspondence, the editor and the publisher agreed on a working plan: Poe would make out a new prospectus and a list of possible subscribers; they would divide the profits equally; the title page would state that the magazine would be published simultaneously in "New York and St. Louis" (the nearest large city to Oquawka, Illinois) but that the actual printing would be done in the plant at Patterson's newspaper. Patterson concluded that if Poe were agreeable to these requirements, he would visit him in New York "during the latter part of July or 1st of August" to complete their arrangements, the first issue of the magazine tentatively slated for release in early January 1850.

To obtain the necessary one thousand subscribers, Poe decided "to take a tour through the principal States—especially West & South— visiting the small towns more particularly than the large ones—lecturing as I went, to pay expenses—and staying sufficiently long in each place to interest my personal friends (old College & West Point acquaintances scattered all over the land) in the success of the enterprize." He asked Patterson to forward an advance of fifty dollars to him in Richmond, where he would start his tour.

Poe had planned to leave for his journey south on June 11, but he was delayed until June 29, probably because he didn't have enough money for the train fare. In early June, Poe went to Lowell, ostensibly to find subscribers for "The Stylus," but probably most likely to visit Annie Richmond. While there, Poe befriended Annie's brother, Bardwell, who was the headmaster of a local school. Bardwell was intrigued with Poe and thought him something of a literary demigod, rarely straying from his presence, so as not to lose "the benefit of his original thoughts, which were continually dripping from his lips." Poe must have felt gratified by Bardwell's puppy-dog behavior, and possibly also grateful to him for introducing him to a twenty-one-year-old teacher at his school, Eliza Jane Butterfield, whom Poe visited at least twice. According to Bardwell, Poe swiftly courted the woman, and he may have proposed marriage. This is not certain; but with the name "Eliza," the woman must have struck Poe's fancy and engaged his psychic memory, both of Eliza Poe and of Virginia Eliza Clemm. Whatever the nature of the relationship, it left Annie fiercely jealous, and by the end of the visit, Poe was again melancholy. The novelist

Elizabeth Oakes Smith found him to be ill at ease and "emaciated." He told Annie, "My life seems wasted—the future looks a dreary blank."

He returned to Fordham to find Stella Lewis helping out the household by doing some chores that Muddy could not handle, and lending her some money. To return the favor, the night before he left, Poe sent Rufus Griswold a long article on Stella to include in the next edition of his anthology, *Female Poets of America*, the current one, Poe told Griswold, not doing justice to Mrs. Lewis. Possibly just before, Poe may have told Muddy that he wanted Griswold to "act as his Literary Executor and superintend the publication of his works," or so Muddy claimed in her preface to Griswold's edition of Poe. Choosing Griswold was logical: the two men had repaired their friendship, and, most important, Griswold had acted as press agent or literary executor for many of Poe's fellow authors, among them Fanny Osgood.

Other things transpired that summer evening. Poe and Muddy spent the night at the Lewises' house in Brooklyn, and Poe told Muddy that he felt he might never see her again. He asked her to write his biography after he passed on. Stella also found Poe to be melancholy, even morose. They dined the following afternoon; then at five o'clock Poe left for Richmond. He took with him a valise of clothing and probably also a trunk of books and manuscripts. Loui Shew reported that he also carried the miniature portrait of Eliza, on the back of which he had written, "My adored Mother! E. A. Poe, New York." Once on the steamboat, however, his mood lightened, and he told Muddy, "God bless you, my own darling mother. Do not fear for Eddy! See how good I will be while I am away from you, and will come back to love and comfort you."

These were the last words he spoke to Muddy, and the last she would hear from him for some time. She returned to Fordham and awaited a letter. One finally arrived, not for her but for Stella, written ten days later from Philadelphia. Its contents could not have cheered her, for Poe wrote that he had been "*so* ill" that he could "hardly hold the pen." Poe described spasms, violent retching, and bodily weakness, and concluded that he had been infected by cholera, part of the vast epidemic that swept across the country that summer; the plague had reached as far west as

California, because the virulent disease was transported by the gold rushers. Poe felt bereft, hopeless: "It is no use to reason with me *now*; I must die. I have no desire to live since I have done 'Eureka.' I could accomplish nothing more. For your sake it would be sweet to live, but we must die together. You have been all in all to me, darling, ever beloved mother, and dearest, truest friend." Other evidence suggests that Poe was not in the grip of cholera but was simply having anxiety attacks that left him delusional and inconsolable, as he often was. Poe could be soothed, but never really comforted. Nothing could completely extinguish the darkness.

Arriving in Philadelphia on 30 June, he at once began drinking and lost the trunk that contained the manuscripts of the lectures he intended to deliver. A couple of days later he showed up, "pale and haggard, with a wild and frightened expression in his eyes" at the studio of John Sartain, a Cockney printer, illustrator, and engraver who had supplied many of the elegant plates for *Graham's Magazine* when Poe was editor there. He asked Sartain for "a refuge and protection" and told him a harrowing tale that began with a confinement in prison and ended with an escape from some assassins who were following him on the train from New York.

Poe contended that he had "overheard some men who sat a few seats back of him plotting how they should kill him and then throw him off from the platform of the car." He said it was only due to his overacute sense of hearing that he could make out their words, as they were speaking in hushed tones. He did not let on that he had heard them, and when the train stopped at an outlying station, he jumped off and gave them the slip. He had then gone on to Philadelphia. When Sartain asked him why the mysterious killers were pursuing him, Poe became evasive, answering first that it was for revenge and then for "a woman trouble."

Sartain thought that Poe was not only delusional, but suicidal as well, for when the author asked for a razor to shave off his moustache, the better to disguise himself from his would-be attackers, Sartain offered only a pair of scissors. The printer cut off Poe's moustache, and this seemed to calm him. Later that night, Poe suddenly expressed a desire to go to the Fairmount Waterworks, a central park overlooking the Schuylkill River.

Complaining that his shoes were worn thin, he borrowed a pair of Sartain's slippers, and his friend accompanied him on the omnibus, still fearing for his safety. They reached their destination and embarked on foot for the park, crossing a bridge—similar to the top of the aqueduct that Poe liked to stroll across near Fordham. Sartain recalled: "I kept on his left side, and on approaching the foot of the bridge guided him off to the right by a gentle pressure, until we reached the lofty flight of steep wooden steps which ascended almost to the top of the reservoir." They sat down briefly to rest, and Poe confided that upon arriving in Philadelphia he had been arrested for drunkenness and confined briefly to the city's massive Moyamensing Prison, although there is no record of this ever happening.

More distressing, Poe told of grotesque and sadistic things that he dreamt were done to him by the prison guards. He said that in one dream a guard asked him if he would like to stroll around the place and that when they came "to a cauldron of boiling spirits," asked him if he wanted a drink. Poe declined, thinking that if he had said yes, "I should have been lifted over the brim and dipped into the hot liquid up to the lip, like Tantalus." Having escaped the guards' snare, in the dream they had then brought to him "my mother," Maria Clemm, "to blast my sight by seeing them first saw off her feet at the ankles, then her legs to the knees, her thighs at the hips, and so on." The horror of the imagined scene, according to Sartain, "threw him into a sort of convulsion."

Poe was disabled by the experience for about ten days. On or about the tenth of July, he recovered, found his missing valise at the railway station and was prepared to continue his journey south but did not have the money for a ticket. So he made the rounds, calling about the city on well-to-do Philadelphians whose slight acquaintance he may have made when he had lived there, asking to borrow money. After several days of being made to wait in offices and anterooms without the prized loans, Poe wearily climbed the four flights of stairs up to the *Quaker City* offices of George Lippard, another old friend from his *Graham's Magazine* days who was editing a weekly newspaper. Poe told Lippard that he had "no bread to eat—no place to sleep." Lippard had just paid his rent and so had no extra funds himself, but he good-naturedly went door to door, trying to locate anyone willing to help. The cholera epidemic had sent many people out to the country or had otherwise scared them into posting notices on their premises that they were receiving no visitors, fearful of contracting the contagion themselves. Finally, however, Lippard was able to scrape together enough for Poe's fare. At 10 p.m. on 13 July 1849, Poe boarded the train for Baltimore, continuing on to Richmond.

Poe arrived in Richmond the next day, the fourteenth of July. In returning for this second extended visit to the scene of his youth, he must have had mixed feelings. This was the place of strained relations with John Allan and jealousy of Allan's second wife and family, the place of the deaths of three women who meant much to him—Eliza Poe, Fanny Allan, and Jane Stanard. Yet it was also the place where he first made his mark as a man of letters, and where he spent the beginning of his married life. He never wavered from his conception of himself as a southerner, and always thought of Richmond as his home. He had told his cousin George Poe some years earlier, "Richmond is my home, and a letter to that City will always reach me in whatever part of the world I may be." He put up at the Swan Tavern, a cheap, two-story hostelry built in the 1780s. He called at the *Messenger* offices and collected two letters from Patterson, with the fifty dollars promised. The weather was hot and humid, and Poe's spirits were low. He was terribly homesick for Muddy: "I never wanted to see any one half so bad as I want to see my own darling mother. . . . When I am with you I can bear anything, but when I am away from you I am too miserable to live."

Some of Poe's homesickness, however, was assuaged by his reuniting with his sister, Rosalie, still living with the MacKenzie family. Rose took him to visit a relative of Fanny Allan's, Susan Archer Talley, a young poet whom he admired and in whom he may have had a romantic interest. Susan idolized Poe, as previous women had done, finding him refined and chivalrous, the very model of the southern gentleman—an image that Poe must have taken comfort in and encouraged, after his nightmarish experiences in Philadelphia.

Susan, however, did not become the object of his affections. Rather, it was his childhood sweetheart, Elmira Shelton nee Royster, whom he began courting. Friends reacquainted them, and by late July Poe had proposed marriage to the recently widowed Elmira—his fifth and final attempt to remarry. As with previous women, Poe's pursuit of Elmira was impetuous and brash. She, however, did not seem to mind the circumstances, and much to Poe's relief and happiness, by late August, reports began to circulate around Richmond that she had consented to marry him.

As with Helen Whitman, however, the path to Elmira's hand in marriage was neither smooth nor easy. Like Helen, Elmira made Poe wait several weeks while she weighed the evidence about his character, and it is something of a wonder that she consented to become his wife, for many people in Richmond that summer witnessed Poe on the binge. Perhaps encouraged (or even required) by Elmira, on 27 August Poe officially joined the local division of the Sons of Temperance, and attended his first meeting. There is little question but that Elmira loved Poe, for in marrying him she moved from financial stability to a much less secure position. Her husband's will provided for her only if she "remained his widow"; her share of his estate decreased by seventy-five percent if she married again.

Poe traveled around the tidewater area giving his lecture, "The Poetic Principle," attended by both Rosalie and Elmira, who, again like Helen before her, dutifully sat in the front row of the lecture hall, taking his measure with her eyes. These lectures, however, brought in very little money. By late September, Poe had made only enough to cover his bill at the Swan Tavern, with two dollars left over. He could not send any money back to Muddy, which he had hoped to do, and although Poe had rapt audiences and also some adoring young women mooning over his renditions of poems like "The Raven" and "Ulalume," the lecture series had not been a success. Most discouragingly, he had rounded up only a few subscribers for "The Stylus."

On or about the twenty-second of September, Elmira formally accepted Poe's offer of marriage, writing Maria Clemm that she felt that their "spirits" would be "congenial" and complimenting Muddy highly, perhaps trying to forestall some frosty reception of her as the replacement of the mother in Poe's life. On 26 September, Poe called on John R. Thompson at the *Messenger* and briskly told him that he was leaving in the morning for New York, via a Baltimore steamer, and was planning to stop in Philadelphia en route in order to spend three days editing the poems of a Philadelphia piano manufacturer's wife for one hundred dollars, hardly a cheering commission, but one which paid handsomely and would defray his travel expenses. To Elmira he was much less businesslike and self-assured. Poe was feverish when he left, and she later recalled that when he said goodbye, "he paused a moment as if reflecting," and then said to her, "'I have a singular feeling, amounting to a presentiment, that this will be our last meeting until we meet to part no more,' then walked slowly and sadly away."

On 27 September Poe left Richmond for Baltimore. The contradictory stories of what happened next are a melange of second- and third-hand reports. Little can be certain, but Poe probably sailed on the *Pocahontas*, which arrived in Baltimore on the twenty-eighth. Five days later, on the third of October, his old friend Joseph Evans Snodgrass received a note from a young printer named Joseph W. Walker who told him he had seen a man "stretched unconscious upon a broad plank across some barrels on the sidewalk" and had recognized him as Poe. Snodgrass raced down to Gunner's Hall, a tavern operated by an Irishman that was being used that day as a polling place for the Fourth Ward. There he found Poe "sitting in an arm-chair, with his head dropped forward, so stupefied by liquor and so altered from the neatly-dressed and vivacious gentleman which he was when I last had the pleasure of a call from him, that, unaided, I should not have distinguished him from the crowd of less-intoxicated men . . . at the tavern." Snodgrass initially intended to take Poe to his residence, but then thought better of it and conveyed him to the nearest hospital, at Washington College.

Poe, his face "haggard" and "bloated," his whole body "unwashed" and "repulsive," was attended by Dr. John J. Moran, who, like Snodgrass and almost everyone else, published his own account of Poe's last days, seeking to cash in on the melodramatic story. Poe remained hospitalized for the next three days, alternately lucid and delirious, sometimes cool to the touch, at other times his whole body feeling like dying coals. Vitality seemed to ebb and flow out of him, in gasps and spasms, the result, almost everyone thought, of alcohol poisoning. Poe's cousin Neilson later wrote Griswold that he was certain Poe's death was attributable to drink; however, Moran, in his account, grandly declared that "enter[ing] upon this work fully prepared, with living testimony, legally indorsed, in proof of all that I shall say," Poe "did not die under the influence of any kind of intoxicating drink," thus rebutting "an oft-repeated slander."

The delirium continued until Saturday evening, when Poe began calling out the name "Reynolds." At three the following morning Poe suddenly became enfeebled, seemed to rest a short time, then gently moved his head and said, "*Lord help my poor Soul!*" He died around 5 a.m., aged forty. Moran listed the cause of death as "congestion of the brain."

As to exactly what Poe died of, possibilities abound, and speculation seems to grow more varied with each passing year: "brain fever"; alcohol poisoning; pneumonia; epilepsy; diabetes; even rabies. Maria Clemm later speculated that when he arrived in Baltimore, he met up with some old West Point buddies who induced him to break his temperance pledge, with the result that he got drunk and beaten up by some ruffians; a favorite cabal of some dockside saloons was to dope a sailor's grog with laudanum, then carry the unconscious man outside, clean out his pockets, and leave him in the street. Another theory has it that Poe was the victim of political violence, since it was election day and he was found near a polling place.

Poe's persisting, diagnosed ailment—some lesion on the brain—was probably the root cause of what killed him, whether a diabetic coma or a bite from a rabid dog. All of the diseases or injuries that have been mentioned would have caused some sort of inflammation of the tissues in the brain, and alcohol would have exacerbated the effect. According to the autopsy and diagnosis made after Poe's death by one of the staff surgeons at Washington College Hospital, as printed in the *Baltimore Sun* on

8 October 1849, Poe's death was caused by congestion of the brain as well as cerebral inflammation, or encephalitis, brought on by exposure. This explanation is consistent with Snodgrass's description of how poorly clothed Poe was when he found him, and with the wintry weather conditions on that day. Whether the brain lesion was independent of Poe's other problems or whether an escape through drugs and alcohol caused the brain lesion will never be known. However, a brain tumor is the best explanation for Poe's peculiar behavior throughout his life.

Poe rarely felt that he was in control of his destiny, but that some insidious fate instead controlled *him*. In his last years, after the death of Virginia, it is clear he felt that some evil destiny was pulling him inexorably down into a vortex of terror and oblivion, like Arthur Gordon Pym at the end of his harrowing tale or the narrator of "MS. Found in a Bottle." Was his death something that he demanded of himself? Charles Baudelaire remarked that it was "almost a suicide . . . a suicide prepared for a long time."

The years after Virginia's death were also filled with foreboding and omens of ill fortune. Poe several times remarked that he felt his life was near an end, that he saw only a blank future ahead. His cheery predictions of success with "The Stylus" were unconvincing to most of his associates. Women saw in him a doomed romantic, someone whose life was spent preparing for a terrible end. And this is the baseline terror in almost all of Poe's imaginative writings—the fear of coming to nothingness, of oblivion.

A fragmentary tale written in the spring of 1849 conveys this in a remarkable, eerily prophetic way. Untitled by Poe but appearing as "The Light House" in most modern editions, the story is narrated by a lighthouse keeper through a fragmentary journal that tells of his circumstances. The narrator is an author who has been given the appointment as a political favor to provide him time to write. He describes himself as a "noble of the realm" who has shunned society, as a light bringer, a guardian of culture and an umpire of taste. He has sought the appointment to be alone, to distance himself from society on "an island in the sea," a description that recalls the scene of "Annabel Lee."

Separated from land by two hundred miles of high, rough seas, the narrator is anxious, sensing danger both within and outside himself ("there is no telling what may happen to a man all alone as I am—"), but believing that the invulnerable lighthouse will protect him ("but why dwell on that, since I am *here*, all safe?"). Yet the story lacks a title and an ending, and is told through gaps and fragments, through to the final sentences, which relate the terrifying truth that the lighthouse keeper is not safe at all:

Jan. 3. . . . *A structure such as this is safe enough under any circumstances. I should feel myself secure in it during the fiercest hurricane that ever raged— and yet I have heard seamen say occasionally, with a wind at South-West, the sea has been known to run higher here than any where with the single exception of the Western opening of the Straits of Magellan. No mere sea, though, could accomplish anything with this solid iron-riveted wall—which, at 50 feet from high-water mark, is four feet thick, if one inch* . . . . *The basis on which the structure rests seems to me to be chalk* . . . . . . *(925)*

Following the discovery of that grim evidence is the date "*Jan. 4.*" and then a blank.

The tale disturbingly images Poe's position as a writer trying to bring order and coherence to a chaotic and ultimately futile existence by protecting himself from the world at large. Like the narrator of "MS. Found in a Bottle," the lighthouse keeper writes to forestall death, yet accedes to its terrible inevitability by laying down his pen on the date of his last day on earth. Recalling Hop-Frog's statement "*this is my last jest,*" Poe vanishes from the page, in what is probably the last piece he ever wrote. Remarkably, the story ends on 3 January 1796, the same day and the same year that Poe's mother arrived in Boston on her crossing from England. Poe's biography obviously begins with Eliza, but does it end with her, too?

By erasing himself from the page, Poe was engaged in the logical extension of his constant rhetorical acts of trying to retrieve the past and then become one with it. He hoped that he could escape one universe and enter a better one, where he would be reunited with lost loves and find peace and amity. If somehow that could have been known to be a certainty, would such knowledge have consoled him, would it have insulated him from the psychic stresses of his life and somehow averted a terrible inevitability?

In death, as in life—contradictions, paradoxes, rumors, and bitter disagreements continued about Poe. Some say that his corpse was tended to with little care and little display of ceremony, but Dr. Moran contended that Poe's body was laid in state "in the large room in the rotunda of the college building adjoining the hospital where it remained from the 7th to the 9th of October." Some family members, friends, and acquaintances visited the body throughout those three days, including a number of women, some of whom snipped a lock of his hair as a keepsake. Henry Herring said that initially, Poe was placed in a coffin made of poplar wood which was stained to resemble walnut; he, however, stepped up to pay for a finer coffin, "a lead-lined oak casket with an inscribed brass plate at the foot."

On Monday, 8 October, at 4 p.m., Poe was conveyed to the Westminster Cemetery of the First Presbyterian Church in Baltimore. Neilson Poe paid for the hearse and for the single carriage that followed it. In the carriage with Neilson were Snodgrass, Herring, Z. Collins Lee, a Baltimore lawyer who had been Poe's classmate at the University of Virginia, and the Reverend W. T. D. Clemm, one of Virgina's cousins. Poe was buried in his grandfather Poe's lot near the center of the graveyard. The brief, three-minute ceremony was described as "cold-blooded and unchristianlike," but that may have been owing as much to the bone-chilling weather as to any disregard for Poe.

Since 1949, the Westminster grave has been visited every year in the early hours of Poe's birthday, January 19, by an unidentified person. This person, described as an elderly gentleman draped in black and carrying a silver-tipped cane, kneels at the grave for a toast of Martel cognac, then leaves behind the half-full bottle and three red roses.

249

Poe's grave has become talismanic, and its effect today is as strong as it was in 1879 when the famed poet Stéphane Mallarmé became entranced and wrote "Tomb of Poe":

Alas, from the warring heaven and earth, if
our concept
cannot carve a bas-relief
with which to adorn Poe's dazzling sepulcher,
calm block fallen down here from some dark
disaster, let this granite forever mark
bounds to dark flights of Blasphemy scarce in the future.

EPILOGUE

Two days after Poe's death, on 9 October 1849, Rufus Griswold published a hastily prepared obituary of the author for the New York *Tribune*. It was reprinted widely in other national papers, and it did incalculable, long-lasting damage to Poe's reputation. Writing pseudonymously as "Ludwig" (Wagner's mad king of Bavaria), Griswold began the piece by misstating Poe's name, then followed with a damning rhetorical flourish:

> *Edgar Allan Poe is dead. He died in Baltimore the day before yesterday. This announcement will startle many, but few will be grieved by it. The poet was known, personally or by reputation, in all this country; he had readers in England, and in several of the states of Continental Europe; but he had few or no friends; and the regrets for his death will be suggested principally by the consideration that in him literary art has lost one of its most brilliant but erratic stars.*

The opening lines paid Poe a backhanded compliment while condemning him in unmitigated terms. The rest of the obituary was even more severe, depicting Poe as a raving lunatic, muttering curses as he stumbled about the streets, drunk and delirious. According to the piece, Poe was unprincipled, immoral, and repugnant.

Muddy could not have known that Griswold was the author of the piece (perhaps she did not even see it), for she gave Griswold power of attorney less than a week after Poe's death, enabling him to contract for a uniform edition of Poe's works, which Griswold told her he was bringing out for no other reason than to benefit her financially. To do so, Griswold would have to find the trunk of manuscripts that Poe had brought along on his last trip, but when Griswold tried to retrieve it from Baltimore, he found that Poe's sister, Rosalie, on legal advice from John R. Thompson, had asserted her right to its ownership and was claiming herself to be Poe's single legal heir. Muddy, with a stroke of a pen that she was soon to regret, denied the legitimacy of Rose's claim and handed over to Griswold all of Poe's remaining literary papers.

Griswold's edition appeared soon thereafter, but the publishers offered Muddy no royalties, only a few free sets for her own use. Pathetically, she then tried to sell them, at a discounted rate, to earn some money, resorting to her usual methods of writing embarrassing letters to acquaintances of Poe's begging them to do her a good turn.

Willis, Graham, John Neal, and others knew of "Ludwig"'s smears, and for the next six months vigorously defended Poe against them in the press, parrying Griswold's accusations with kind statements about Poe's genius and generosity to others, and mourning him as an underrated author whose life of poverty should be an object lesson about the effects on artists of living in a philistine society. Several other friends rose to the occasion in print, defending Poe against Griswold's accusations. But, as Lambert Wilmer noted, "the whole press of the country seemed desirous of giving circulation and authenticity to the slanders." Rumor mongering in the sensational press, after all, was still the norm.

Striking back, Griswold rebutted Willis's and others' claims in a lengthy "Memoir" he prepared for his third edition of the *Works*, published in 1850. If, as some have thought, it seemed that Griswold had pulled his punches in the "Ludwig" piece, then that was nothing compared to the torrent of abuse that he unleashed in the "Memoir." He stated, either directly or by inference, that Poe had been expelled from the University of Virginia, that he had seduced Allan's second wife, that he had physically beaten Virginia and was thus responsible for her untimely death, that he was a deserter from the army, and that he had been arrested on multiple occasions. Gallingly, Griswold took Poe's letters to different friends and colleagues and revised them so that many of the original sentences, either complimentary or just innocuous, became insults and slanders. In one of the more lurid stories Griswold circulated—this one by word of mouth rather than in print—Poe and Muddy had been lovers.

When Muddy read Griswold's "Memoir," she was traumatized, and she "nearly sunk" under the burden of its scabrous lies. Confined to bed from this emotional blow, and having no resources of her own, Muddy could do nothing but accept that the letters Poe allegedly had written were genuine. She spent the rest of her life in bewildered disbelief, defending Poe whenever she could and embarking on a nomadic, penniless existence as an old woman that no one wanted. Left by Poe's death with no immediate family and no income, in the years that followed, Muddy moved around, staying with friends who would take her in for a while, then, wearing out her welcome, going on to stay with someone else. For about a year and a half, she lived with the Richmonds in Lowell, almost as an adjunct member of the family, for they cared for her well, taking her on vacations and providing for all her needs. In Lowell, she received many letters of condolence from admirers of Poe, and had a visit from Longfellow, who made her promise to come see him in his home in Cambridge, and who spoke of Poe as the greatest author of his time.

She eventually wore out her welcome at the Richmonds', however, and for the next dozen years or more she wandered about the country, living off the generosity of others, including Stella Lewis and Loui Shew. She wrote Helen Whitman for a place to stay, but Helen was ill and was at the time caring for other members of her family, also infirm. The two women never met. In the spring of 1863, with the Civil War raging all around her, she sought shelter and was given a place at the Episcopal Church Home in Baltimore. She died there on 16 February 1871.

Rosalie Poe fared no better than Muddy. She continued to live in Richmond with the MacKenzies throughout the Civil War. The family then fell on hard times, their money vanishing with the collapse of the Confederacy in 1865. Rose eventually made her way north to Baltimore, eking out a scant existence by selling photographic likenesses of her famous brother. Eventually she moved into the Epiphany Church Home in Washington, D.C., a refuge for the indigent run by the Episcopal Church. She remained there until her death on 22 July 1874.

Neilson Poe died in January 1884. He had been indifferent to his cousin's literary career when Poe was alive but suddenly became very knowledgeable about it after his death, granting interviews and speaking about Poe on some of the public occasions when the author was remembered. Neilson corresponded at great length with Poe's early biographers, and he continued his distinguished legal career; he was eventually appointed chief judge of the Orphans' Court of Baltimore.

Both Nancy Locke ("Annie") Richmond and Stella Lewis cared for Muddy at different times after Poe's death. Although she was divorced in 1858, Stella Lewis very often took Muddy in and gave her free room and board. She lived in London the last years of her life, where she had a personal relationship with Poe's first authoritative biographer, John Ingram, whom she tried earnestly to convince of her importance in Poe's life. After her husband's death in 1873, Mrs. Richmond had her first name legally changed to "Annie," and she too corresponded with John Ingram. He published some of Poe's letters to her without her consent and greatly without her wishes. She died in Lowell on 9 February 1898.

Fanny Osgood died at age thirty-nine, only eight months after Poe, of tuberculosis.

Helen Whitman, the most prominent love of Poe's life after Virginia, became his most steadfast defender and champion, her efforts culminating in the 1860 publication of *Edgar Poe and His Critics*. Poe had supplied Helen with the chief romantic experience of her life. She always held that "Annabel Lee" was his message to her, and she guarded his public image faithfully. She even wrote in memory (and imitation) of her suitor. In her *Poems*, published posthumously in 1879, sixteen are associated with Poe, and many others echo the cadences and language of his own verse. Helen left a detailed account of her 1848 romance with the poet with John Ingram, who worked it into his account of Poe's life.

After expressing her anguish over Poe's death in the October letter to Muddy, Poe's last love, Elmira Royster Shelton, entered into a discreet silence on all matters about the author for twenty-six years. She broke it only in 1875, when she granted an interview to Edward V. Valentine, of Richmond, who tape-recorded her statements. After Elmira's death on 11 February 1888, the recording was placed in the Valentine Museum in Richmond, where it remains today.

On Nassau Street and in other quarters of literary New York, most of Poe's friends and enemies continued their careers, many trading on their association with Poe for some time after his death, a number of them writing books and articles on him—some fanciful, others earnest. The Poe legend was alive and well.

Rufus Griswold, who played Dr. Moriarity to Poe's Sherlock Holmes, fared no better than the adversary that he felt he had conquered in print. Griswold, in fact, led much more of a double life than Poe had; he was a former Baptist minister who had remade himself from a swampland hick into a sophisticated Manhattanite. But Griswold's last years were miserable, marred by illness and tragedy. In 1849, while taking the ferry to Brooklyn, he was seized by an epileptic fit and sunk twice in the water, nearly drowning, before he was rescued. His old malady, tuberculosis, recurred several times before his death, making it impossible for him to work on two ambitious and unfinished projects, a life of George Washington and a vast biographical dictionary. In 1853, his fifteen-year-old daughter was riding on a train that jumped the tracks and plunged into a Connecticut river. He rushed there from New York and viewed forty-nine corpses by moonlight before finally finding her pinned underwater. Incredibly, she was revived by a physician, and she survived. But that same year, a gas explosion in his home severely burned his face and caused other injuries. His third wife deserted him, moving to Maine and leaving him alone in New York in his tubercular condition, made worse by nightmares and neuroses. It was said that his only comforts were the portraits of Fanny Osgood and Edgar Poe that decorated his room.

The revival of interest in Poe began with the 1874 rededication of his gravesite and the memorial ceremony, organized by Sara Sigourney Rice, that accompanied it. Letters of praise arrived from Whittier, Bryant, Longfellow, Holmes, Tennyson, Swinburne, and others. Helen Whitman mounted an earnest defense of Poe's character in *Edgar Poe and His Critics*. In France, Poe posthumously found an ardent champion in Charles Baudelaire, who translated his works and interpreted Poe's tragic life as that of a victim of a philistine society. Poe's reputation in France soared, puzzling many later American writers, whose assessment of the author was mixed.

In 1878, Henry James condescendingly remarked that "An enthusiasm for Poe is the mark of a decidedly primitive stage of reflection." In 1880, Walt Whitman, the poet closest to Poe in the unconventionality of his life and views, opined that Poe was "probably . . . among the electric lights of imaginative literature, brilliant and dazzling, but with no heat." George Bernard Shaw was unstinting in his praise of all facets of Poe's literary achievement: "this finest of fine artists, this born aristocrat of letters. . . . He was the greatest journalistic critic of his time, placing good European work at sight when the European critics were waiting for somebody to tell them what to say. His poetry is so exquisitely refined that posterity will refuse to believe that it belongs to the same civilization as the glory of Julia Ward Howe's lilies or the honest doggerel of Whittier." Later writers as varied as Hemingway and T. S. Eliot demurred. Hemingway belligerently concluded that Poe was "a skillful writer," but that his writing was "skillful, marvelously constructed, and . . . dead." Eliot sarcastically contended that Poe's intellect was that of "a highly gifted young person before puberty." D. H. Lawrence and William Carlos Williams were more complimentary: Lawrence called Poe "an adventurer into vaults and cellars and horrible underground passages of the human soul. He sounded the horror and warning of his own doom"; in *In the American Grain*, Williams argued that Poe "was in no sense the bizarre, isolate writer, the curious literary figure. On the contrary, in him American literature is anchored, in him alone, on solid ground. . . . On him is FOUNDED A LITERATURE."

Despite these many laudatory assessments, and despite the revival of interest in American literature following World War One, Poe's reputation was not firmly fixed until the 1940s, when Arthur Hobson Quinn, a professor of English at the University of Pennsylvania, published the first authoritative, scholarly biography of Poe. After much diligent research, Quinn uncovered Griswold's forgeries of Poe's correspondence, and new interest in Poe surged after that, accompanying the widespread legitimization of American literature as a subject for literary study in university classrooms after World War Two. As *Moby-Dick* and *The Scarlet Letter* became firmly positioned in the canon of widely taught works, so too did Poe's complex tales of psychic conflict and ratiocination take their rightful place in the list of American masterpieces. Today, Poe's prominence in the academy has spawned a small industry of scholarship about him, and with the introduction of postmodern critical methodologies, which open up new avenues of interpretation in Poe's multilayered tales, his position not only seems entrenched, but shows little sign of ever eroding.

CHRONOLOGY

1809   Edgar Poe is born on 19 January in Boston to actors David and Elizabeth Arnold Poe. He is the second of three children.

1810   David Poe abandons his family.

1811–14   Eliza dies on 11 December 1811 in Richmond Theatre fire. The three children—Henry, Edgar, and Rosalie—are taken in by foster families. Poe lives with the Allans in Richmond. He is baptised Edgar Allan Poe, although he is not legally adopted by Allan.

1815   Allan, a merchant, takes his family to live in London. Poe is educated at private schools there.

1820   The family returns to Richmond. Poe continues his schooling. Earns distinction in athletics, languages, and military exercises.

1825   John Allan's uncle, the wealthy William Galt, dies, leaving his vast fortune to Allan.

1826   Goes to the University of Virginia, but is forced by Allan to withdraw when he runs up gambling debts and is rumored to be behaving badly.

1827   Works for a while in Richmond as a bookkeeper. Poe quarrels with Allan and runs away to Boston, where he publishes his first book, *Tamerlane and Other Poems.* Enlists in U.S. Army under the alias "Edgar A. Perry." Is transferred to Fort Moultrie on Sullivan's Island, South Carolina.

1828   Is reconciled with Allan after the death of Allan's wife, Fanny, on 28 February.

1829   Hatch and Dunning publish *Al Aaraaf, Tamerlane, and Minor Poems.*

1830   Wins appointment to West Point. In October, Allan remarries.

1831 Poe gets himself expelled from West Point, goes to New York and publishes *Poems . . . Second Edition.* He then travels to Baltimore to live with his father's sister, Maria Clemm, her daughter, Virginia, and his brother, Henry, who dies on 1 August.

1832–33 Publishes various stories in Philadelphia *Saturday Courier* and wins contest sponsored by Baltimore *Saturday Visiter.* Is befriended by attorney and author John Pendleton Kennedy.

1834 Allan dies on 27 March.

1835 Moves to Richmond in August to take up editorial post at *Southern Literary Messenger,* garnering national attention for his bold and somewhat abrasive book reviews.

1836 On 16 May, marries his cousin Virginia, age thirteen, in public ceremony.

1837 In January falls out with Thomas White over severity of book reviews, editorial content of the magazine, and questions about Poe's character. Moves to New York with Maria and Virginia.

1838 Settles in Philadelphia sometime in the spring. *The Narrative of Arthur Gordon Pym* is published 30 July.

1839 Ghost-writes geology textbook, *The Conchologist's First Book.* Accepts job offer to edit *Burton's Gentleman's Magazine* and publishes therein many of his most famous tales, including "The Fall of the House of Usher" and "William Wilson." Stories collected in *Tales of the Grotesque and Arabesque,* published 3 December.

1840–41 *Gentleman's Magazine* put up for sale. Poe circulates plan for his own journal, "The Penn," but fails to find financial backers. Accepts post at *Graham's Magazine.* Continues to publish tales of the supernatural and psychic conflict. Also writes popular series on cryptography and autography. Refines literary theories through examination of current books in his critical reviews.

1842 Resigns from *Graham's* over disagreement with content. Prepares new prospectus for "The Penn" and becomes acquainted with Rufus W. Griswold.

1843 Continues to circulate prospectus for "The Penn." Applies unsuccessfully for government post in Philadelphia Custom House. In July, *The Prose Romances of Edgar A. Poe* is published. Achieves renown with detective story "The Gold-Bug," which also wins a hundred-dollar prize in *Dollar*

Newspaper contest. On 21 November delivers first lecture, "American Poetry."

1844   Relocates to New York. "The Balloon-Hoax" published in *Sun*. The series "Doings of Gotham" appears in *Columbian Spy*.

1845   "The Raven" appears on 29 January and is immediately popular. Poe's fame swells but is then deflated quickly through a series of quarrels and ill-advised publications like "The Literati," accusations of plagiarism against Longfellow, and biting lectures on American poetry. Consorts with circles of literary ladies. Wiley and Putnam bring out *Tales* on 25 June and *The Raven and Other Poems* on 19 November. Attacks Longfellow again in Boston Lyceum lecture, 16 October. Acquires financial interest in *Broadway Journal* but cannot sustain it financially.

1846   Begins to be recognized in Europe but is troubled at home by series of dalliances with literary women. Successfully sues Thomas Dunn English for libel.

1847   On 30 January, Virginia dies. Poe nursed back to mental health by Loui Shew, Mary Gove Nichols, and others.

1848   Continues to try to drum up support for magazine, now renamed "The Stylus." Liasions with several literary women, most seriously Sarah Helen Whitman, of Providence, Rhode Island. Proposes marriage to her but is rejected. Delivers lectures, "The Universe," published by Putnam on 11 July as *Eureka*.

1849   Woos Annie Richmond, of Lowell, Massachusetts, again unsuccessfully. Is contacted by Edward H. N. Patterson of Illinois, who wishes to underwrite "The Stylus." Travels south to interest subscribers in the magazine, stopping en route in Philadelphia, where he undergoes delusional episode. Lectures in and around tidewater Virginia on "the poetic principle" and proposes marriage to former childhood sweetheart, Elmira Royster Shelton, who accepts. Joins Sons of Temperance. On 27 September leaves Richmond aboard steamer for New York to bring Maria down to Richmond. Disembarks in Baltimore and disappears for five days. Discovered in semiconscious, feverish state near a polling place and is taken to Washington College Hospital, where he dies of "congestion of the brain" on 7 October. Buried in Westminster Cemetery the following day. Pseudonymous obituary published by "Ludwig" in New York *Tribune* on 9 October deeply damages Poe's personal and literary reputation.

NOTES

Sources used in this book are identified by excerpts from the text, followed by the reference. References to Poe's own writings—fiction, poetry, and criticism—are to one or the other of the authoritative Library of America editions. References to critical writings are to *Edgar Allan Poe: Essays and Reviews*, ed. G. R. Thompson (New York: Library of America, 1987), and references to fiction and poetry are to *Edgar Allan Poe: Poetry and Tales*, ed. Patrick F. Quinn (New York: Library of America, 1984). Page numbers to these editions are cited parenthetically within the text.

Almost all references are to published sources, and abbreviations are used in the notes which follow.

Harrison   James A. Harrison, ed., *The Complete Works of Edgar Allan Poe.* 17 vols. New York: T. Crowell, 1902. Rpt., New York: AMS Press, 1965.

Letters   John Ward Ostrom, ed., *The Letters of Edgar Allan Poe.* 2 vols. 1948. Rpt. with suppl., New York: Gordian, 1966.

Log   Dwight Thomas and David K. Jackson, *The Poe Log: A Documentary Life of Edgar Allan Poe.* Boston: G. K. Hall, 1987.

Mabbott   Thomas Ollive Mabbott, ed., *The Collected Works of Edgar Allan Poe* (Vol. 1, *Poems*; Vols. 2–3, *Tales and Sketches*). Cambridge, MA.: Belknap Press of Harvard University Press, Vol. 1, 1969; Vols. 2–3, 1978. Edition continued by Burton Pollin, below.

Meyers   Jeffrey Meyers, *Edgar Allan Poe: Life and Legacy.* New York: Scribners, 1992.

Miller   John Carl Miller, *Building Poe Biography.* Baton Rouge: Louisiana State University Press, 1977.

Pollin   Burton R. Pollin, ed., *The Collected Writings of Edgar Allan Poe* (Vol. 1, *The Imaginary Voyages: Pym, Hans Pfaall, Julius Rodman*; Vol. 2, *The Brevities: Pinakidia, Marginalia and Other Works*; Vol. 3, *The Broadway Journal, Non-fictional Prose, Part I: Text*; Vol. 4, *The Broadway Journal, Non-fictional Prose, Part II: Annotations*; Vol. 5, *Writings in the Southern Literary Messenger*). Vol. 1, Boston: Twayne Publishers, 1981, reprinted by Gordian Press. Vols. 2–5, New York: Gordian Press, 1985, 1986, 1997.

Quinn   Arthur Hobson Quinn, *Edgar Allan Poe: A Critical Biography.* New York: Crowell, 1941.

Silverman Kenneth Silverman, *Edgar A. Poe: Mournful and Never-ending Remembrance.* New York: HarperCollins, 1991.

Symons   Julian Symons, *The Tell-Tale Heart: The Life and Works of Edgar Allan Poe.* New York: Penguin, 1978.

Walker   Ian Walker, ed., *Edgar Allan Poe: The Critical Heritage.* London: Routledge, 1986.

Woodberry George Woodberry, *The Life of Edgar Allan Poe.* Boston: Houghton Mifflin, 1909.

Introduction

"Literature is the most noble of professions": Poe to Frederick W. Thomas, 14 Feb. 1849, *Letters* 2:426.

alcoholism among writers: Tom Dardis, *The Thirsty Muse: Alcohol and the American Writer* (New York: Ticknor and Fields, 1989).

"a source of quiet fascination": J. Gerald Kennedy, *Poe, Death, and the Life of Writing* (New Haven: Yale University Press, 1987), 5.

CHAPTER 1

Childhood: Boston, Richmond, England

"On this night": *Log* 13.

Poe's mother: Geddeth Smith, *The Brief Career of Eliza Poe* (Newark: University of Delaware Press, 1988).

Theatre scene in America: Brooks McNamara, *The American Playhouse in the Eighteenth Century* (Cambridge: Harvard University Press, 1969), esp. 122–25.

Federal Street Theater: John Alden, "A Season in Federal Street," *Proceedings of the American Antiquarian Society,* April 1955 (Worcester, MA: American Antiquarian Society, 1955), 11–12.

General Poe: Mary E. Phillips, *Edgar Allan Poe the Man* (Chicago: John C. Winston, 1926), 29.

"a more wretched Alonzo": *Log* 7.

death of David Poe: Susan Archer Weiss, "Reminiscences of Edgar Allan Poe," *The Independent* (25 Aug. 1904): 447.

death of Eliza Poe: Quinn 732–41. See also *Log* 13.

Richmond Theatre fire: *Log* 16.

"For my little son Edgar": Quoted in Hervey Allen and Thomas O. Mabbott, *Poe's Brother: The Poems of William Henry Leonard Poe* (New York, 1926), 41.

Descriptions of Richmond: Agnes M. Bondurant, *Poe's Richmond* (Richmond, 1942), esp. 7–16; passim.

Poe taken in by Allans: Charles Marshall Graves, "Landmarks of Poe in Richmond," *Century* 67 (Apr. 1904): 914–15.
"never turned a beggar": Poe, *Letters* 1:48.
Fanny frequently ill: George E. Woodberry, *The Life of Edgar Allan Poe* (1909; rpt., New York, 1965), 1:360.
DuBourg and Bransby schools: Quinn 73; *Log* 42, 36.
Schooling by Joseph Clarke: Richard Beale Davis, *Intellectual Life in Jefferson's Virginia 1790–1830* (Chapel Hill: University of North Carolina Press, 1964), 29 ff.
"capping verses": *Log* 53.
swimming in James River: Quinn, 82–83.
"first, purely ideal love": Poe to Sarah Helen Whitman, 1 Oct. 1848, *Letters* 2:385.
"not a Spark of Affection": Weiss, *The Home Life of Edgar Allan Poe* (New York: Broadway, 1907), 86; *Log*, 61–62.
"He has had little else": Weiss, 86.
Death of William Galt: G. Melvin Herndon, "From Scottish Orphan to Virginia Planter: William Galt, Jr., 1801–1851," *Virginia Magazine of History and Biography* 87 (1979): 326–27.
Description of Moldavia: Samuel Mordecai, *Virginia, Especially Richmond, in By-Gone Days* (2d ed.; rev. 1860; rpt., Richmond: Dietz, 1946), 131–32.

CHAPTER 2

The Byronic Youth: University, the Army, and West Point

University of Virginia: James Southall Wilson, "Poe at the University of Virginia," *Alumni Bulletin, University of Virginia* 16 (Apr. 1923): 167.
"I saw the arm": *Letters* 1:5–6.
Poe's studies: John Ingram, *Edgar Allan Poe: His Life, Letters, and Opinions* (1886; rpt., New York, 1965), 76.
Poe's mood swings: Ingram 351.
"with a piece of charcoal": *Log* 75; Wilson, "Poe at the University," 166–67.
"Invisible Spirit of Wine": *Log* 75.
"Poe's passion for drink": Thomas Holley Chivers, *Life of Poe* (1852), ed. Richard Beale Davis (New York, 1952), 57; Charles Kent, "Poe's Student Days at the University of Virginia," *Bookman* 44 (Jan. 1917): 523.
"spoke with regret": William Wertenbaker, "Edgar A. Poe," *Virginia University Magazine* 7 (Nov.–Dec. 1868): 114–17.
"I will boldly say": *Letters* 1: 40.
card-playing: Ingram 92.
expensive lifestyle: *Log* 73.
Allan went up to Charlottesville: Floyd Stovall, *Edgar Poe the Poet* (Charlottesville: University Press of Virginia, 1969), 18.

"You suffer me": *Letters* 1:7–9.

"tone of lofty resolve": Kenneth Silverman, *Edgar A. Poe: Mournful and Never-ending Remembrance* (New York: HarperCollins, 1991), 35.

"It is true I taught you to aspire": Mary Newton Stanard, ed., *Edgar Allan Poe Letters Till Now Unpublished, in the Valentine Museum, Richmond, Virginia* (Philadelphia: Lippincott, 1925), 67–68.

Underfunding Poe at Virginia: Jeffrey Meyers, *Edgar Allan Poe: Life and Legacy* (New York: Scribner, 1992), 28.

Henry: *Log* 77.

Sea: *Log* 78.

Poe in the army: J. Thomas Russell, *Edgar Allan Poe: The Army Years* (West Point, 1972).

Letters between Poe and John Allan: *Letters* 1:9, 11–12.

Death of Fanny Allan: Ingram 494.

Entering West Point: Col. James House to "General Commanding the E. Dept.," Fortress Monroe, 30 Mar. 1829, *Selected Military Service Records Pertaining to Edgar Allan Poe*, National Archives microfilm, 1987.

Publication of poems: Ian Walker, *Edgar Allan Poe: The Critical Heritage* (London: Routledge, 1987), 175–76.

"I no longer look": Poe to William Gwynn, 6 May 1831, *Letters* 1:45.

"I *earned*, myself": Poe to Allan, 3 Jan. 1831, *Letters* 1:41.

Debts at West Point: *Log* 114.

Children who lose their parents: Silverman 76–77.

Culture of death in Victorian America: Kennedy, *Poe, Death, and the Life of Writing*, chaps. 1–2.

CHAPTER 3

Baltimore: Early Tales and Satires

Description of Baltimore: Lawrence C. Wroth, "Poe's Baltimore," *Johns Hopkins Alumni Magazine* XCII, no. 4 (June 1929), esp. 301–2.

"entirely given up to drink": Poe to Allan: *Letters* 1:29–30.

Henry Poe: Hervey Allen and Thomas O. Mabbott, *Poe's Brother: The Poems of William Henry Leonard Poe* (New York: Doran, 1926), esp. 29–33.

Death of Henry Poe: Quinn 187–88.

Muddy to Thomas Kell: *Log* 124.

"the ever-vigilant guardian": Reid, "A Dead Man Defended: Being Some Reminiscences of the Poet Poe," *Onward* 1 (Apr. 1869): 308.

"I feel deeply interested in him": Mary Newton Stanard, *Edgar Allan Poe Letters Till Now Unpublished, in the Valentine Museum, Richmond, Virginia* (Philadelphia: Lippincott, 1925), 295–97.

Letter not posted: Silverman 95; *Log* 123–24.

Lambert Wilmer's recollections: Wilmer, *Merlin, Baltimore, 1827: Together with "Recollections of Edgar A. Poe."* Ed. Thomas O. Mabbott (New York: Scholars' Fascimiles & Reprints, 1941), 29–32.

"carried himself erect and well": Sara Signourney Rice, ed., *Edgar Allan Poe: A Memorial Volume* (Baltimore: Turnbull Brothers, 1877), 60–61.

Mary Starr: Starr's own account, presented in Augustus Van Cleef, "Poe's Mary," *Harper's New Monthly Magazine* 78 (Mar. 1889): 634–40.

Elizabeth Herring: J. H. Whitty, ed., "Memoir" of Poe in *The Complete Poems of Edgar Allan Poe* (Boston: Houghton Mifflin, 1911), xxxiii.

Interest in Virginia's advancement: "Poe's Literary Baltimore," esp. 307–11.

"fraught with the treasure of thought": *Log* 119. Thomas and Jackson speculate that this review was penned by either George P. Morris or Theodore S. Fay, in the *New-York Mirror*. Poe would later launch personal attacks on these figures through his book reviews in the *Southern Literary Messenger*.

"in promotion of the Cause of LITERATURE": *Log* 120.

"the creation of a literary personality": Jay B. Hubbell, "Edgar Allan Poe," *Eight American Authors*, ed. James Woodress, rev. ed. (New York: Norton, 1971), 14.

"the ludicrous heightened into the grotesque": *Letters* 1:57–58.

fistfight with Hewitt: Hewitt, *Recollections of Poe.* Ed. Richard Barksdale Harwell (Atlanta: Emory University Library, 1949), 19. Poe's abrasive, combative personality was much like Hemingway's. As dissimilar as these two writers' prose styles were, in temperament they could have been twins: the exaggerated physical prowess and athleticism, the thrill-seeking binges, the enormous ego and easily hurt pride, and the wrangling—both through words and actions—with their editors and competitors.

John Pendleton Kennedy: *Dictionary of American Biography*, Vol. 10 (New York: Scribners, 1933), 333–34.

Carey to Kennedy: *Log* 142.

"drudging upon whatever may make money": Rufus Wilmot Griswold, "Memoir of the Author," Vol. 3 of Griswold's 4-volume edition of Poe, *The Literati . . . by Edgar A. Poe* (New York: J. S. Redfield, 1850), xiii.

"in a state of starvation": George E. Woodberry, *The Life of Edgar Allan Poe, Personal and Literary*, 2 vols. (1909; rpt., New York: Biblo and Tannen, 1965), 2:350.

"For God's sake pity me": *Letters* 1:29–30.

"When I look back": *Letters* 1:46.

"Apl 12, 1833": Stanard 268.

Death and burial of John Allan: Mary E. Phillips, *Edgar Allan Poe: The Man*, 2 vols. (Chicago: John C. Winston, 1926), 1:456.

Poe's visits to Allan: *Log* 127, 137.

Revision of Allan's will: *Log* 126, 128.

CHAPTER 4
Return to Richmond: Marriage, the *Southern Literary Messenger*, and *The Narrative of Arthur Gordon Pym*

Magazines: Frank Luther Mott, *A History of American Magazines*, Vol. 1, 1741–1850 (Cambridge, MA: Belknap Press of Harvard University Press, 1938), 341.

"rush of the age": "Marginalia," *Graham's Magazine* (Dec. 1846), 499.

White and the *Southern Literary Messenger*: *Dictionary of American Biography*; David K. Jackson, *Poe and the* Southern Literary Messenger (Richmond, VA: Dietz Press, 1934; rpt., New York: Haskell House, 1970).

"the latter financed in part": *Log* 130, 139.

"[Poe] was engaged": Quoted in Meyers 80.

"irresistible interest": *Log* 160.

"the chief interest": Poe, "Richard Adams Locke," part of an unpublished MS section of "Literary America," Poe's 1848 series for *Godey's Lady's Book*. This incomplete manuscript, called Version C, was reprinted by Griswold in his *Works*.

oral violence in "Berenice": To note the long reach of Poe's influence on later, much different writers, one might point out how this incident resembles the pervasive oral brutality in Frank Norris's *McTeague* (1899).

"embroidering the whole": Silverman 112–13.

examples of Gothicism: Michael S. Allen, *Poe and the British Magazine Tradition* (New York: Oxford University Press, 1969).

"the history of all Magazines": *Letters* 1:57–58.

"bizarre behavior": see John F. Jebb, "Ligeia," *Beacham's Encyclopedia of Popular Fiction*, Vol. 10, ed. Kirk Beetz (Osprey, FL: Beacham, 1998), 5889–98; see also Silverman 216.

possible marriage of Poe and Virginia: A license was issued by the clerk of the Baltimore County Court on 22 September (*Log* 171), but proof of an actual ceremony taking place is not extant. For opposing views, see Quinn 227–28, and Mabbott, ed., *Collected Works of Edgar Allan Poe, Volume I: Poems* (Cambridge, MA: Harvard University Press, 1969), 546.

"My dearest Aunty": *Letters* 1:69–71.

"endlessly susceptible": Symons 51.

"of the full age": *Log* 207.

"Poe hinted to him": Meyers 86.

"effeminate" demeanor: Wilmer 32.

"appeared in its most beautiful light": Frances Sargent Osgood, in Griswold, "Memoir of the Author," xxxvi–xxxvii.

Poe's compositional manner: Ostrom 14.

"the most remarkable body of criticism": Wilson, "Poe at Home and Abroad," *New Republic* 49 (8 Dec. 1926): 79. Reprinted in *The Shores of Light* (New York: Farrar, Straus, and Young, 1952), 179–90. It was natural that Wilson should

have admired Poe's reviews, for Wilson's own critical precepts were as
unyielding and high-minded as Poe's were. The Auden remark is from the
poet's "Introduction" to *Edgar Allan Poe: Selected Prose, Poetry, and Eureka*
(New York: Rinehart, 1950), v–xvii.
"a child, techy and wayward": "Literature of the Nineteenth Century," *Athenaeum* 8
(Jan. 1835): 10. For a full discussion of literary nationalism and the campaign of
the American periodicals against the British, see Mott; also, Benjamin T. Spencer,
The Quest for Nationality: An American Literary Campaign (Syracuse: Syracuse
University Press, 1957), and Perry Miller, *The Raven and the Whale: The War of
Words and Wits in the Era of Poe and Melville* (New York: Harcourt, 1956).
fanciful autobiographical memorandum: 25 February 1834 autobiographical piece
written by Poe for the Philadelphia *Saturday Museum*. See Burton R. Pollin,
"Poe's Authorship of Three Long Critical and Autobiographical Articles of 1843
Now Authenticated," *American Renaissance Literary Report* 7 (1993): 139–71.
"We wish, if possible": *Letters* 1:93.
"I mention this *merely*": *Letters* 1:104.
"man with the tomahawk": Silverman 122.
"utter want of *keeping*": Harrison 8:42.
"from beginning to end": Symons 57.
Norman Leslie incident: The definitive account is Sidney P. Moss, *Poe's Literary
Battles* (Durham, NC: Duke University Press, 1963).
slashing reviewing styles: Allen 47–50.
label of "tomahawk critic" undeserved: *Letters* 1:100.
unity: Edd Winfield Parks, *Edgar Allan Poe as a Literary Critic* (Athens: University
of Georgia Press, 1964), 18.
Schlegel: Albert Julius Lubell, "Poe and A. W. Schlegel," *Journal of English and
Germanic Philology* 52 (1953): 7.
debt to Scottish aestheticians: Robert D. Jacobs, *Poe: Journalist and Critic*
(Baton Rouge: Louisiana State University Press, 1969), 112.
"right hand man": *Log* 190.
"exceedingly kind": *Letters* 1:83–84.
Poe's stipend: *Letters* 1:81–82.
very little cash: *Log* 196.
"The situation was disagreeable to me": *Letters* 1:141.
"cramped . . . in the exercise": Quoted in Jackson 110.
White's problems: *Dictionary of American Biography*, 499.
"no man is safe who drinks before breakfast": White to Poe, 29 Sept. 1835, Harrison
17:20–21.
"bread soaked in gin": Quoted in Susan Archer Weiss, "The Sister of Edgar A. Poe,"
Continent 3 (27 June 1883): 817.
temperance movement: A good general history is W. J. Rorabaugh, *The Alcoholic
Republic: An American Tradition* (New York: Oxford University Press, 1979).

See also Nicholas O. Warner, *Spirits of America: Intoxication in Nineteenth-Century American Literature* (Norman: Oklahoma University Press, 1997).

anagrammatic names: Silverman, 126, 135, 173, passim.

Poe was let go: Letter of White to Beverly Tucker, *Log* 236.

Gowans recollection: *Log* 242.

Benjamin Franklin satirized by Poe: See J. A. Leo Lemay, "Poe's 'The Business Man': Its Contexts and Satire of Franklin's *Autobiography,*" *Poe Studies* 15, no. 2 (Dec. 1982): 29–37.

Conchologist's First Book: Log 259.

Narrative of Arthur Gordon Pym: The scholarship on this novel is copious. A good sampling of the divergent opinions about Poe's intentions in the book can be found in Richard Kopley, ed., *Poe's Pym: Critical Explorations* (Durham, NC: Duke University Press, 1992). For the composition of the novel, see Joseph V. Ridgely and Iola S. Haverstick, "Chartless Voyage: The Many Narratives of Arthur Gordon Pym," *Texas Studies in Literature and Language* 8 (1966): 63–80. For analysis of the author-identity question, see J. Gerald Kennedy, "The Preface as a Key to the Satire in Pym," *Studies in the Novel* 5 (1973): 191–96 and "'The Infernal Twoness' in Arthur Gordon Pym," *Topic:* 30 (1976): 41–53. For autobiographical echoes, see Silverman and Kopley, "The Hidden Journey of Arthur Gordon Pym," *Studies in the American Renaissance 1982*: 29–51.

"impart a tone": Kennedy, "The Preface as a Key to the Satire in Pym," 195.

"single and connected story": Quoted in Quinn 251.

analysis of *Pym:* The ideas presented here generally follow the psychoanalytic reading of the novel presented by Silverman, 133–36, although numerous critics before Silverman have noted the themes of illusion, the journey motif, and the concern with feeding and nourishment.

CHAPTER 5

Philadelphia: *Burton's Gentleman's Magazine* and the Great Tales

"cut your mutton": *Log* 262.

Burton: *Dictionary of American Biography.*

"were I to detail my daily avocations": Quoted in Silverman 142.

"keen visaged": John M. Daniel, *The Semi-Weekly Examiner,* 21 August 1849, quoted in *Log* 827.

"a face to rivet one's attention": *Log* 577–578.

"the expenses of the Magazine": *Log* 261–62.

"poetry has been not a purpose . . . ": "Preface," *The Raven and Other Poems* (1845).

"I send the Gent's Mag": *Letters* 1:118.

"To render Burton's Magazine": *Log* 277.

extra revenue: *Log* 294.

report to Congress: David K. Jackson, "A Poe Hoax Comes Before the U.S. Congress," *Poe Studies* 7 (Dec. 1974): 47–48.
"merely penning an occasional paragraph": *Letters* 1:118–19.
"negative merit": Harrison 10:42.
"easy lies and half truths": Silverman 142.
Longfellow review as prelude to "The Poetic Principle": Kenneth Alan Hovey, "Critical Provincialism: Poe's Poetic Principle in Antebellum Context," *American Quarterly* 39 (1987): 341–54.
"understanding of Poe's epistemology": Eric W. Carlson, "New Introduction," *Selections from the Critical Writings of Edgar Allan Poe*, ed. F. C. Prescott (New York: Gordian, 1981), xi.
"It is upon the South": *Letters* 1:141.
"a beauty no truth could invade": Hovey 349.
"The Business Man" as attack on John Allan: Lemay, "Poe's 'The Business Man.'" Horatio Nelson: Meyers 110.
Tate comment: "The Angelic Imagination: Poe as God." In *The Man of Letters in the Modern World* (1936; rpt., New York: Meridien, 1995), 118.
"in a morally profounder manner": Quoted in Benjamin Lease, *Anglo American Encounters: England and the Rise of American Literature* (New York: Cambridge University Press, 1981), 77, 78.
sources for "William Wilson": Lease 77–78. Irving source: Thomas O. Mabbott, "An Unwritten Drama," *Americana Collector* 1 (Nov. 1935): 64–66. Ironically, another source for "William Wilson" may have been Hawthorne's "Howe's Masquerade," which appeared in the *Democratic Review* in 1838. It was later collected in *Twice-Told Tales*, and in Poe's favorable review of that book for *Graham's Magazine* in 1842, he laid out the similarities in precise detail, perhaps in ignorance of the fact that Hawthorne's story predated his own. However, Poe wrote off the similarity as merely "a very flattering coincidence of thought" (575).
"the lives of Meason": Melville, *The Confidence-Man* (1857), Northwestern-Newberry edition, ed. Harrison Hayford et al. (Evanston, IL: Northwestern University Press, 1984), 4; criminal narratives: David Reynolds in *Beneath the American Renaissance* explores criminal literature, but, curiously, touches very little on this element in Poe's work. For Lippard in particular, see 459–63.
structure of the spiritual autobiography: See Roger Sherrock, introduction to John Bunyan, *Grace Abounding to the Chief of Sinners* (Oxford: Clarendon Press, 1962), esp. xxix. Also see William C. Spengemann, *The Forms of Autobiography* (New Haven: Yale University Press, 1980), 44–51.
dual impulses: A good elaboration of this theory is in Symons 70. In a 13 April 1869 letter to George Wolff Fahnestock, John Pendleton Kennedy said, "I have never known, nor heard of any one, whose life so curiously illustrated that twofold existence of the *spiritual* and the *carnal* disputing the control of the man, which has often been made the theme of fiction. His was debauched by the most grovelling

appetites and exalted by the richest conceptions of genius" (quoted in Thomas Bohner, "The Poe-Kennedy Friendship," *Pennsylvania Magazine of History and Biography* 82 [Apr. 1958]: 220–22).

"very Poe-esque protest": Silverman 150, 151.

"glory of the Ancient Dominion": review of Benjamin Blake Minor's "Address on Education," in the *Southern Literary Messenger* for Dec. 1835.

Virginia dynasty: Dana Nelson, *The Word in Black and White: Reading "Race" in American Literature, 1638–1867* (New York: Oxford University Press, 1992), 91.

"person of any literary distinction": Quoted in Hovey 349.

racism in *Pym*: Nelson 102ff.

Poe's possible authorship: An unsigned review of two pro-slavery books, the anonymous *The South Vindicated from the Treason and Fanaticism of the Northern Abolitionists*, attributed to William Drayton, and *Slavery in the United States*, by James Kirke Paulding, appeared in the April 1836 *Messenger*. The authorship of this review was traditionally ascribed to Poe (it appears in Harrison 8:265–75) until William Hull rejected it from the Poe canon in his 1941 doctoral dissertation and argued that the review was the work of Nathaniel Beverley Tucker, professor of law at William and Mary College, a well-known apologist for slavery and frequent contributor to the *Messenger*. The review was generally accepted as Tucker's until 1974, when in *Poe Studies* Bernard Rosenthal reexamined the authorship question and concluded in a long and intricate argument that the review was Poe's. However, the most recent treatment of the question, by Terence Whalen in *Edgar Allan Poe and the Masses: The Political Economy of Literature in Antebellum America* (Princeton: Princeton University Press, 1999), 113–21, seems to lay the matter to rest, Whalen concluding almost definitively that the piece could not have been written by Poe.

"storm of business": Poe to Joseph Evans Snodgrass, 20 Jan. 1840, *Letters* 1:127.

"at their own risque and expense": Quinn 288–89.

Reviews of *Tales of the Grotesque and Arabesque:* In Ian Walker, ed., *Edgar Allan Poe: The Critical Heritage* (London: Routledge, 1986).

Neal comment: *Log* 267–68.

"We very much regret": *Log* 338.

St. Louis Commercial Bulletin comment and "In your private ear": *Letters* 1:120.

"You see that I speak plainly": *Log* 262.

"regain a wholesome activity": Quoted in Silverman 144.

earlier harsh review: *Log* 254.

"very silly book": *Letters* 1:130.

"Had I written": Quoted in Symons 67.

"You do me a gross injustice": *Letters* 1:130.

"I would go down": *Letters* 1:138.

CHAPTER 6
Graham's Magazine, "The Penn," and the Red Death

funding for "The Penn": See Poe to Nicholas Biddle, 6 Jan. 1841, Letters 2:693–95.
financial crisis: Log 318.
"Across the pages": American Literary Magazines: The Eighteenth and Nineteenth
    Centuries, ed. Edward E. Chielens (Westport, CT: Greenwood, 1986), 156.
"at least as liberal": Quoted in Silverman 162.
"the little garden in summer": Quoted in Symons 71.
"precisely as if the little fellow": Poe to Hiram Haines, 24 Apr. 1840, Letters 1:128–29.
"morbid": Meyers 123.
"more perfect in its proportions": Log 265.
"These tales of ratiocination": Poe to Cooke, 9 Aug. 1846, Letters 2:328.
Echoes of Poe in Native Son: This similarity has gone unremarked. Thomas P. Riggio,
    however, notes the Poe influence on an author who influenced Wright: Theodore
    Dreiser. In An American Tragedy (1925), one sees Gothic landscapes that seem to
    exert a malign influence on the protagonist and a "psychic evil genie" that also
    tempts him. Moreover, there is an ambivalent feeling toward the murderer in that
    book which, as in Poe, the author brings out by calling into question the
    character's true criminal intent. Dreiser read Poe intensively during the 1920s and
    several times commented on his literary genius. See Riggio, "American Gothic: Poe
    and An American Tragedy," American Literature (Jan. 1978): 515–31. And at least
    three later writers seem prominently to have borrowed from "Usher" the conceit of
    the house as metaphor for the body: Charlotte Perkins Gilman in "The Yellow
    Wall-Paper"—which was repeatedly described in contemporary reviews as Poe-
    esque when it appeared in 1891; the southern author Ellen Glasgow—who
    acknowledged a debt to Poe in the preface to one of her story collections—in such
    tales as "Dare's Gift" and "Jordan's End"; and, perhaps most obviously, William
    Faulkner, whose southern Gothic mansion in "A Rose for Emily" closely resembles
    the Usher house as a symbol for the family that inhabits it. (The tableau vivant
    image of Miss Emily in her bedroom window, lit from behind by a lamp, is also
    similar to the image of Helen in a niche in "To Helen.") Faulkner was well
    acquainted with Poe's work, especially the grotesque element in many of his stories.
    Very Poe-esque characters appear in the Snopes novels (especially Eula in The
    Hamlet); and several critics have noted resemblances between Quentin Compson in
    The Sound and the Fury and the speaker of Poe's "The Raven"—both are lovers
    mourning the loss of their cherished beauties and both are "visited"—oddly so for
    the Faulkner novel—by a bird.
"more perfect in its proportions": Log 265.
doubling and homosexuality in "The Rue Morgue": J. A. Leo Lemay, "The
    Psychology of 'The Murders in the Rue Morgue,'" American Literature 54, no. 2
    (May 1982): 165–88.

Poe and Griswold: See Killis Campbell, "The Poe-Griswold Controversy,"
Publications of the Modern Language Association (PMLA) 34 (September 1919):
436–464; and B. Bernard Cohen and Lucien A. Cohen, "Poe and Griswold Once
More," *American Literature* 34 (March 1962): 97–101.
"make war to the knife": Poe to Daniel Bryan, 6 July 1842, *Letters* 1:206.
"constitutional infirmity"; Ann Sophia Stephens, quoted in Silverman 216–17.
"careless, erratic": Jacob Neu, "Rufus Wilmot Griswold," *University of Texas Studies in
English* 5 (1925): 164–65. A full-length biography of Griswold is Joy Bayless,
Rufus Wilmot Griswold: Poe's Literary Executor (Nashville, TN: Vanderbilt
University Press, 1943).
"I speak to her": Quoted in Silverman 217.
Dickens interviews: Gerald Grubb, "The Personal and Literary Relationships of
Dickens and Poe," *Nineteenth-Century Fiction* 5 (1950): 1–22, 101–120, 209–221;
and Sidney P. Moss, "Poe's 'Two Long Interviews' with Dickens," *Poe Studies* 11,
no. 1 (June 1978): 10–12.
"Did any one read such nonsense?": Harrison 11:220–243.
"namby-pamby character": Poe to Frederick Thomas, 25 May 1842, *Letters* 1:197.
"labored solely for the benefit": Poe to Robert R. Conrad, 22 January 1841,
Letters 1: 154.
Prospectus of "The Penn": *Log* 300–301.
"I must now do or die": *Letters* 1:152, 192.
writing to American authors: See *Letters* 1:184 ff.
"I am ugly enough": Poe to Frederick W. Thomas, 25 Feb. 1843, *Letters* 1:223.
Thomas Holley Chivers: See Charles Henry Watts, *Thomas Holley Chivers: His
Literary Career and His Poetry* (Athens: University of Georgia Press, 1956).
"How would you like to be an office holder": Thomas to Poe, 20 May 1841, quoted
in Symons 75.
Poe's interview with Smith: Poe to Thomas, 19 Nov. 1842: *Letters* 1:218–19.
"*un homme blasé*": Quoted in Meyers 145.
"He exposes himself here": Quoted in Symons 83.
"a little sick": *Letters* 1:228.
"She lay abed": Mrs. A. B. Harris, "Edgar A. Poe," *Hearth and Home* (9 Jan.
1875): 24.
"anxious solicitude": In Walker 381.
"suggestive poetic effects": Silverman 206. This story in particular—among
others—seems to have influenced Stephen Crane in a little-known but
technically expert tale entitled "Manacled." In this macabre fable, a popular
actor is performing onstage when the players are suddenly interrupted by cries
of "Fire!" The actor is handcuffed with real manacles and leg irons and cannot
escape. His painfully slow progress as he squirms, gropes, and fumbles his
way toward the exit is reminiscent of the similar impeded movements of the
character in "The Pit and the Pendulum." The theatre is also plunged into

darkness, and the actor is further hampered by fire and smoke, which cut off his ability to see, hear, and breathe—he too is deprived of his senses. Crane, who had read Poe as a schoolboy, may even have been imaginatively recalling the legend during this time that Poe's mother, Eliza, had died during the Richmond Theatre fire.

lyceum movement: See Carl Bode, *The American Lyceum* (New York: Oxford University Press, 1956) and Merton M. Sealts, Jr., *Melville as Lecturer* (Cambridge: Harvard University Press, 1957).

"highly philosophical": *Log* 441–47.

CHAPTER 7

New York: Triumphs and Troubles—"The Raven" and the Longfellow War

"My dear Muddy": *Letters* 1:251–52.
"well known to the Literary public": *Log* 461–62.
"manufacturer of hoaxes": *Log* 460.
"far more intense sensation": *Log* 458.
"every intelligent reader": *Log* 461.
"ill in health": Poe to N. P. Willis, 21 May 1844. Woodberry and Stedman, eds., *The Works of Edgar Allan Poe*, 1894–95, Vol. 4 (New York: Scribners, 1914), 153.
"a living soul": Poe to Thomas, 8 Sept. 1844, *Letters* 1:262.
"deeply conscious": Poe to J. R. Lowell, 2 July 1844, *Letters* 1:257.
"magnetic sleep": *Log* 498.
"awake, at last": Poe to Lowell, 2 July 1844, *Letters* 1:256.
"he was not half": Quoted in Symons 94.
"rather a step downward": *Log* 473.
Poe's description of Willis: *Godey's Lady's Book*, May 1846, 199.
"unvarying deportment": In Walker 307–8.
"I am glad to see": *Log* 474.
"a host of small troubles": *Log* 475.
"among a class of readers": *Log* 476.
reviews of "The Raven": Silverman 237–38.
"a highly gifted young person": Quoted in Carlson, *The Recognition of Edgar Allan Poe*, 212.
Harrison recollection: *Log* 472.
night Poe's mother died: Silverman 241.
remark to William Ross Wallace: *Log* 495–96.
remark to Frederick W. Thomas: Poe to Thomas, 4 May 1845, *Letters* 1:287.
Longfellow War: The commentary on this episode is voluminous. A good overview with reasonable arguments appears in Kent Ljungquist and Buford Jones,

"The Identity of 'Outis': A Further Chapter in the Poe-Longfellow War,"*American Literature* 60 (Oct. 1988): 402–15.

"asleep on velvet": Quoted in T. O. Mabbott, "Annals," *Poems*, 1969, 557.

"The harshness of his criticisms": Samuel Longfellow, *Life of Henry Wadsworth Longfellow* (Boston: Ticknor and Fields, 1886), 2:150.

"It was an occupation peculiarily suited": *Graham's Magazine* 44 (Feb. 1854): 222.

"Plagiarism—see the works of Thomas Moore": *Al Aaraaf*, 71. Facsimile available at http://www.eapoe.org/works/poems/fairylc.htm.

"Campbell is a plagiarist": Recollection by Thomas W. Gibson, quoted in *Log* 108.

Poe and plagiarism: See Nelson F. Adkins, " 'Chapter on American Cribbage': Poe and Plagiarism," *PBSA* 42 (1948): 169–210.

"There are points at which you do me in justice": Poe to Hunt, 17 March 1845, *Letters* 1:283.

"She was dressed in black": *Log* 553.

"Miserrimus": *Log* 553–54.

"dreadfully unwell": *Letters* 1:290.

Quarrel with L. G. Clark: *Log* 544–54.

Poe satirized by Briggs: *Log* 692.

"fell into a sort of eloquent monologue": Joseph Wood Krutch, *Edgar Allan Poe: A Study in Genius* (New York: Knopf, 1926), 154.

"true imagination": "Frances Sargent Osgood," *Southern Literary Messenger* (Aug. 1849), 514.

"sitting pale and smiling": Quoted in Symons 106.

"maintained a correspondence": Griswold, "Memoir of the Author," xxxvii.

"characterless character": Charles F. Briggs to James Russell Lowell, Woodberry 2:145.

"a sort of persistent . . . flattery": *Log* 578.

"pursued Poe in print": *Log* 579.

"the basest ingratitude": Quoted in Quinn 487–88.

L. G. Clark attack: *Log* 587.

Simms's comments: *Log* 588.

"utterly impossible to conceive": *Letters* 1:302.

Poe's income: See John Ostrom, "Edgar A. Poe: His Income as a Literary Entrepreneur," *Poe Studies* 15 (June 1982): 1–7.

"deliberate attempt to . . . ruin": Poe to Halleck, 1 Dec. 1845, *Letters* 1:304.

"awakened from some horrible dream": *Letters* 1:300.

"the poor boy is deranged": Quoted in Meyers 187.

"unexpected engagements": Quoted in Symons 107.

"transferred the Journal": Quoted in Silverman 277.

"from publisher to publisher": "The Late Edgar Allan Poe," *Graham's Magazine* 36 (March 1850): 224–26; rpt. in Walker 382.

CHAPTER 8
Quarrels, Loves, and Losses

fight with English: *Log* 623–24; Francis Desmond, "Poe's Libel Suit Against T. D. English," *Boston Public Library Quarterly* 5 (1953): 31.
"gave E. a flogging": Poe to Henry B. Hirst, 27 June 1846, *Letters* 2:322.
"labors under mental derangement": *Log* 635.
"a woman whose loathsome love": Poe to Sarah Helen Whitman, 18 Oct. 1848, *Letters*, 2:393.
"continued ill health": *Letters* 2:316.
speaking engagements: *Log* 646.
Description of Fordham cottage: Reminiscences of Mary Gove Nichols (1863), quoted in *Log* 644.
"a sort of universal Providence": Ibid.
"are both dangerously ill": *Log* 672.
"with no symptoms of ordinary intoxication": Quoted in William F. Gill, "Some New Facts About Edgar A. Poe," *Laurel Leaves* (Boston: William F. Gill and Co., 1876), 383.
"Even in the city of New York": *Log* 677.
"the final sanctification": Edward H. Davidson, *Poe: A Critical Study* (Cambridge, MA: Belknap Press of Harvard University Press, 1957),184.
visits to Jesuits: *Log* 644; Meyers 194.
all matter was "God": Poe to Chivers, 1:259–60.
"all rigamarole": *Log* 564.
Evening Mirror notice: *Log* 641.
"pilgrimage to Bloomingdale": *Log* 642.
"forehead rather broad": *Log* 643.
"generous offer to hammer Poe": *Log* 645–46.
Fuller's preface: *Log* 648.
newspaper comments: *Log* 649, 651, 654, 655.
English's rejoinder: *Log* 653.
Morgan book: See James E. Ruck, "Conflict and Motive in 'The Cask of Amontillado,'" *Poe Studies* 5 (1972): 50–51.
"Bringing authors 'before the public . . .'": *Log* 654.
"I am rather ashamed": *Log* 655.
"sumptuous delicacies": Moss, *Poe's Literary Battles*, 238.
"A poor creature": *Log* 656.
"flocks of little birds of prey": *Letters* 2:325–27.
"Domain of Arnheim": The Belgian painter Magritte gave this same title to a 1949 canvas. His picture presents nothing like the paradise that Poe describes in his story; but Magritte, like other visual artists, was profoundly influenced by Poe, especially regarding each man's interest in the contradiction between the familiar and the strange.

Gove recollection: *Log* 644.

"machinery of [their] own thoughts": Review of Bland's *Reports, Southern Literary Messenger* (Oct. 1836).

"expressed a desire": Shew to Ingram, 28 March 1875, in Miller 1977, 116.

Portrait of Virginia: Michael Deas, *The Portraits and Daguerreotypes of Edgar Allan Poe* (Charlottesville: University Press of Virginia, 1988), 168.

assembled mourners: *Log* 686.

"I hope and believe": Miller 1977, 23–24.

Christmas Eve service: *Log* 711.

"Can you *hint* to me": *Letters* 2:356.

"plaything of a lying . . . Overlord": Silverman 404.

"I found him sitting": Shew to Ingram, 3 Apr. 1875, Miller 1977, 120.

"be a friend": Augustus Van Cleef, "Poe's Mary," *Harper's Monthly* 78 (March 1889): 639.

"in passionate terms": Henry Harrington, "Poe Not To Be Apotheosized," New York *Critic* (3 Oct. 1885): 158.

"as a souvenir": Quoted in Neu, "Rufus Wilmot Griswold," 141.

"extremely civil": Silverman 332–333.

"As regards the Stylus": Poe to George W. Eveleth, 15 Dec. 1846, *Letters* 2:333.

"will . . . revolutionize the world": Ibid.

"elaborate and profound": *Log* 721.

"a mountainous piece of absurdity": *Log* 722.

"used to walk up and down": Woodberry 301–2.

"Newton's discovery of gravitation": Putnam recollection, quoted in Meyers 218.

"it makes no deep impression": Eliot, quoted in Carlson, *Recognition*.

"the beginning of the great era of the unification of force": Limon 72; quoted in Dana Nelson, *The Word in Black and White*.

Discussions of *Eureka*: See in particular Barbara Cantalupo, "Eureka: Poe's 'Novel Universe,'" *A Companion to Poe Studies*, ed. Eric W. Carlson (Westport, CT: Greenwood Press, 1996), 323–44, and Richard P. Benton, ed., *Poe as Literary Cosmologer: Studies in Eureka. A Symposium* (Hartford, CT: University of Connecticut, 1975).

"the most *passionless*": Wilmer, *Our Press Gang* (Philadelphia, 1859), 284.

"crying in laps": Auden, "Edgar Allan Poe," 218.

composition of "The Bells": Shew to John Henry Ingram, 23 Jan. 1875, quoted in Miller 98–99.

"the Raven in his eyrie": *Log* 730.

"You may remember": Poe to Whitman, 1 Oct. 1848, *Letters* 2:384–85.

"Judge, then,": *Letters* 2:385.

"Simultaneously both arose": Phillips 2:1316.

"I *must* now speak": Poe to Whitman, 18 Oct. 1848, *Letters* 2:393.

"my own sweet *sister*": Poe to Richmond, 16 Nov. 1848, *Letters* 2:401.

"I remember nothing": Ibid., 401–2. Unlike a strikingly similar incident in the life of the French symphonist Hector Berlioz which had occurred fifteen years earlier, Poe's suicide attempt was half-hearted—meant to arouse compassion in both women and to convince one or both of them of the depths of his love. Berlioz (1803–1869), whose dark temperament and melancholic bitterness toward the world seem to have run parallel with Poe's, swallowed a near-fatal dose of opium in a determined effort to convince a woman of his love for her. When she then acceded to his challenge, he drank an emetic and, like a Poe character, lived to tell the tale of his survival.

"very French": *Baudelaire on Poe*, trans. and ed. Lois and Francis E. Hyslop, Jr. (State College, PA: Bald Eagle Press, 1952).

"terrible excitement": Poe to Whitman, 22 Nov. 1848, *Letters* 2:405.

"You allude": Poe to Whitman, 24 Nov. 1848, *Letters* 2:407.

"Helen sat in the front row": James A. Harrison and Charlotte Dailey, "Poe and Mrs. Whitman: New Light on a Romantic Episode," *Century Magazine*, n.s., 55 (Jan. 1909): 447.

"on Tuesday": Poe to Clemm, [23 Dec. 1848], *Letters* 2:412.

"cautioning me": Stanley T. Williams, "New Letters about Poe," *Yale Review*, n.s., 14 (July 1925): 762–63.

"In commencing": Poe to Whitman, [21 ? Jan. 1849], *Letters* 2:420–21.

CHAPTER 9

The Journey and the Lighthouse

"there is *nothing*": *Letters* 2:414–15.

"to consult your happiness": Poe to Richmond, [18] Feb. 1849, *Letters* 2:431.

"Only think of your Eddy": *Letters* 2:425.

"Literature is the most noble of professions": *Letters* 2:427.

"not doubting that even a cheap Magazine": Patterson to Poe, 4 May 1849, Harrison 17:352–55.

"such a mag.": *Letters* 2:440.

"the benefit of his original thoughts": Frederick W. Coburn, "Poe as Seen by the Brother of 'Annie,'" *New England Quarterly* 16 (Sept. 1843): 474–75.

"emaciated": Smith, "Autobiographic Notes. Edgar Allan Poe," *Beadle's Monthly* 3 (Feb. 1867): 156.

"my life seems wasted": Poe to Richmond, after 5 [?] May 1849, Harrison 17:345–46.

"act as his Literary Executor": Harrison 1:347.

"My adored Mother!": Shew recollection, quoted in Silverman 414.

"God bless you": Miller 199.

"It is no use to reason": Poe to Clemm, 7 July 1849, *Letters* 2:452.

"lost the trunk": Poe to Clemm, [14 July 1849], *Letters* 2:453–54.

"pale and haggard": Sartain, *The Reminiscences of a Very Old Man* (1899; rpt., New York: Blom, 1969), 207–12.

"no bread to eat": Lippard's reminiscence in the *Sunday Mercury*, before 3 Oct. 1849; rpt., T. C. Duncan Eaves, "Poe's Last Visit to Philadelphia," *American Literature* 26 (March 1954): 46–47.

"Richmond is my home": 1966 rpt. with supplement to Ostrom's *Letters* (New York: Gordian Press, 1966), 686.

"I never wanted": *Letters* 2:453.

Shelton's husband's will: F. Meredith Dietz, "Poe's First and Final Love," *Southern Literary Messenger*, n.s., 5 (March 1943): 38–47.

"I have a singular feeling": Sartain 213.

"stretched unconscious": Snodgrass, "The Facts of Poe's Death and Burial," *Beadle's Monthly* 3 (March 1867): 283–87.

Moran's statement: *A Defense of Edgar Allan Poe* (Washington, DC: Boogher, 1885; rpt., New York: AMS, 1966), 22, 18.

Autopsy and diagnosis: Phillips 1508.

"almost a suicide": Baudelaire, "Edgar Allan Poe: His Life and Works," introduction to *Les Histoires extraordinaires*. Quoted in Walker 409.

"in the large room": Moran 78.

"a lead-lined oak casket": Charles Scarlett, Jr., "Tale of Ratiocination: The Death and Burial of Edgar Allan Poe," *Maryland Historical Magazine* (1978): 370.

"cold-blooded": George P. Clark, "Two Unnoticed Recollections of Poe's Funeral," *Poe Studies* 3 (June 1970): 1–2.

Epilogue

Ludwig article: Harrison 1:348–59.

"the whole press": Wilmer, *Merlin*, 26.

"nearly sunk": Quoted in Silverman 440.

"An enthusiasm for Poe": James, *French Poets and Novelists*, 1878; quoted in Carlson, *Critical Essays on Edgar Allan Poe* (Boston: G. K. Hall, 1987), 82.

"probably . . . among the electric lights": Whitman, "Edgar Poe's Significance" (1880); quoted in Carlson, *Critical Essays* 83.

"this finest of fine artists": Shaw, "Edgar Allan Poe" (1909); quoted in Carlson, *Critical Essays* 86.

"a skillful writer": Hemingway, *The Green Hills of Africa*, in *The Hemingway Reader*, ed. Charles Poore (New York: Scribner, 1953), 466.

"a highly gifted young person": Eliot, quoted in Carlson, *Recognition*, 212.

"an adventurer into vaults": Lawrence, *Studies in Classic American Literature* (1923; rpt., New York: Viking, 1964), 81.

"against the grain": Williams, in *Recognition*, 132–33.

INDEX